Essentials of Music Technology

Mark Ballora

Penn State University

Prentice
Hall

Upper Saddle River, New Jersey 07458

Library of Congress Cataloging-in-Publication Data

Ballora, Mark.
   Essentials of music technology / Mark Ballora.
      p. cm.
   Includes bibliographical references and index.
   ISBN 0-13-093747-9 (paper)
   1. Sound—Equipment and supplies. 2. Music—Performance. I. Title.

TK7881.9 .B35 2002
780´.285—dc21

                                        2002031267

VP/Editorial Director: Charlyce Jones-Owen
Acquisitions Editor: Christopher T. Johnson
Managing Editor: Jan Stephan
Production Liaison: Joanne Hakim
Project Manager: Gail Gavin
Editorial Assistant: Evette Dickerson
Prepress and Manufacturing Buyer: Ben Smith
Art Director: Jayne Conte
Cover Designer: Bruce Kenselaar
Cover Art: The Image Bank
Director, Image Resource Center: Melinda Reo
Manager, Rights and Permissions: Zina Arabia
Interior Image Specialist: Beth Boyd-Brenzel
Image Permission Coordinator: Joanne Dippel
Marketing Manager: Chris Ruel

This book was set in 10/12 Souvenir Light by The Clarinda Company and was printed and bound by Courier. The cover was printed by Phoenix Color Corp.

 © 2003 by Pearson Education, Inc.
Upper Saddle River, New Jersey 07458

Printed in the United States of America

10 9 8 7 6 5 4 3 2 1

ISBN 0-13-093747-9

Pearson Education Ltd., London
Pearson Education Australia, PTY. Limited, Sydney
Pearson Education Singapore, Pte. Ltd
Pearson Education North Asia Ltd, Hong Kong
Pearson Education Canada, Ltd., Toronto
Pearson Educacion de Mexico, S.A. de C.V.
Pearson Education—Japan, Tokyo
Pearson Education Malaysia, Pte. Ltd
Pearson Education, Upper Saddle River, New Jersey

Contents

Preface

What Is Music Technology?

This newly defined component of music education means many things to many people. Music technology, a broad subject, has meanings that may differ for music educators, composers, performers, audio producers, electrical engineers, computer programmers, or perceptual psychologists. All of the music activities in these fields intersect in the personal computer. Within the span of the last decade or so, computers in music have gone from being a niche subject to becoming a ubiquitous presence that all music students are bound to encounter in their professional lives. Furthermore, the new and varied role of the computer in music making brings about surprising overlaps with all of these fields.

Prior to the 1980s, "music technology" (if the term was used at all) would most likely have referred to audio engineering, the conversion (*transduction*) of musical material into electricity for purposes of amplification, broadcasting, or recording. The first step in the process was the microphone, which performed the acoustic-to-electronic conversion. Once the musical material existed in the form of electrical current, it could be sent to an amplifier that would drive a set of speakers, thus relaying the material over a public address system. Alternatively, the electromagnetic radiation that resulted from the electrical current could be broadcast from an antenna for television or radio reception. Or, if the signal were to be recorded, the musicians were likely to be assembled in a recording studio, with a number of microphones strategically placed for optimal sound capture. The signals from the various microphones were combined in a mixer, which allowed a technician to adjust the relative volumes and stereo positions of each microphone's signal. With a mixer, it was also possible to send the signal to processing devices to adjust the character of the sound, making it, for example, sound as though it were occurring in a large room. Following effects processing, the mixed signals could be sent to tape for storage.

Other possible meanings for "music technology" might have included the use of synthesizers for composing electronic music, an activity attractive to musicians who had a penchant for electrical assembly or who had the means to employ technicians to create and maintain the machinery. Perhaps least known to the general public were those who worked in high-end research institutions who had access to computers, sharing time on these mysterious machines with engineers and rocket scientists and programming them to emit sounds and music.

The personal computer has generalized and expanded these models and affected every area of education. Music technology, implying "the use of computers as an aid to music making" is now a subject that all music educators must address in some way. Small desktop computers may now be part of every step of the musical production process just described, acting as performer, mixer, processor, and storage medium. This development has implications for all practitioners of music, regardless of their specialty. Whether they find themselves working at a school, a recording studio, or concert hall, musicians can count on finding computers at work in the production of musical activity. Performers are often expected to send CDs of their performances as part of applications for jobs. Educators are expected to employ the resources of the Internet and multimedia technology to teach students about music rudiments. Composers are expected to provide performers with laser-printed scores and parts. Thus, knowledge of music technology is becoming a core skill of musical training, along with history, figured bass, and Roman numeral notation.

Purpose of This Book

> Things should be made as simple as possible, but no simpler.
> —Albert Einstein

With any learning endeavor, it is typically the basics that are most difficult to master. This book is meant to provide an overview of essential elements of acoustics, MIDI, digital audio, and sound recording so that students may understand what musical elements may be stored in a computer and what type of manipulations and representations of musical information are possible. It is written in an attempt to find a balance between simple and straightforward presentations and descriptions that are thorough enough to explain the material without "dumbing it down."

The book is not meant to be a substitute for a qualified instructor. A performer cannot master an instrument without the help of an experienced musician, just as an athlete cannot excel at a sport without the guidance of a coach. But even experienced performers and athletes find it useful to consult a fingering chart or a rule book as a reference. This book is intended to play a similar role for a student learning some aspect of music technology. Different sections will be relevant for different types of projects or different levels of learning. It is broken into short sections in order to allow an instructor to assign reading selectively to focus on areas that are important for a given group of students.

The only assumptions are that students are familiar with a computer operating system and fundamentals of music. Certain concepts are best presented with equations, but no advanced mathematical training is necessary to understand the main points. Computers deal with information in the form of numbers, and different programs may require information to be entered differently. A given program may ask for frequency values or musical pitches, for loudness in decibels or in arbitrary units. Mathematics is not presented for its own sake, but rather to give students alternative views of how to understand and work with music in a computer environment. The cognitive psychologist Marvin Minsky has stated that a thing or idea seems meaningful only when we have a variety of different ways to represent it, providing different perspectives and different associations. Viewing music through the lenses of acoustics, physics, or computer science has the potential to yield rich rewards in the form of new perspectives and associations that they bring to the meaning of music.

Acknowledgments

I am only able to write this book due to a series of mentors who have led me along and patiently tolerated my persistent questions and all-too-frequent impenetrability. It is due to the efforts of Alan Wasserman, Kenneth J. Peacock, Robert Rowe, Bruce Pennycook, and Philippe Depalle that I gained the knowledge that is laid out here.

My students at McGill University and Penn State University clarified my understanding on many of these concepts through their questions and efforts.

My friend and colleague Geoff Martin was an invaluable consultant in the formation of the book's contents. Geoff has always kept me honest, and this time was no exception.

Richard Green, Director of the Penn State School of Music, brought me to PSU with a mandate to bring these concepts to the music curriculum, with the solid support of Richard Durst, Dean of the Penn State College of Arts and Architecture. I hope that seeing these topics in print offers them some gratification for their efforts.

Christopher Johnson, my editor at Prentice Hall, has nurtured this project to completion and endured all the bumps along the way.

My wife, Jui-Chih Wang, has seen me through the creation of this book and much more. Someday, somehow, I intend to make it up to her.

Mark Ballora
Penn State University

CHAPTER 1

Basic Acoustics

Subjective terms typically predominate in descriptions of music. A piece might be described as "sweet," "lively," "bright," "good," "bad," or with any one of a number of creative descriptors. But computers, being nothing more than fast idiots, lack the ability to derive anything meaningful from such poetic terms. They are made to store and manipulate numbers. Thus, for computers to encode and manipulate sound, acoustic information has to be translated into numerical values. Subsequent chapters will deal with what properties of sound a computer can and cannot work with. An essential preliminary step is to cover basic acoustic measurements that form the basis of music technologies.

The Nature of Sound Events

Imagine a set of light wind chimes. You approach the wind chimes, lean in close, and blow on them sharply, as though you were trying to blow out a candle or remove a speck of dust from a surface. The gust of air causes the chimes to move, first in one direction, and then the other. They oscillate back and forth for several moments until they settle again to their initial state.

Air behaves somewhat like these wind chimes. Simply put, sound consists of vibrations of air molecules. For purposes of this discussion, air molecules may be visualized as tiny superballs hovering in space. When a sound event occurs, such as when people clap their hands, molecules are pushed together, just as the wind chimes were in the example. After the molecules collide, they bounce away from each other, then collide with other molecules. This second collision causes them to ricochet back toward their initial location, where they again collide and ricochet, oscillating back and forth until the energy of their motion dissipates.

Thus, sound occurs when air molecules are disturbed and made to ricochet off of each other. These ricochets cause the density of the air molecules to oscillate. The density of air molecules is also termed *air pressure*. When air molecules are undisturbed, the air is said to be at a normal state of density (or at normal pressure level). When they are pushed together, the pressure level is greater than normal, in a *compressed* state. When they ricochet away from each other, the pressure level is lower than normal, and the molecules are said to be in a *rarefied* state. The three states are illustrated in Figure 1–1.

The changes in air pressure that humans perceive as sound are the same as the air pressure changes that are discussed regularly by meteorologists on television

Figure 1–1

Molecular Density Oscillations

During a sound event, atmospheric density oscillates among three states: normal, compressed, and rarefied.

Normal

Compressed

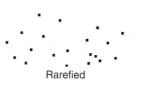
Rarefied

time

news and elsewhere. High air pressure typically implies a sunny day, whereas low air pressure implies rain and wind. These air pressure changes that determine the weather are at a much greater magnitude and change far more slowly than pressure changes that result in sound. Thus, the pressure changes discussed by a TV weatherperson are normally termed *atmospheric pressure,* and pressure changes discussed by an acoustician or recording engineer are normally termed *sound pressure.*

The energy of a sound event occurring at an isolated point expands in a sphere, moving away from the sound source (try to imagine an expanding, spherical slinky). Figure 1–2 shows a two-dimensional slice of this expanding sphere. Thus, energy is transported through the medium of air molecules. When energy is transported through a medium, the medium often oscillates as a result. The energy is transported by means of the medium's oscillations, which are called *waves.*

Figure 1–2

Expanding Sphere of Energy

Two-dimensional slice of expanding sphere of compressed and rarefied atmospheric pressure resulting from a vibrating tuning fork.

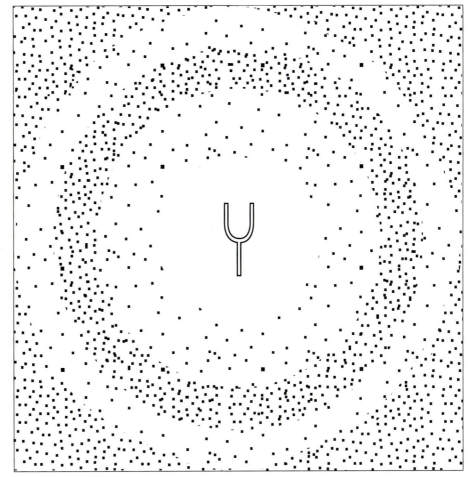

The expanding pressure wave does not consist of individual molecules moving away from the sound source and surfing along with the pressure front. What spreads is the energy of the wave. The individual molecules simply oscillate about their original position. This is a general characteristic of many waves: they consist of energy moving from one place to another through a medium, while the medium itself is not transported.

Sound waves are an example of *longitudinal* waves, which are waves that oscillate back and forth along the same axis as the wave's propagation. In contrast, water waves are *transverse* waves, which are waves that oscillate back and forth along an axis perpendicular to the wave's propagation (Figure 1–3).

Sound waves are often illustrated on a graph in which sound pressure is plotted as a function of time. This is the type of representation obtained from an oscilloscope. An example is shown in Figure 1–4. The horizontal line represents an undisturbed level of molecular density. It is sometimes called the *zero line,* as it represents a pressure change level of zero from the undisturbed pressure level. Points above the zero line represent pressure levels higher than equilibrium (compressions in air molecules); points below the zero line represent pressure levels lower than equilibrium (rarefactions in air molecules). Since this type of graph illustrates changes over time, it is also called a *time domain plot.*

Figure 1–3

Transverse and Longitudinal Waves

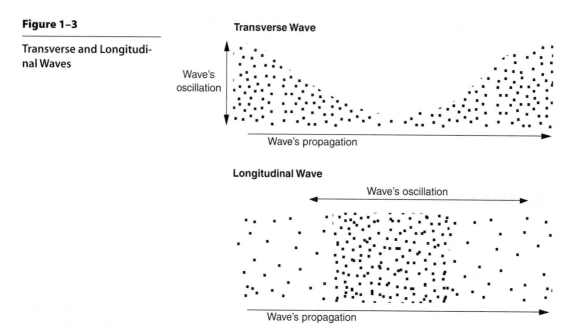

Transverse Wave

Wave's oscillation

Wave's propagation

Longitudinal Wave

Wave's oscillation

Wave's propagation

Wave Propagation

Simple Harmonic Motion

Sound waves are an example of a *vibrating system.* Everyday life provides many other examples of vibrating systems: waves in water, tides, oscillating springs, pendulums, and so on. Vibrating systems share a number of common properties. Their motion is repetitive, which means that the vibrating body returns to a particular position at regular, predictable time intervals. These intervals are called the *period* of the vibration. As the body vibrates, a tension is created within it as it is displaced from its position of rest, and a *restoring force* acts to return the body to its equilibrium position. The farther the object moves from equilibrium, the stronger the restoring force in the opposite direction. Thus, the restoring force may be described as being *proportional* to the displacement of the object. This relationship

Figure 1–4

Time Domain Plot

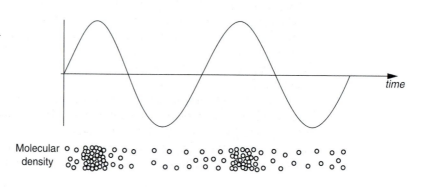

time

Molecular density

between force (F), tension (K), and displacement (y) is known as *Hooke's law* and may be written as the following equation:

$$F = -Ky \hspace{4cm} \text{1–1}$$

The level of displacement over time for most vibrating systems follows the shape of a sine wave curve like the one shown in Figure 1–4. Vibrating systems that move in this way are said to exhibit *simple harmonic motion.* The word *harmonic* will appear repeatedly in the study of sound and music; for now, simply consider it to mean "moving in a sinusoidal fashion."

Characteristics of Waves

Waves may be described by several characteristics:

1. *Wavelength:* the distance between corresponding points (for example, the extreme high or low point) from cycle to cycle as the wave repeats itself; the wavelength is often notated with the Greek letter lambda, λ.
2. *Frequency:* how often the wave repeats itself. Frequency is the inverse of wavelength; a higher frequency implies a shorter wavelength, and a lower frequency implies a longer wavelength.
3. *Amplitude:* how high and low the wave's oscillations are. This characteristic is completely independent of frequency. Two waves may vibrate at the same frequency but have different amplitudes.
4. *Wave shape:* the wave shape in Figure 1–4 is that of a *sine wave,* but most actual sound waves exhibit far more complex pressure changes.

Each of these characteristics will be discussed in greater detail in the next chapter (Properties of a Musical Sound).

Refraction and Reflection

Waves cannot travel undisturbed forever. Sooner or later, they are bound to come into contact with obstacles. Water waves in a swimming pool eventually come into contact with the pool walls, swimmers, floating rafts, etc. Air pressure oscillations similarly come into contact with buildings, mountains, people, and so on. The behavior of a wave when it comes into contact with an obstacle depends on the wavelength and the dimensions of the object. If the height and width of a surface are significantly smaller than the wavelength, the wave *refracts* (bends) around the object and continues to propagate. If the dimensions of a surface are significantly larger than the wavelength, the wave is *reflected* away from the object. In the same way that a billiard ball reflects away from the edge of the table, a wave reflects away from an obstacle at the same angle with which it struck the object (Figure 1–5).

Furthermore, any change in the medium functions as an obstacle. Imagine holding one end of a rope and giving the rope a flick. A pulse results that travels down the rope and then travels back to you. The nature of the reflection differs depending on whether the other end of the rope is fixed or free. If the other end is fixed, as would be the case if the other end were secured to a wall, the reflection is "flipped":

Figure 1–5

if the original pulse was upward in orientation, the reflection is downward in orientation. A wave's up or down orientation is termed its *polarity.* In the case of a pulse propagating along a rope with a fixed end, the wave's polarity is opposite on reflection. However, if the other end of the rope is free, as would be the case if you were standing on a ladder and holding the rope down toward the floor, the wave's polarity does not change on reflection. If the incident pulse is upward in orientation, so is its reflection. These two conditions are illustrated in Figure 1–6.

These reflective properties are equivalent in the case of a sound wave propagating within a tube. Imagine holding a tube to your mouth and producing an impulsive sound by smacking your lips or clicking your tongue. The pulse is translated into a region of greater air pressure that travels down the tube and is reflected back when it reaches the opposite end. The other end of the tube functions in the same manner as does the opposite end of a string. If the tube's opposite end is closed, the pulse reflects back at opposite polarity, just as does a wave from a fixed end of a string. If the tube's opposite end is open, the reflection is at the same polarity, just as in the case of a string with an open end. Reflections within a tube are illustrated in Figure 1–7.

Figure 1–6

Wave Reflection on a String

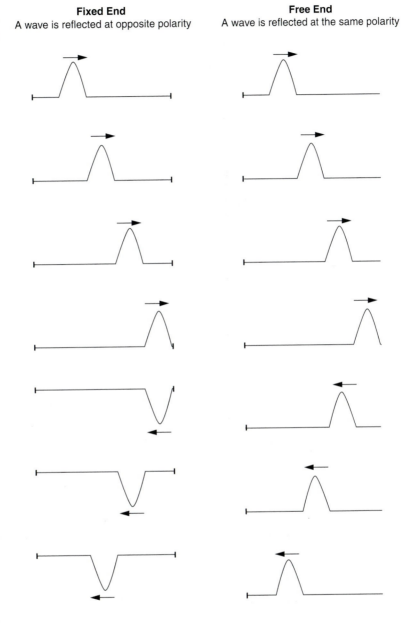

Fixed End
A wave is reflected at opposite polarity

Free End
A wave is reflected at the same polarity

Superposition

Now return to the example of the rope. Imagine holding one end of the rope while a friend holds the opposite end. You both give your ends a flick, sending pulses toward each other. Somewhere in the middle the two waves meet and their displacement patterns are momentarily combined, after which the two waves pass each other and continue, completely unchanged by their encounter with each other. This property of waves—that they may meet, be combined, and then separate again with their original characteristics intact—is known as *superposition*. Superposition is illustrated in Figure 1–8. When two waves of similar polarity

Figure 1–7

Wave Reflection within a Tube

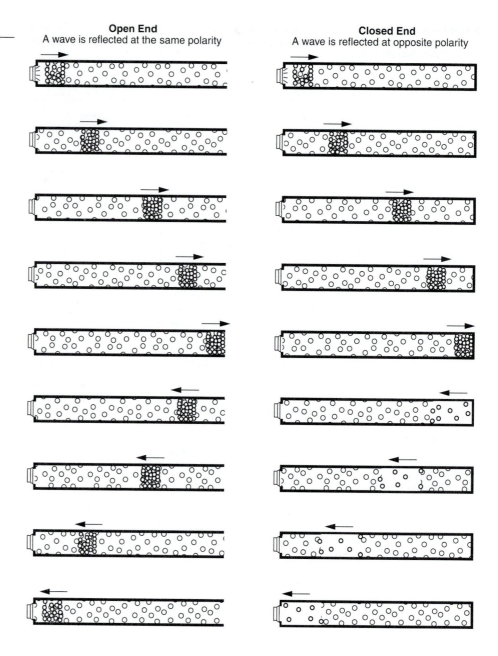

combine, they are said to exhibit *constructive interference* (a wave of greater amplitude is momentarily constructed). When two waves of opposite polarity combine, they exhibit *destructive interference* (their opposite amplitudes cancel each other out).

Standing Waves, Resonant Frequencies, and Harmonics

Imagine securing one end of your rope to a wall again. Now, instead of giving the rope a single, impulsive flick, you move your hand up and down at a regular frequency, creating a wave pattern in the rope. You can observe the combination of

Figure 1-8

Wave Superposition

Superposition of two waves
at the same polarity

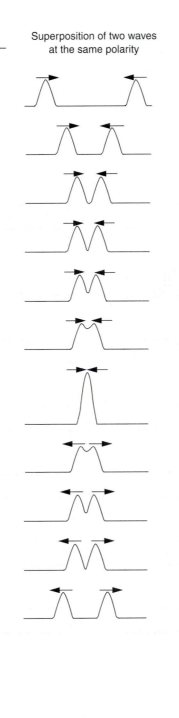

Superposition of two waves
at opposite polarity

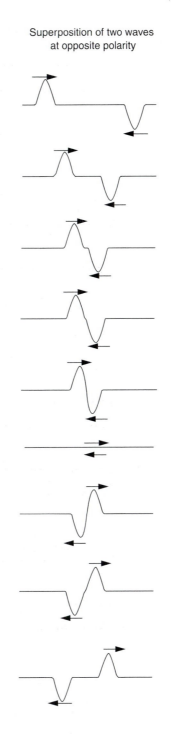

reflection and superposition as waves travel down the rope, are reflected back, and, on the way back, are superposed with waves traveling in the opposite direction.

Suppose you shake the rope at just the right frequency to create a pattern with a wavelength that is an integer subdivision of the rope (one-half of the rope's length, one-third of its length, or one-fourth the length, etc.). The superpositions of the waves, moving in opposite directions at opposite polarities, create a series of constructive and destructive interferences. A combination wave is produced that does not appear to propagate at all, but rather oscillates in one place. Such a combination wave is called a *standing wave* (Figure 1–9). There are a series of points that remain motionless at all times, called *nodes;* halfway between each node are points of maximum deviation up and down, called *antinodes.*

In general, for a string bound at both ends with a length L, standing waves may be produced that have wavelengths at:

$$\lambda = \left(\tfrac{2}{n}\right)L \qquad n = 1, 2, 3, \ldots \quad \text{(Figure 1–10)} \qquad\qquad 1\text{–}2$$

The set of frequencies that produce standing waves in a string are called the string's *characteristic frequencies* or *resonant frequencies.* Seen in terms of frequency, the inverse of wavelength, each successive standing wave in the figure is an integer multiple of the frequency represented by the top wavelength. This frequency is called the *fundamental* frequency of the string. If the fundamental in the figure oscillates once per second, then, moving down the figure, the frequencies below it oscillate twice per second, three times per second, four times per second, and so on. The set of oscillating frequencies that is based on integer multiples of the fundamental is called the *harmonic series,* and each of the standing waves may be called a harmonic of the fundamental.

Standing waves and harmonics may also be produced in tubes. Consider first a tube that is closed at both ends. Granted, such a tube would not be terribly effective as a musical instrument, but the example serves to introduce wave behavior. (In Chapter 11 it will be shown that small rooms can act as closed tubes in the way they treat sound waves.) As longitudinal sound waves oscillate back and forth within the tube, the ends of the tube act as obstacles that prevent any further oscillation outward. Thus, the pressure level is always greatest at the closed end of a tube. A standing wave may be created if pressure oscillations are generated at a wavelength that produces pressure antinodes at the tube ends, as shown in Figure 1–11. The longest wavelength corresponds to twice the tube length, and additional resonant frequencies may be also be created according to Equation 1–2.

$$\lambda = \left(\tfrac{2}{n}\right)L \qquad n = 1, 2, 3, \ldots \qquad\qquad 1\text{–}2$$

The same set of standing waves may be created within a tube that is open at both ends, with the difference that the pressure nodes and antinodes are reversed. At the open end of a tube, any pressure changes introduced within the tube are equalized with the pressure level outside of the tube. The result is that the pressure level is always lowest at the open end of a tube (Figure 1–12).

Thus, the length of a tube that is either open or closed on both ends is one-half the wavelength of the lowest standing wave (fundamental frequency) it may support. Such tubes, therefore, are sometimes called *half-wave resonators.* A flute is a half-wave resonator, as it is a pipe that is open at both ends (the embouchure hole may be considered an open end). Notice from Figures 1–11 and 1–12 that half-wave resonators produce frequencies at all harmonics of the fundamental.

For a tube that is closed on one end and open on another, the fundamental frequency has a wavelength that is four times the length of the tube. All standing waves possible within such a tube have a pressure antinode on the closed end and a pressure node on the open end (Figure 1–13). Standing waves may be created according to

$$\lambda = \left(\tfrac{4}{2n-1}\right)L \qquad n = 1, 2, 3, \ldots \qquad\qquad 1\text{–}3$$

Figure 1–9

Standing Waves

——— Wave traveling from left to right
——— Wave traveling from right to left
━━━ Combination (sum) of the two waves

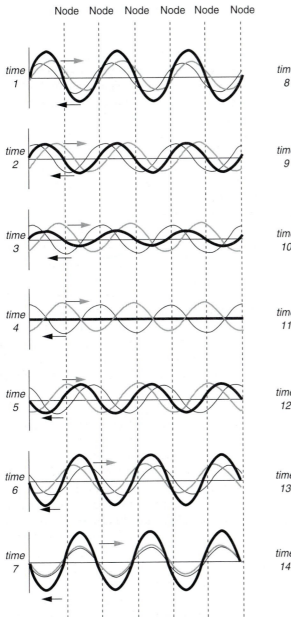

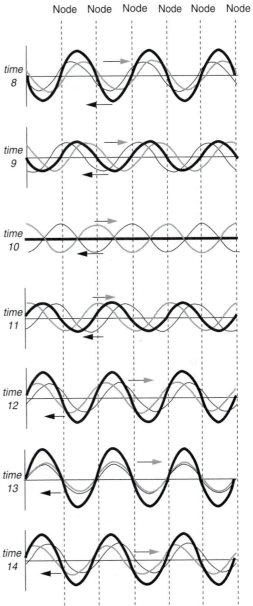

Figure 1–10

Characteristic Frequencies
of a String Bound at Both
Ends

Wavelength
(times string length)

Frequency
(times fundamental)

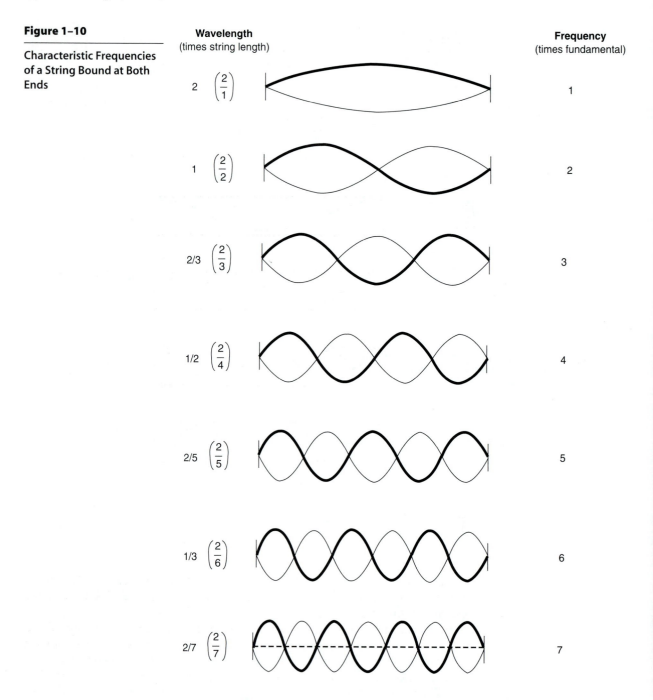

Wavelength		Frequency
2 $\left(\frac{2}{1}\right)$		1
1 $\left(\frac{2}{2}\right)$		2
2/3 $\left(\frac{2}{3}\right)$		3
1/2 $\left(\frac{2}{4}\right)$		4
2/5 $\left(\frac{2}{5}\right)$		5
1/3 $\left(\frac{2}{6}\right)$		6
2/7 $\left(\frac{2}{7}\right)$		7

Notice that the fundamental frequency of the type of resonator shown in Figure 1–13 is half the fundamental frequency of a half-wave resonator, because the fundamental wavelength is twice as long. Since the length of a tube that is open on one end is one-fourth the wavelength of the fundamental, such tubes are sometimes called *quarter-wave resonators*. The figure shows that due to the absence of a pressure node on one end of the tube, even harmonics of the fundamental frequency cannot be sustained, so quarter-wave resonators can support

Figure 1–11

First Five Characteristic Frequencies of a Tube Closed at Both Ends

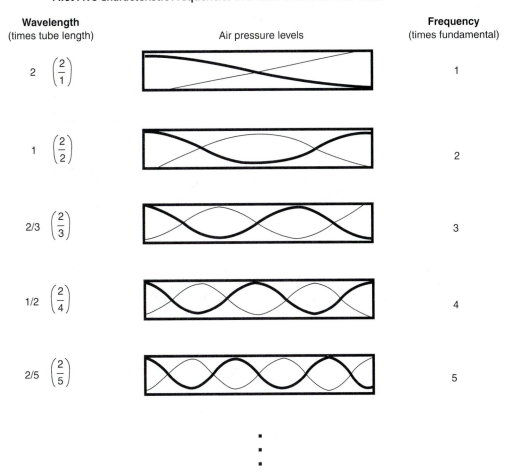

Wavelength (times tube length)	Air pressure levels	Frequency (times fundamental)
2 $\left(\frac{2}{1}\right)$		1
1 $\left(\frac{2}{2}\right)$		2
2/3 $\left(\frac{2}{3}\right)$		3
1/2 $\left(\frac{2}{4}\right)$		4
2/5 $\left(\frac{2}{5}\right)$		5

resonant frequencies at odd harmonics only. Reed instruments such as the clarinet or oboe are examples of quarter-wave resonators, as the reed effectively closes one end of the instrument body.

The examples thus far have examined one frequency at a time within a medium. However, due to the properties of wave superposition discussed earlier, multiple standing waves may be active simultaneously within a tube or on a string. Put another way, simultaneous sets of nodes may coexist within a vibrating medium. This capability is an important aspect of the vibrations produced by musical instruments.

Phase

Phase means "the position of a wave at a certain time." It is an important characteristic of multiple waves traveling within a medium. The interaction of the waves can create a shape that is a composite of the respective waves. If the waves do not start at precisely the same time, the composite shape can appear quite different from any of the individual waves.

Figure 1–12

First Five Characteristic Frequencies of a Tube Open at Both Ends

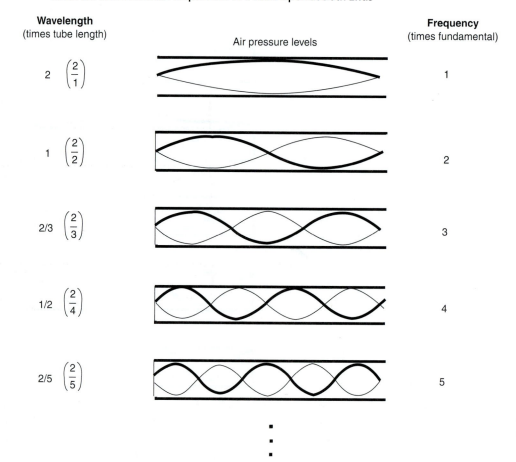

Wavelength (times tube length)	Air pressure levels	Frequency (times fundamental)
2 $\left(\dfrac{2}{1}\right)$		1
1 $\left(\dfrac{2}{2}\right)$		2
2/3 $\left(\dfrac{2}{3}\right)$		3
1/2 $\left(\dfrac{2}{4}\right)$		4
2/5 $\left(\dfrac{2}{5}\right)$		5

If two waveforms at the same frequency do not have simultaneous zero-crossings, they are said to be "out of phase." Figure 1–14 shows an example of two sine waves at the same frequency but at different phases. The dark line shows the superposition of these two waves (their sum). The superposition wave is at the same frequency as the other two but out of phase with them. A phase shift of one-half wavelength results in a reversal of polarity. If the waves in Figure 1–14 were one-half wavelength out of phase, their combined positive and negative polarities would cancel each other out entirely, and the result would be an absence of displacement.

Speed and Velocity

The *speed of sound* in air is approximately 1000 feet per second, or 344 meters per second, with slight variances due to altitude, humidity, and temperature (the speed increases approximately 0.6 meters per second for each increase of 1 degree Celsius). The speed of sound refers to the speed at which sound waves propagate. *Air*

Figure 1–13

First Four Characteristic
Frequencies of a Pipe
Closed at One End

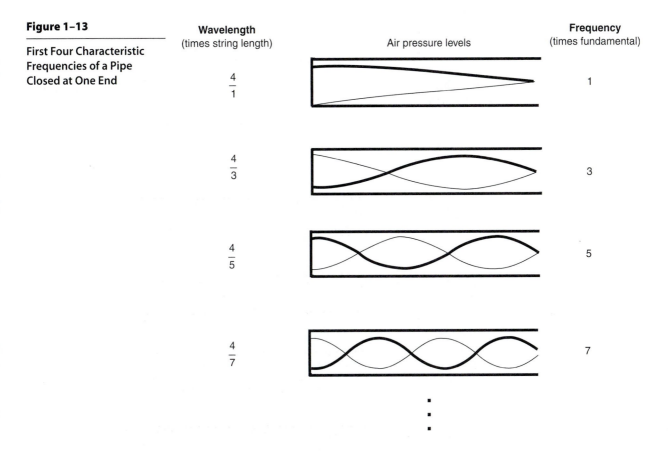

Wavelength (times string length)	Air pressure levels	Frequency (times fundamental)
$\frac{4}{1}$		1
$\frac{4}{3}$		3
$\frac{4}{5}$		5
$\frac{4}{7}$		7

particle velocity refers to the speed at which individual molecules oscillate. Unlike the speed of sound, air particle velocity is not constant, but increases when there is an increase in amplitude and/or frequency—two topics that will be discussed shortly.

There is a precise relationship between air particle velocity and air pressure level. At maximum pressure levels, when air molecules are most compressed, there is little room for air particles to interact, and thus the particle velocity is at a minimum. Similarly, at minimum pressure levels, when the molecules are most rarefied, there is greater empty space between the molecules that also prevents their interaction. Thus, particle displacement is at a minimum when pressure levels are at maximum and minimum. When pressure levels are zero, there is the greatest opportunity for molecules to interact, so the particle displacement is greatest when the air pressure level is at its equilibrium level.

Figure 1–14

Phase

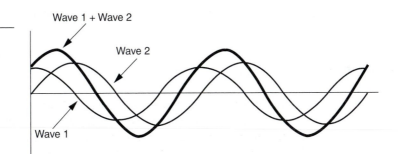

Wave 1 + Wave 2

Wave 2

Wave 1

Figure 1–15

Air Pressure and Air Particle
Velocity

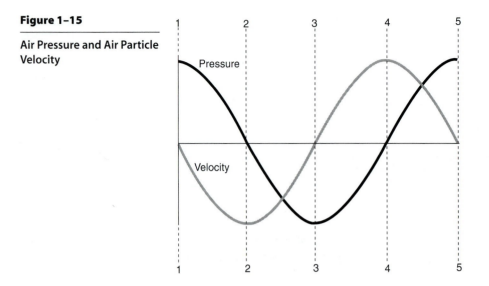

Speed of displacement and direction combined refer to *velocity,* which implies speed in a given direction. The relationship between air pressure and air particle velocity is plotted in Figure 1–15. One period of a harmonic oscillation of pressure is described by a cosine curve; the corresponding oscillations in velocity are described by an inverted sine wave. Thus, it may be said that the velocity curve matches the pressure curve, but with a lag of 90° (one-quarter wavelength).

Notice that when the velocity curve is below the zero line, the pressure curve is moving down, meaning that the pressure level is decreasing and the molecules are moving away from each other. When the velocity curve is above the zero line, the pressure curve is moving up, meaning that the pressure level is decreasing and the molecules are moving toward each other. At point 1, the pressure level is at maximum. The molecules are at their tightest level of compression, and no interaction is possible among the air molecules, meaning that their velocity is zero. As the pressure decreases, the molecules move rapidly away from each other. As the pressure reaches its equilibrium level at point 2, the molecules are at their maximum velocity moving away from the earlier point of high pressure. As the pressure level drops into a state of rarefaction, the speed of the molecules away from each other slows as their greater relative distance lessens their level of interaction. At point 3, the pressure reaches its lowest level and the velocity level is once again zero, as the maximally rarefied molecules are momentarily stopped in their motion away from each other. As the pressure level begins to increase, the molecules reverse direction to move quickly toward each other. As the pressure level reaches equilibrium at point 4, the velocity level is highest as molecules are moving at maximum speed toward each other. The velocity level slows as the molecules begin to pack together until the pressure level reaches its maximum again at point 5, and the velocity slows to zero.

In short, the air particle velocity represents the slope of the pressure curve. (This is what they meant in Calculus I when they taught you that the derivative of a cosine curve is a negative sine curve.)

The figures showing waves within a pipe illustrated pressure changes. Some sources illustrate the same phenomenon in terms of velocity changes, in which case the nodes and antinodes are reversed.

CHAPTER 2

Music and Acoustics

What Is the Difference Between Musical Sound and Noise?

Although every generation has a subjective answer to this question, the difference can also be quantified. Musical sounds typically have a pitch; pitched wave forms are *periodic*, which means that the sound wave generated by a musical instrument repeats regularly. Noise is *aperiodic,* which means that there is no repeating pattern to the wave form and no perceptible pitch to the sound. Both types of sound are illustrated in Figure 2–1. The periodic wave is a *sine wave,* which was discussed in the last chapter. The noise wave shows a type of noise called *white noise,* meaning that all values are completely random. As opposed to a periodic wave, there is no correlation from one point to another in a white noise wave.

Although sine waves are helpful as demonstrations due to their simple harmonic behavior, sine wave sounds are virtually nonexistent in nature. Soft whistling comes close. So do the sounds from tuning forks, high notes played on the recorder, and the tone that accompanies test patterns displayed when television stations stop broadcasting at night.

Properties of Musical Sound

A musical event can be described by four properties. Each can be described subjectively or objectively.

Subjective	Objective
Pitch	Frequency
Volume	Amplitude/power/intensity
Timbre	Overtone content/frequency response/spectrum
Duration in beats	Duration in time

This chapter focuses on each of these properties.

Figure 2-1

Music and Noise

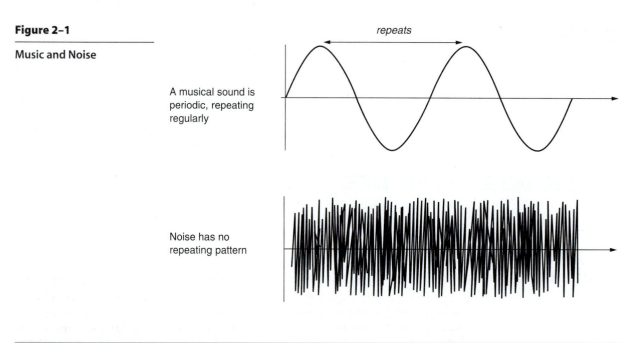

A musical sound is periodic, repeating regularly

Noise has no repeating pattern

Frequency/Pitch

Frequency describes how often a periodic wave repeats itself. It is measured in *cycles per second* or *hertz* (Hz), named after the physicist, Heinrich Hertz (1857–1894). *Pitch* is correlated with frequency: higher frequencies produce higher perceived pitches, while lower frequencies produce lower perceived pitches.

The *wavelength* (λ) or *period,* the distance between corresponding points on the wave, is the inverse of frequency. In Chapter 1, the speed of sound was defined as 1000 feet per second (344 meters per second). The wavelength can be calculated by dividing the speed of sound, *c,* by frequency, *f:*

$$\lambda = \frac{c}{f}$$

2-1

An example is shown in Figure 2–2. As another example, the pitch middle A is 440 Hz (λ = 2.3 ft).

Thus, longer wavelengths correspond to lower frequencies and pitches, while shorter wavelengths correspond to higher frequencies and pitches. This relationship is seen often: longer piano strings are used for the bass notes, longer organ pipes are used for lower notes, larger bells produce lower pitches than small bells, and so on. The maximum frequency range audible to humans is from 20 Hz (λ = 50 ft) to 20,000 Hz, or 20 kHz (λ = 0.05 ft). This upper limit lowers with age; 16–17 kHz is closer to the norm for most adults who do not have hearing impairments.

As an aside, sound wavelengths are significantly larger than light wavelengths. This explains why people can hear sounds around corners but cannot see objects around them. Recall the discussion in the last chapter on reflection and refraction of waves. The long wavelengths of sounds, particularly those in lower ranges, can easily refract around corners, thus remaining audible. Light wavelengths, in contrast, are far too small to refract around any visible surface, and thus objects normally are not visible if they are behind an obstacle.

Figure 2–2

Wavelength

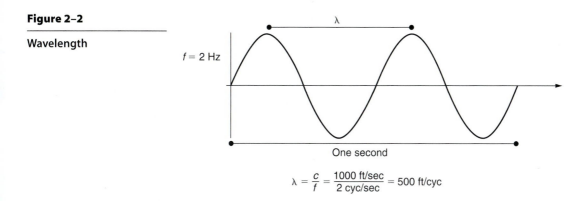

$f = 2$ Hz

λ

One second

$$\lambda = \frac{c}{f} = \frac{1000 \text{ ft/sec}}{2 \text{ cyc/sec}} = 500 \text{ ft/cyc}$$

Frequency Is Objective, Pitch Is Subjective

Frequency is a precise and objective measurement. In contrast, pitch, the assignment of a note name to a frequency, is arbitrary. While 440 Hz is commonly equated with the pitch middle A, many orchestras tune to a frequency of 444 for added "bite" to the sound. In the appendix of Hermann Helmholtz's seminal *On the Sensations of Tone*, there is a table titled "Historical Pitches from Lowest to Highest" in which European church bells that sound the pitch A are listed according to frequency, date, and country. The range of frequencies ranges from 370 Hz to 567.3 Hz, showing that tuning references are a matter of convention, and not a fixed measurement.

Human Pitch Perception Is Logarithmic

This is a critical point concerning the relationship of perceived pitch to frequency. Equivalent pitch intervals are not perceived over equivalent changes in frequency (such as adding a certain number of cycles per second to any given frequency), but rather by equivalent changes in the value of an exponent that describes a frequency. Logarithms will be described more completely in the section "Loudness." For now, simply consider a logarithm to be the same as an exponent, with the distinction that an exponent is an *integer*, while a logarithm may be a decimal value. Integers are numbers within the set of positive whole numbers (1, 2, 3), negative whole numbers (−1, −2, −3), and zero (0).

The top part of Figure 2–3 shows an example of this relationship with one of the primary axioms of music, which is that humans hear an equivalent pitch class with *every* doubling of frequency (the interval of an octave). That is, an octave is traversed whenever the value of a descriptive exponent is increased by 1. Another example is shown in the bottom part of Figure 2–3, which illustrates the construction of the chromatic scale used in Western music. "Twelve-tone equal temperament" refers to the frequency span of an octave being divided into 12 logarithmically (and perceptually) equal increments.

Thus, an equally tempered octave may be constructed by the following steps:

- Choose a starting frequency.
- Multiply it by $2^{n/12}$ for $n = 0$ to 11.
- Higher octaves may be created by doubling each frequency.
- Lower octaves may be created by halving each frequency.

Figure 2–3

The Relationship of Perceived Pitch to Frequency

Frequencies of Successive Octaves of Concert A

55	110	220	440	880	1760	3520
$55 \times 2^{0*}$	55×2^1	55×2^2	55×2^3	55×2^4	55×2^5	55×2^6

Twelve-Tone Equal Temperament

A	A#	B	C	C#	D	D#	E	F	F#	G	G#
$220 \times 2^{\frac{0*}{12}}$	$220 \times 2^{\frac{1}{12}}$	$220 \times 2^{\frac{2}{12}}$	$220 \times 2^{\frac{3}{12}}$	$220 \times 2^{\frac{4}{12}}$	$220 \times 2^{\frac{5}{12}}$	$220 \times 2^{\frac{6}{12}}$	$220 \times 2^{\frac{7}{12}}$	$220 \times 2^{\frac{8}{12}}$	$220 \times 2^{\frac{9}{12}}$	$220 \times 2^{\frac{10}{12}}$	$220 \times 2^{\frac{11}{12}}$
220	233	247	261.6	277	293.6	311	329.6	349.2	370	392	415.3

*Any number to the power of zero equals one.

Loudness

Loudness is correlated with three related but distinct measurements:

- Power
- Amplitude
- Intensity

Power

Recall that as a sound wave travels, molecules themselves are not traveling with the sound wave. What is traveling is an expanding sphere of kinetic energy that displaces molecules as it passes over them. The amount of energy contained in this wave, its *power,* correlates to its perceived loudness.

Air molecules, like any object, are set into motion when *force* is applied to them. The unit of measurement for force is the *newton* (N), named after the mathematician and scientist Sir Isaac Newton (1642–1727). A force of 1 newton applied to an object having a mass of 1 kilogram causes the object to increase its speed (accelerate) by 1 meter per second for as long as the force is applied.

When an object has force applied to it and is displaced, *work* is performed, with work being defined as force times the distance the object moves:

$$\text{work} = \text{force} \times \text{distance}$$

2–2

Work, however, is irrespective of the time involved. Whether an object is moved quickly or slowly, the amount of work done is the same. The term *power* brings time into the equation. For example, when a book is pushed across a tabletop, it may be moved slowly or quickly. In both cases, the same amount of work is done.

But when the book is pushed quickly, more power is applied since the movement is completed in less time.

The unit of measurement for power is watts, W, named after the engineer James Watt (1736–1819). One watt corresponds to 1 newton of work performed per second. Power is defined as

$$\text{power} = \frac{\text{work}}{\text{time}} \qquad\qquad 2\text{--}3$$

Now, since velocity is defined as

$$\text{velocity} = \frac{\text{distance in a given direction}}{\text{time}} \qquad\qquad 2\text{--}4$$

power may be rewritten in terms of velocity by combining Equations 2–2, 2–3, and 2–4:

$$\text{power} = \frac{\text{work}}{\text{time}} = \frac{\text{force} \times \text{distance}}{\text{time}} = \text{force} \times \text{velocity} \qquad\qquad 2\text{--}5$$

Creating a useful scale of sound power levels is complicated by two factors. For one thing, molecules are never completely motionless. There is always some degree of activity among neighboring molecules; there is no level of zero motion by which a given sound's power level may be described in absolute terms. Thus, power levels are measured *comparatively*. The measurement is derived from a ratio that compares the power of a given sound event to a threshold level of little-to-no power.

However, even after determining a threshold, further complications result due to the wide range of audible power levels. The difference in wattage between the softest perceptible sound and the threshold of pain is on the order of a millionfold. To make a more manageable scale of measurement, the scale is therefore not only comparative but also *logarithmic*. The unit of measurement is the *decibel* (dB). The next section will discuss logarithms and the nature of the decibel scale.

The Decibel Scale

Any units of measurement are chosen as a matter of convenience, depending on the scale of what is being measured. The distance from Los Angeles to New York could be described accurately in terms of inches or centimeters, but such small units are not terribly convenient to describe distances of this magnitude; miles or kilometers are usually employed because that scale results in a more manageable number. This is not the case when the distance between stars is measured. For distances of that scale, a larger unit of measurement, the light-year, is commonly employed. By the same token, the distance between hair follicles may also be described in miles, but the resulting fractional number would be too small to have any intuitive value. On smaller scales, inches, centimeters, millimeters, or micrometers are more convenient.

Measurement on a logarithmic scale was discussed briefly in the section on pitch. It was explained that equivalent perceptual pitch changes correspond to equivalent changes in an exponent that describes the difference between two frequencies. Thus, a logarithmic perception of pitch is built into the human auditory system. This section will detail further the nature of a logarithmic scale and how it can make certain measurements more convenient by condensing a large range of values to a smaller range of values. A brief overview of logarithms will explain how this condensing occurs.

Overview of Logarithms   Any number can be expressed in exponential terms, for example:

$$10^2 = 100 \quad \text{or} \quad 10^3 = 1000$$

The subject of logarithms focuses on the exponent. A logarithm is an exponent, with the distinction that an exponent is an integer value, whereas a logarithm may be a decimal value. The two preceding equations ask the question, "This number, raised to that power, results in what value?" When people speak of logarithms, the question is being posed in reverse. Starting with the value, this question is asked: "This value is the result of what power applied to that number (base)?"

The two examples may be rewritten as

$$\log_{10} 100 = 2 \quad \text{and} \quad \log_{10} 1000 = 3$$

(Read: "log to base 10 of 100 equals 2" and "log to base 10 of 1000 equals 3.") Now consider the range of numbers *between* 100 and 1000. With logarithms, exponents that are decimal numbers, any number may be expressed. Two further examples may be written as

$$10^{2.60205999} = 400 \quad \text{or} \quad \log_{10} 400 = 2.60205999$$

$$10^{2.79588002} = 625 \quad \text{or} \quad \log_{10} 625 = 2.79588002$$

Before the age of calculators, logarithms were extremely useful to mathematicians because principles of logarithms simplified a variety of operations. Today's scientific calculators can readily provide values for logarithms, but mathematicians and scientists used to rely on thick books of tables for logarithms ("what power of 10 results in this number?") and *antilogarithms* ("10 to this power results in what number?"). The simplifications that they provided are shown next.

Property 1

$$\log_a(M \times N) = \log_a M + \log_a N$$

(i.e., multiplication can be performed with addition)

Examples:

a. $\log_{10}(1000 \times 10) = \log_{10} 1000 + \log_{10} 10$
$$= 3 + 1$$
$$= \underline{\underline{4}}$$

antilog: $10^4 = 10,000$

b. $\log_{10}(400 \times 625) = \log_{10} 400 + \log_{10} 625$
$$= 2.60205999 + 2.79588002$$
$$= \underline{5.39794001}$$

antilog: $10^{5.39794001} = 250,000$

Property 2

$$\log_a \frac{M}{N} = \log_a M - \log_a N$$

(i.e., division can be performed with subtraction)

Examples:

a. $\log_{10} \dfrac{1000}{10} = \log_{10} 1000 - \log_{10} 10$

$$= 3 - 1$$
$$= \underline{\underline{2}}$$

antilog: $10^2 = 100$

b. $\log_{10} \dfrac{400}{625} = \log_{10} 400 - \log_{10} 625$

$$= 2.60205999 - 2.79588002$$
$$= \underline{\underline{-0.19382}}$$

antilog: $10^{-0.19382} = 0.64$

Property 3

$$\log_a M^n = n \log_a M$$

(i.e., an exponential operation can be performed with multiplication)

Examples:

a. $\log_{10} 100^3 = 3 \log_{10} 100$

$$= 3 \times 2$$
$$= \underline{\underline{6}}$$

antilog: $10^6 = 1{,}000{,}000$

b. $\log_{10} 625^4 = 4 \log_{10} 625$

$$= 4 \times 2.7958002$$
$$= \underline{11.1835201}$$

antilog: $10^{11.1835201} = 152{,}588{,}000{,}000$

Notice from the examples of 400 and 625 expressed as logarithms (2.60205999 and 2.79588002, respectively), the value range from 100 to 1000 may be expressed with values that are between 2.0 and 3.0, thus compacting the terms that express a large range of numbers. In addition to the three properties just listed, this exemplifies another advantage of using a logarithmic scale. Compacting numeric ranges this way is particularly valuable when the range is large, as is the case with audible sound power levels.

Definition of the Decibel   To make the wide range of measurable sound power level values more manageable, Bell Labs created a logarithmic unit of measurement called the bel (named after the inventor of the telephone, Alexander Graham Bell [1847–1922]; hence the unit is abbreviated with a capital *B*).

It was discussed earlier that the scale used for measuring sound power is comparative. In laboratory settings, the lowest audible sine tone at 1 kHz has been found to have a power level of 2×10^{-12} watts, a power threshold notated as W_0, which would cause a mass of 1 kilogram to move 0.000000000002 meters. While power at this magnitude is infinitesimal on a visual scale, it is the threshold level of excitation for a healthy human eardrum.

A sound's power level, *L,* in bels is derived by dividing a measured value, W, by a threshold value, W_0, and then taking the logarithm to base 10 of this ratio:

$$L_W(B) = \log_{10}(W/W_0) \qquad\qquad 2-6$$

However, it turns out that measuring sound power levels in bels tends to result in fractional values, so as a convenience the result is multiplied by 10 and termed the *decibel* (dB).

$$L_W(dB) = 10 \log_{10}(W/W_0) \qquad\qquad 2-7$$

Note that a doubling of power results in an increase of approximately 3 dB, as shown by determining the power level of a sound at twice the level of the threshold:

$$L_W(dB) = 10 \log_{10}\left(\frac{4 \times 10^{-12}}{2 \times 10^{-12}}\right) = 10 \log_{10}(2) = 3.01 \text{ dB}$$

A sound at 13 dB has twice the power of a sound at 10 dB. The level is doubled again at 16 dB, and so on.

Amplitude

Amplitude refers to the degree of fluctuation present in a vibrating object. In the case of a sound, the oscillations are in sound pressure level (SPL), or molecular density. As shown in Figure 1–4, the sound pressure level is in a constant state of variation. The *peak amplitude* refers to the highest point on these curved plots—the maximum change in sound pressure level (or, more generally, the maximum displacement from equilibrium position in a vibrating system). The unit of measurement for sound pressure level is newtons per square meter (N/m^2), also called *pascals* (Pa). In general, any pressure level may be described as

$$\text{pressure} = \frac{\text{force}}{\text{area}} \qquad\qquad 2-8$$

Peak amplitude, however, is not often used as a perceptual reference because sound waves in real life are rarely as regular as the tidy sinusoidal waves in the figures illustrating molecular density. (The complex shapes of real sound waves will be covered in detail in the section on timbre). Sound waves, both in nature and also in audio systems that are prone to occasional electrical inconsistencies, tend to contain spurious peaks and irregularities that may or may not be perceptible. The auditory system does not respond instantaneously to pressure changes, but rather to the average power of a sound over time.

Sound power levels and pressure levels are closely related, but not synonymous. Amplitude, the degree of oscillation of air particles, is for many an easier concept to visualize than acoustic power, which describes how much work oscillating air particles perform on the eardrum. An oscillating object contains a certain amount of energy within its oscillation. How does this oscillation level translate into an energy level? Asked another way: if the energy contained in the object's oscillations (or, in the case of a sound wave, in the air molecules' oscillations) were rechanneled into a forward thrust, how powerful would this thrust be?

The relationship between amplitude and power may be derived by returning to Equation 2–5

$$\text{power} = \text{force} \times \text{velocity} \qquad \qquad 2\text{--}5$$

Recalling that amplitude refers to changes in sound pressure, this equation may be rewritten to reflect the relationship between power and amplitude. First, recall Equation 2–8:

$$\text{pressure} = \frac{\text{force}}{\text{area}} \qquad \qquad 2\text{--}8$$

Provided the area in question remains constant, Equation 2–8 indicates that an increase in pressure results in an increase in force. Thus, pressure is *proportional to* force, which may be written as:

$$\text{pressure} \propto \text{force} \qquad \qquad 2\text{--}9$$

Equation 2–5 may therefore be rewritten by substituting pressure for force, and by changing the equality to a proportionality:

$$\text{power} \propto \text{pressure} \times \text{velocity} \qquad \qquad 2\text{--}10$$

As discussed in the last chapter (Speed and Velocity), air particle velocity increases with amplitude (pressure change). Thus, velocity is proportional to pressure:

$$\text{velocity} \propto \text{pressure} \qquad \qquad 2\text{--}11$$

Making this substitution in Equation 2–10 results in

$$\text{power} \propto \text{pressure} \times \text{pressure} \propto \text{pressure}^2 \qquad \qquad 2\text{--}12$$

Simply put, power is proportional to amplitude squared.

More generally, for any propagating wave—be it mechanical, electrical, or acoustic—the power contained in the wave is proportional to the wave's amplitude squared. The relationship can be similarly derived for other wave types with the factors involved in their propagation.

Since, as has been stated, perceived loudness corresponds to average power over time, a useful measurement of amplitude should also be expressed as an average over a period of time. But a simple averaging of a wave that is regularly positive and negative results in a value of zero. For this reason, amplitude measurements are commonly expressed in terms that equate them with power levels. To do this, amplitude meters give a reading of *rms* (root-mean-square) pressure changes. That is, each periodic amplitude reading is squared so that all values are positive. The mean of these values over a period of time is taken. The square root of the mean then gives a useful measurement of average amplitude. (Readers familiar with statistics may be reminded of the *standard deviation* of a sequence of values, which is derived by a similar process.)

A sine wave has a mean power level over one period of 0.5. (This may be verified by creating a sine wave in a spreadsheet as described in Appendix 1, squaring the values of one period, and taking the mean of these squared values.) The square root of 0.5 is 0.707. Thus, the rms of a sine wave is its peak amplitude value multiplied by 0.707. This rms value is a common acoustical reference.

Amplitude is also measured in decibels, as in Equation 2–7, but with a modification that reflects the equivalent power level. The threshold stimulus is the same as that used to determine the threshold of audible power levels. The power threshold level used in Equation 2–7 translates into a pressure threshold level of 2×10^{-5} Pa, notated p_0. Recalling that power is proportional to the amplitude squared, decibels in watts may be equated to decibels in amplitude by using logarithmic property three:

$$L_W(dB) = 10 \log_{10}(W/W_0) = 10 \log_{10}(p/p_0)^2 = 20 \log_{10}(p/p_0) \qquad 2\text{–}13$$

Thus, Equation 2–13 is used to determine amplitude levels, and Equation 2–7 is used to determine power levels. A doubling of pressure level results in a change of approximately 6 dB in pressure, as can be shown by returning to the example of a pressure level at twice the threshold value:

$$SPL(dB)20 \log_{10}\left(\frac{4 \times 10^{-5}}{2 \times 10^{-5}}\right) = 20 \log_{10}(2) = 6.02 \text{ dB}$$

The following are some typical pressure levels of everyday events:

Soft rustling leaves	10 dB
Normal conversation	60 dB
Construction site	110 dB
Threshold of pain	125 dB

In audio parlance, loudness is frequently equated with amplitude because a volume control adjusts the amplitude (level) of electrical current sent to an amplifier. In terms of perception, power is more closely correlated with perceived loudness than amplitude. However, the quantification of perceived loudness is refined further when the distance of the listener from the sound event is considered.

Intensity

A sound wave is a sphere of energy expanding outward from the sound source. The wave's power corresponds to the energy contained in the sphere's surface. The power remains constant, spread evenly over the surface of the sphere. As the sphere expands to greater distances from the sound event, the power at any given square meter on its surface is less than it was at closer proximity to the source. Thus, perceived loudness depends not only on the sound power level but also the distance of the listener from the sound event.

Power combined with distance is expressed as *intensity, I,* and is measured in watts per square meter (W/m^2). Intensity is also measured in decibels:

$$L_I(dB) = 10 \log_{10}(I/I_0) \qquad 2\text{–}14$$

where $I_0 = 10^{-12}$ W/m^2

Intensity is proportional to power; therefore, intensity is also proportional to amplitude squared.

Timbre

Timbre has historically been the most difficult sound property to describe. Although computer analysis of sounds has brought about more precise definitions, problems remain in creating a definitive description of timbre. Until the 1960s, timbre was most commonly described by what it is not. A typical explanation went along the lines of: "The perceived difference in sound quality when two different instruments play at the same pitch and loudness." Computer analysis has resulted in a definition of timbre based on frequency content.

Figures 1–4, 1–14, 2–1, and 2–2 relied on illustrations of sine waves, even though it was also noted that such wave shapes rarely occur in nature. Sine waves are useful as demonstrations because they represent a wave consisting of only one frequency component. For this reason they are often termed *pure tones.* Natural sounds are more typically composed of a multitude of frequencies. To understand how a wave can be composed of multiple frequencies, consider the behavior of a wave in a bounded medium, such as a string secured at both ends (or air vibrating within a pipe).

When a string is plucked, wave motion is initiated.

The wavelength is twice the length of the string, as shown in Figure 2–4.

The perceived pitch corresponds with the *fundamental frequency,* the speed of sound divided by the wavelength.

The curved shape shown in the figure represents an averaging of the string's maximum deviation. But a more accurate conception of a string's motion is to consider the string as consisting of a number of suspended masses (like popcorn strung together to hang from a Christmas tree, but with masses heavier than popcorn kernels). Imagine a string with only one suspended mass, halfway along its length. When the string is plucked, the mass moves up and down, and the string may be described as having one *mode of vibration.* Now, imagine a string with two suspended masses. When this string is plucked, there are two possibilities: the two masses may move up and down together, or they may move in opposition to each other. (In fact, the string's total motion is likely to be some combination of these two modes of vibration.) Each time a mass is added to the string, another mode of vibration is introduced.

Now, consider a string to consist of an extremely large number of small masses. When the string is excited, there are many simultaneous and independent vibrations and frequencies occurring along the string. When the string is set into motion, the initial frequency content is theoretically infinite. However, the bounded nature of the string eventually limits the range of frequencies the string can support. The only stable mode of vibration for a string is one that consists of frequencies that have wavelengths that correspond to standing wave nodes. All other frequencies are cancelled out. Thus, only the string's resonant frequencies, or harmonics, based on integer subdivisions of the wavelength (or inversely, on integer multiples

Figure 2–4

Wavelength of a Vibrating String

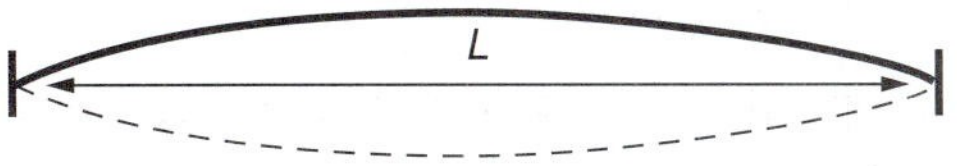

$\lambda = 2L; f = 330/2L$

of the fundamental frequency) can continue to propagate, as shown in Figure 2–5 (notice the similarity with Figure 1–10).

Harmonic frequencies create a *linear* progression, being successive multiples of the fundamental. Because equivalent pitches are produced by successive exponential intervals, harmonics are not all at the same pitch. Thus, the natural result of vibrations in a bounded medium is a complex vibration consisting of a number of component frequencies and pitches.

The Harmonic Series and Intonation

Harmonics are numbered beginning with the fundamental. The fundamental is considered the first harmonic. The first six harmonics are usually the strongest:

220	440	660	880	1100	1320
Fundamental	Octave	Perfect fifth	Octave	Major third	Perfect fifth

People can learn *analytic listening,* which involves learning to "hear out" the individual harmonics of a plucked string.

The intervals of the harmonic series, shown in the bottom row of the table, are obtained by *normalizing* each frequency so that it lies between the fundamental, f (220 Hz in the table), and an octave higher, $2f$ (440 Hz in the table). Pitch class identity is maintained when a frequency is transposed by octaves, either by raising it an octave with a multiplication of 2 or by lowering it an octave with a multiplication of $1/2$.

In the harmonic series, intervals may be identified by halving each frequency as many times as is necessary for the frequency to fall between the fundamental and the next octave, in this case between 220 and 440 Hz. Treating the third and sixth harmonics in this fashion, they are transposed to a frequency of 330 Hz, a ratio of $3/2$ to the fundamental, corresponding to a perfect fifth. Treating the fifth

Figure 2–5

Four Harmonics of a Plucked String

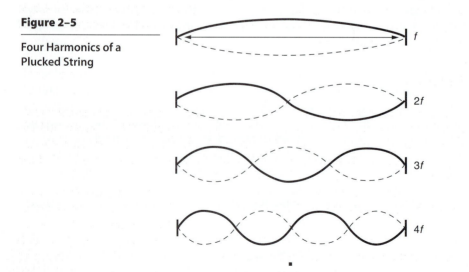

harmonic in this fashion transposes it to a frequency of 275 Hz, a ratio of 5/4 to the fundamental, corresponding to a major third.

These ratios are an example of *just intonation,* a tuning system that relies on simple integer ratios to derive each interval of a musical scale. (*Temperament* refers to a scale in which the ratios of each pitch to the fundamental are irrational numbers; tuning or *intonation* refers to a scale consisting of simple integer ratios such as those mentioned.) These intervals are approximated by the system of equal temperament shown in Figure 2–3. But the difference between an interval in just intonation and in twelve-tone equal temperament may be audible. Just intervals are noticeably more consonant than equal-tempered intervals. The major third, in particular, is nearly a quarter tone sharper in twelve-tone equal temperament than its just ratio. However, just intervals do not represent equal subdivisions of the octave, and thus it becomes difficult to modulate keys in just intonation. Equal temperament represents a compromise in consonance that allows composers to modulate freely from one key to another, a hallmark of Western common practice music.

Harmonics in Performance

Harmonics are well known to many instrumentalists. String players are taught to dampen strings to produce harmonics. Dampening a string at half its length is not the same as pressing the finger fully onto the string, which effectively shortens it and causes it to vibrate at a higher fundamental frequency. By dampening the string with more gentle pressure from the finger, the string as a whole continues to vibrate, but the fundamental vibration is suppressed due to the dampening, and therefore only frequencies from the second harmonic sound. Dampening the string at one-third its length dampens all frequencies below the third harmonic, and so on.

Brass instruments are constructed to produce tones that are harmonics of the tube that composes the instrument. Through embouchure and breath control, a player produces successive harmonics of the tube length. By depressing the instrument's valves, extra lengths of tube are opened, thus lengthening the total tube length. The pitch is lowered and a set of harmonics based on this lower fundamental becomes possible.

A Partial by Any Other Name . . .

The discussion of harmonics shows one reason why instruments and natural sounds usually contain many frequencies above the fundamental. These additional frequencies, as part of the total sound, are termed *partials.* The first partial is the fundamental. The relative levels of the partials that compose an instrument's tone play a large part in creating an instrument's timbre.

Harmonics refer to that set of partials that are integer multiples of the fundamental frequency. Partials are not necessarily harmonic. Bell sounds, for example, typically contain a number of inharmonic partials that are determined by the size and composition of the bell. Another term, *overtones,* refers only to partials above the fundamental, thus the first overtone corresponds to the second partial. The set of frequencies produced by an instrument (or any vibrating object) is called its *spectrum.*

Resonance

An instrument's partials originate not only from harmonics of its fundamental vibration but also from the vibrations of the instrument's body. It is these vibrations that enable the sound of an instrument to fill a concert hall.

Any object, when struck, vibrates at a characteristic (resonant) frequency, as discussed earlier ("Standing Waves"). This frequency is said to be the *characteristic frequency,* or *resonant frequency,* of the object. But objects do not have to be struck to begin vibrating. Any disturbance of air molecules near an object causes molecules to vibrate against it. Normally, these vibrations have no effect on a stationary object. However, if the air near the object is made to vibrate at the object's resonant frequency (or at a harmonic of the resonant frequency), the vibrations striking the object at its special characteristic frequency cause the object to fall into *sympathetic vibration* with the air molecules. The cliché of an opera singer's voice breaking a glass is a reference to the resonant frequency of the glass. In theory, if a singer were able to maintain a clear and consistent tone at the resonant frequency of a thin glass, the glass would fall into sympathetic vibration with the singer's tone and shatter.

The reason that a Stradivarius violin sounds different from a cheap dime-store fiddle has primarily to do with the choice of materials and the craft that went into its assembly. A Stradivarius was constructed with surgical precision, with the finest woods cut to particular shapes and thicknesses and joined with special adhesives. The result is that different areas of the violin's body have different resonant frequencies that join the strings in vibration when they are played. It is the spectrum of frequencies that is activated by playing the instrument that creates its characteristic sound. These frequencies are a constant presence in the instrument's tone. Regardless of the pitch being played, the spectrum of the instrument always has these fixed spectral peaks. Fixed spectral peaks of this type are also called *formants.*

The Fourier Analysis

The mathematician Jean Baptiste Fourier (1768–1830) is responsible for the proof of a critical tenet of wave theory that underlies much of the physics of music:

> All complex periodic waves may be expressed as the sum of a series of sinusoidal waves.
>
> These sinusoidal waves are all harmonics of the fundamental.
>
> Each harmonic has its own amplitude and phase.

The decomposition of a complex wave into its harmonic components, its *spectrum,* is known as a *Fourier analysis.* Because the process is labor-intensive mathematically, this text treats Fourier transform as a "black box": put a periodic, complex wave in, and a spectrum comes out. It is analogous to directing white light through a prism and observing the rainbow that comes out as the white light is broken into its spectral components. A Fourier analysis is completely reversible. A second "black box" is an *inverse Fourier transform,* which does the same thing in reverse: put a spectrum in, and the original complex wave is reproduced.

Spectral Plots

Given that sounds are typically composed of many frequencies, it is often more useful to represent complex waveforms with a *spectral* plot as opposed to a time domain plot. A comparison is shown in Figure 2–6. In the top left portion of the figure, a time domain plot shows amplitude changes over time, similar to those shown earlier. But this wave is more complex than the sine waves shown earlier, and it is difficult to describe the wave in terms of its frequency content. The top right portion of the figure shows the spectrum of the waveform. From the spectrum it is easy to see that the complex wave consists of the fundamental, the third harmonic at one-third the amplitude of the fundamental, and the seventh harmonic at one-half the amplitude of the fundamental.

The time domain and spectral domain plots are both two-dimensional, showing one property as a function of another. The two may be combined in a *spectrogram* plot, where both frequency and amplitude are shown as a function of time. A spectrogram plot is shown in the bottom portion of the figure. In a spectrogram, frequency is illustrated as a function of time, with higher frequencies appearing at higher vertical positions. Amplitude is represented by darkness level. In this plot, three predominant horizontal bands represent the three harmonics of the

Figure 2–6

Comparison of Time Domain and Spectral Domain Plots

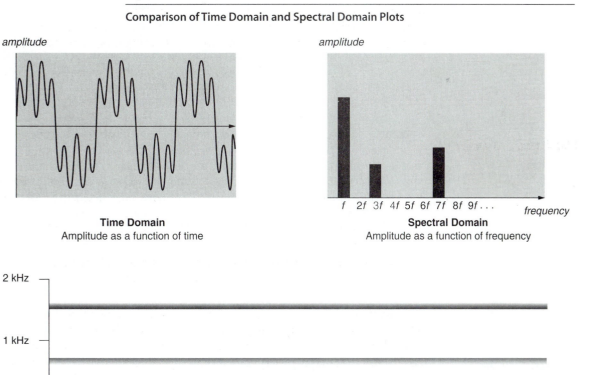

amplitude

Time Domain
Amplitude as a function of time

amplitude

f   2f   3f   4f   5f   6f   7f   8f   9f . . .   *frequency*

Spectral Domain
Amplitude as a function of frequency

Spectrogram
Frequency + amplitude as a function of time

complex wave. The bottom band, representing the fundamental, is darkest, as this is the spectral component with the highest amplitude. The next band, representing the third harmonic, is lighter as it has one-third the darkness of the fundamental. The highest band, representing the seventh harmonic, is one-half the darkness of the fundamental.

What Is the Difference Between Consonance and Dissonance?

This subjective question may also be addressed quantitatively with the aid of spectral plots. When pure tones of differing frequencies are sounded simultaneously, the perceptual effect differs depending on the frequency difference between the tones. When the frequencies are close together, usually within 10 Hz of each other, only one pitch is perceived. The perceived frequency is the average of the two tones, and the volume oscillates at a rate that corresponds to the frequency difference. For example, when a frequency of 440 Hz is combined with a frequency of 444 Hz, the perceived frequency is 442 Hz, and there is a perceptible volume oscillation at 4 Hz.

If the frequency difference between two tones is increased, the volume oscillation becomes more rapid. Eventually, it becomes impossible to perceive them as oscillations; instead, there is a perceptual "roughness." This range of frequency proximity, characterized by oscillations and roughness, is known as the *critical band*. As frequency differences move outside of the critical band, the two tones become autonomous and are perceived as two separate pitches. This quality of beating and roughness is why composers generally do not write thick chords in the bass ranges. At lower pitches, the frequency proximity of pitches is much closer, and the resultant beating and roughness often produces a "muddy" sound. The same pitches in combination in higher ranges, however, have greater frequency separation and thus sound clearer when combined.

A physical definition of consonance and dissonance, based on the perceptual effects of frequency proximity, is illustrated in Figure 2–7. When two tones are separated by an octave, all harmonics coincide. When two tones are separated by a perfect fifth, many of their harmonics coincide. It is easy to see why these intervals are considered consonant. There is a smooth aural blend between the two tones due to their overlap in harmonic content. When two tones are separated by a major second, few (if any) harmonics coincide. But harmonics from the two tones frequently fall within each other's critical band, the result being a beating or roughness that is perceived as dissonance.

Before the invention of electronic tuning devices, piano tuners tuned instruments by listening for beats between simultaneous pitches. They obtained the desired pitch relationships by counting the beats per second when two notes were played in combination, and made the necessary adjustments until all intervals were correct. Some musicians still prefer the work of tuners who work primarily by trained listening skills.

Making Waves: Building Blocks of Sound Synthesis

Classic sound synthesis relies on building blocks that are typically expressed in terms of wave type and spectrum. Synthesizers produce sound waves with *oscillators*. In addition to oscillators that produce noise and sine waves, four other basic

Figure 2-7

Spectra of Coincident Tones

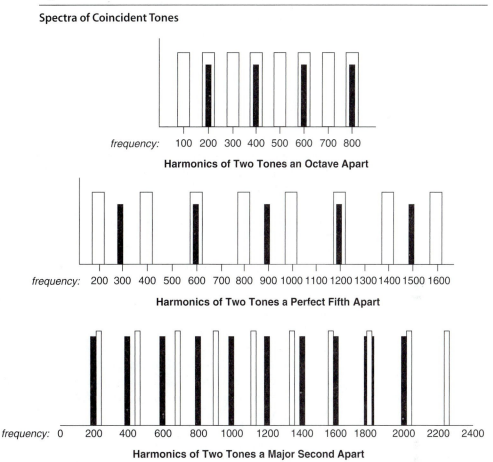

frequency: 100 200 300 400 500 600 700 800

Harmonics of Two Tones an Octave Apart

frequency: 200 300 400 500 600 700 800 900 1000 1100 1200 1300 1400 1500 1600

Harmonics of Two Tones a Perfect Fifth Apart

frequency: 0   200   400   600   800   1000   1200   1400   1600   1800   2000   2200   2400

Harmonics of Two Tones a Major Second Apart

oscillators produce sawtooth, square, triangle, and impulse train waves. These wave shapes and their spectra are shown in Figure 2–8. With the invention of the modular analog synthesizer in the 1960s, these waveforms were produced by audifying changes in electrical voltage. A sine wave oscillator produced a sine tone via a voltage that alternated according to a sine-shaped pattern. A sawtooth oscillator's change in voltage over time was linear in one direction, immediately returned to its original position, and then returned to a linear rate of change. A square wave oscillator's current moved at a constant speed in one direction, then reversed. A triangle wave oscillator's voltage alternated between high and low levels, similar to a sine wave except that the voltage change over time was linear rather than sinusoidal. Computer-based sound synthesis also employed the impulse train oscillator, which produced periodic, instantaneous amplitude bursts with zero amplitude between them.

The wave shapes in Figure 2–8 are idealized. For one thing, all harmonics are in phase. Their waveforms would look very different if the harmonics were not in phase, although they would not sound any different (a topic that will be discussed in Chapter 3). Also, large changes in voltage cannot occur instantaneously.

Figure 2–8

Waveforms Used in Classic Sound Synthesis

Sawtooth

Wave shape

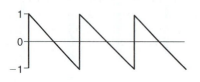

Spectrum

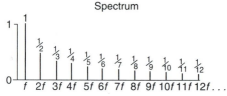

All harmonics, at amplitudes that are the
inverse of the harmonic number

Square*

Wave shape

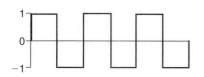

Spectrum

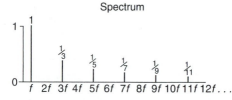

Odd harmonics, at amplitudes that are the
inverse of the harmonic number

Triangle

Wave shape

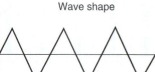

Spectrum

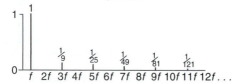

Odd harmonics, at amplitudes that are the
inverse square of the harmonic number

Impulse Train

Wave shape

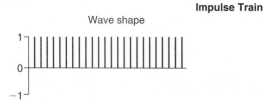

Spectrum

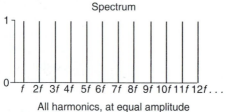

All harmonics, at equal amplitude

*A square wave is an example of a *pulse wave*, which alternates regularly between positive and negative values. A pulse wave is described by its *duty cycle*, which is the ratio of the positive part of each cycle to the entire cycle. In general, a duty cycle of 1 : *n* produces harmonics with amplitudes that are the inverse of the harmonic number, with every *n*th harmonic removed. A square wave is a pulse wave with a duty cycle of 1 : 2, which produces a spectrum with every second harmonic absent.

Thus, the vertical lines in reality have a finite slope. Lastly, such idealized shapes illustrate a series of harmonics that extends to infinity. The waves look somewhat different when there is a limit to their frequency range. Figures 2–9 and 2–10 show square and sawtooth waves that are sums of their first five component partials. Both shapes show pronounced ripples. As more harmonics are added, the ripples lessen and the overall shape approaches the angularity shown in Figure 2–8, but in practical terms there is always some degree of ripple in any synthesized waveform. Synthesis techniques will be discussed in Chapter 13.

Figure 2–9

The First Five Partials of a Square Wave

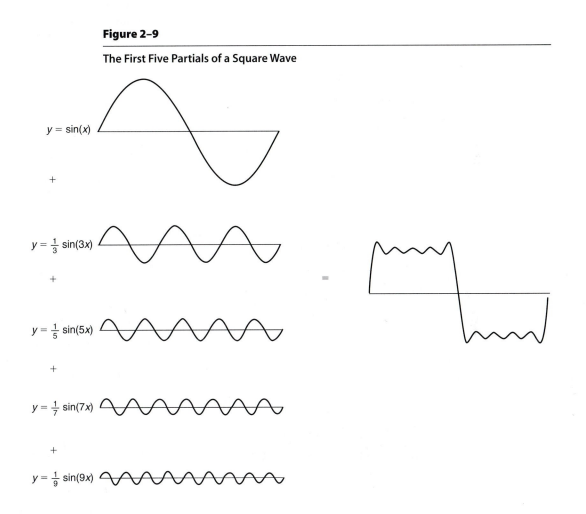

Figure 2–10

The First Five Partials of a Sawtooth Wave

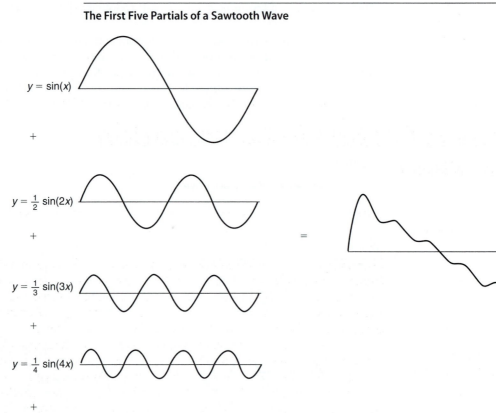

CHAPTER 3

Acoustic Factors in Combination

Perceptual Issues

Sound in Time

Human perception of sound and music events is largely determined by the behavior of frequencies and their amplitudes over time. The plots in Figure 2–6 represent unchanging complex waves with a set of harmonics at a constant level. Real sounds are not so consistent. The presence or absence of partials changes over the duration of a sound event, as do the amplitudes of these partials.

The shape of the amplitude changes over time in the sound of a particular instrument is known as the *amplitude envelope.* An approximation of the amplitude envelopes of three different instruments is shown in Figure 3–1. The sound of most instruments begins with an initial *transient,* or *attack,* portion. The transient is characterized by many high partials mixed with noise. For example, the scraping of a bow on a violin or the *chiff* of breath from a flute both have high noise content. Eventually, the instruments begin to vibrate and a pitch becomes audible. An instrument's distinctive sound is determined primarily by this transient portion. A common exercise in electronic music classes used to be for students to record the sound of a note from the piano. Students were then instructed to take a razor blade and remove the attack portion of the sound from the tape. The lesson of listening to the sound without the attack was that it was very difficult to identify the sound as originating from a piano when it was missing its attack segment.

Following the transient, instruments usually produce a *steady-state,* or *sustained,* sound. In contrast to the attack, the steady state is characterized by periodicity. From the Fourier theorem, this implies that the steady state is composed of a harmonic spectrum. Figure 3–2 shows the spectrogram of a tone from a vibraphone at a pitch of A at 440 Hz. It is easy to recognize the additional harmonics and noise that characterize the attack that results from the mallet strike and the small number of harmonics that constitute the steady-state segment.

Localization of Natural Events

The auditory system localizes everyday sound events using three factors: *interaural time delay, spectral shadows,* and *pinnae filtering.* Interaural time delay is most active for frequencies below 1500 Hz. When a sound occurs directly from the front, there

Figure 3–1

Amplitude Envelopes

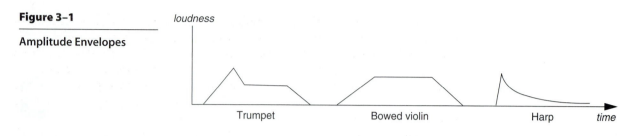

is an equal distance from the sound source to both ears. When a sound occurs to one side, the wavefront must travel a greater distance to reach the farther ear. This delay, on the order of microseconds, between the near and the far ear is the cue used by the auditory system to make an estimation of a sound's point of origin.

When sounds occur at frequencies over 1500 Hz, the wavelength is shorter than the width of the human head (7″ or 17 cm). Frequencies below 1500 Hz refract around the head to reach the farther ear, while higher frequencies are reflected off the head. The result is a spectral shadow at the farther ear in which there is less high-frequency content. This shadowing effect is the predominant localization cue for higher frequencies.

Elevation is judged by changes in a sound's frequency content that are due to reflections off the outer ears (the pinnae). As sound wavefronts reflect off the shoulders, reflections off the outer ear cause a series of reflections at varying delays before the wavefront enters the ear canal. The superposition of these reflections causes *filtering,* a shaping of the overall spectrum that enters the ear. The elevation level of the sound determines the type of spectral shaping that occurs.

Simulated Localization in Audio Systems

In theory, stereo audio systems could re-create the effects of localization by delaying a signal in one stereo channel. Time delay would be impractical, however, because it would require that listeners remain in a "sweet spot" equidistant between the speakers, a degree of care only exercised by the most stringent of audiophiles.

Figure 3–2

Spectrogram of a Vibraphone at 440 Hz

The instrument's sound is characterized by the fundamental at 440 Hz and the third harmonic at 1320 Hz. The attack also contains noise below 2 kHz, the seventh harmonic at 3080 Hz, and the eleventh harmonic at 4840 Hz. Once the steady-state portion sets in, the third harmonic fades first, followed by a fading of the fundamental.

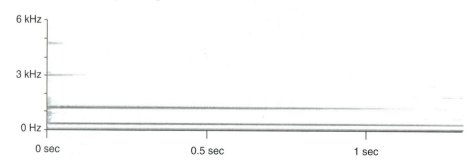

Instead, localization effects are simulated through differences in loudness between two channels. In a multispeaker system, a sound emanating from one speaker sounds as though it originates from that speaker. A sound produced at equal volume from two speakers is perceived as a "phantom image" placed in space between them. Changing the volume balance between two speakers causes the phantom image to "drift" toward the louder speaker. Thus, the perceived sound stage may span the area between the speakers.

Volume controls on audio equipment adjust the amplitude level of the signal. The perceived loudness, however, is based on the power of the signal at the listener's position. For certain types of effects, the relationship between amplitude and power becomes critical. One such effect is that of apparent motion, a sound moving from one side to the other. This is achieved by a volume crossfade between stereo channels, which is controlled by a *panning potentiometer* (*pan pot* for short), a knob that may be rotated to the right or left to indicate a desired stereo placement. Typically, the desired effect is to simulate motion of an object that appears to maintain a constant distance from the listener, as shown in Figure 3–3.

For the perceived distance to remain constant, the total power emitted by the two speakers must remain constant during the crossfade. The total power of the soundfield consists of the sum of each speaker's amplitude level squared (recall Equation 2–12). As shown in the top portion of Figure 3–3, this is achieved by amplitude changes that correspond to a quarter period of a sinusoidal pattern, rather

Figure 3–3

Constant Power vs. Linear
Panning Effects

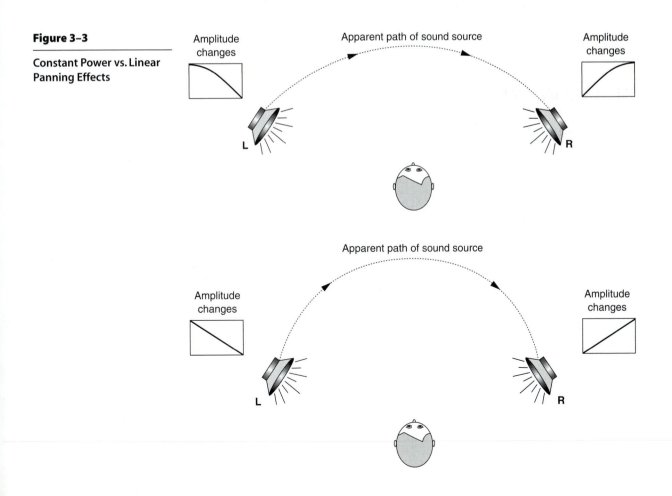

Amplitude changes

Apparent path of sound source

Amplitude changes

Apparent path of sound source

Amplitude changes

Amplitude changes

than a linear crossfade pattern. The sinusoidal amplitude pattern ensures that the total power remains at the full desired level (100% of the level, or a constant value of 1), due to the trigonometric identity

$$\sin^2 \theta + \cos^2 \theta = 1 \qquad\qquad 3\text{--}1$$

On the other hand, a linear crossfade creates a dip in the overall power level at the midpoint of the fade. At the midpoint, the total power, being the sum of the two speakers' amplitudes squared, is

$$\left(\frac{1}{2}\right)^2 + \left(\frac{1}{2}\right)^2 = \frac{1}{2}$$

This decreased power level has implications for the perceived distance of the object.

The perceived distance is dependent on the intensity at the listener's position. Assuming the listener remains stationary during the power changes just described, the change in intensity corresponds to the change in power. Perceived distance is determined by *the inverse square law,* which in this case states that the change in intensity, *I,* is proportional to 1 over the change in distance, *D,* squared:

$$I \propto \frac{1}{D^2} \qquad\qquad 3\text{--}2$$

A change in intensity of one-half implies that

$$\frac{1}{2} \propto \frac{1}{D^2} \quad \text{ or } \quad D^2 \propto 2$$

Thus, the perceived distance at the midpoint of a linear pan is $\sqrt{2}$, or 1.414 . . ., times the perceived distance at the beginning and end points of the crossfade. The apparent path of a linear fade is shown in the bottom portion of Figure 3–3. This nonuniform rendition of distance is known as the "hole in the middle" effect. Stereo panning controls on audio equipment produce a sinusoidal change in amplitude between channels to maintain a uniform perceived distance.

Mismatches Between Measurement and Perception

Having discussed basic acoustic properties in isolation, their perceptual effects in combination may now be considered. It is the combination of these elements that characterizes what is heard. Yet many times auditory events are perceptually more than the sum of their parts. Some of these aspects will now be reexamined, with an emphasis on how their effects may vary according to the context in which they are heard.

Phase

Figure 2–8 illustrates examples of wave shapes that correspond to various spectra. If the relative phases of a steady-state tone—such as in Figure 2–6—are altered, there is usually no perceptible change in sound, although the shape of the wave may change noticeably. Thus, adding spectral components to a sound changes the shape of the wave, but a change in wave shape does not necessarily produce a change in spectral content. This phenomenon, while it may be counterintuitive, makes sense when viewed from an evolutionary perspective. Consider the example of two musicians playing a duet on the same instruments. If one of them should take a step backwards or forwards, the phase relationship of the sounds emanating from these instruments would change. If this change in phases were to result in a significant change in the character of the sound, a concert could be a very inconsistent auditory event unless the musicians were careful to remain motionless during the performance. Generalizing this phenomenon, life would be extremely confusing if combinations of sounds in the environment changed along with slight changes of distance among sound sources. So it is likely that evolution is responsible for this characteristic of phase being imperceptible for steady-state sounds.

The previous paragraph might suggest that phase is perceptually inconsequential. But this is not the case. The behavior of spectral components during the attack segment of a sound is likely to be far more complex than in the steady-state segment. Changing the phase of attack components can change the character of the attack. Solo performance sounds different from group performance because no two players can ever sound at exactly the same time; thus the attack from the two instruments is blurred. Because an instrument's characteristics are defined primarily by its attack (as discussed in the section "Sound and Time"), the phase of attack components is critical to the character of the sound. In Chapter 9 it will be seen that the treatment of a signal's phases is critical in the evaluation of audio filters.

Timbre

Timbre has been discussed as being the result of spectral content. But in truth this is only part of the explanation. Timbre is also the result of a sound's envelope. Research in sound synthesis has shown the envelope shape to be more definitive to a synthesized instrument's verisimilitude than an exact match of spectral content. When creating simulations of instrumental tones, it is far more important to synthesize an accurate facsimile of the instrument's envelope. Once that is achieved, a simple approximation of the instrument's partials will suffice for listeners to recognize the imitation of an instrument.

In the section "Sound and Time," it was mentioned that the attack portion is critical to the definition of a sound. Research has shown that sounds with a faster attack are often described as "brighter," a quality that also is described for tones possessing power in high-frequency overtones. Thus, a fast attack can be perceptually confused with the presence of high partials.

Considerable research has gone into the creation of "timbre space," a multidimensional plot in which timbres are placed according to overtone content, envelope, and attack time. Despite these efforts, a precise definition of timbre remains elusive, and there is no definitive scale of measurement for timbral characteristics. Timbre is best described as an *emergent property,* meaning that is not a single parameter in and of itself, but arises as a consequence of a number of other parameters working in combination.

Loudness

The perception of loudness is also an emergent property that eludes precise definition. While intensity is the measurement most closely correlated to loudness, the perception of volume is based on a number of factors, not all of them entirely measurable.

One factor is that perceived loudness is frequency dependent. Figure 3–4 shows a set of Robinson-Dadson curves (an update to the set of equal loudness curves first presented by Fletcher and Munson in the 1930s) that illustrates perceived equal loudness of sine tones. It is clear from the figure that the auditory system is more responsive to changes in power with frequencies near 1 kHz. (This corresponds to the range of human speech.) At higher and lower frequencies, a far greater change in power is required to create a perceptually equivalent change in loudness. This is why many stereo receivers have a loudness knob. It is meant to give added boost to low frequencies so that when music is played at low volumes the bass ranges are not perceived at disproportionately low levels.

Another curiosity is that within close frequency ranges, perceived loudness is proportional to the cube root of intensity. For example, two violins playing the same pitch generate twice the intensity of one violin, but do not sound twice as loud. To achieve twice the volume, eight violins are required (since $2^3 = 8$). If two instruments are playing two different pitches, however, the perceived loudness matches the doubling of intensity.

Adding to the perceptual mix is the fact that perceived loudness is also *bandwidth* dependent. Increasing the bandwidth (frequency content) of a synthesized sound often results in listeners describing the sound as "louder," even if the intensity is kept constant.

Psychologists have experimented with a variety of scales in attempts to classify perceived loudness. But despite these efforts, no one has succeeded in creating a definitive perceptual scaling system for loudness. Some have argued that estimation of loudness is not automatic (measurable), but depends on a number of higher-

Figure 3–4

Robinson-Dadson Curves

From *Principles of Digital Audio*, 3rd ed., by Ken Pohlmann (1995), McGraw-Hill. Reprinted with the permission of McGraw-Hill Companies.

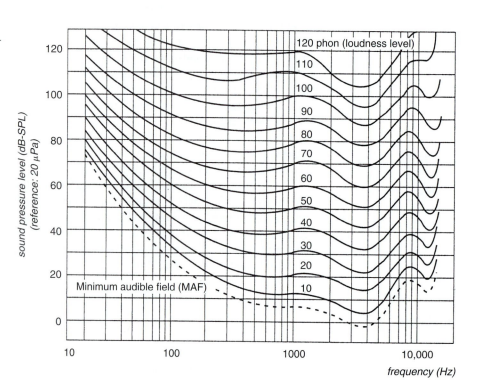

level estimations of distance, import, context, etc. B. C. J. Moore recalls a citation of Hermann Helmholtz:

> . . . we are exceedingly well trained in finding out by our sensations the objective nature of the objects around us, but we are completely unskilled in observing these sensations per se; and the practice of associating them with things outside of us actually prevents us from being distinctly conscious of the pure sensations.

Conclusion

Objective measurements can describe a great deal about sound events, but, as discussed above, they can also fail to describe many perceptual issues. Therefore, a grasp of objective measurements not only increases knowledge of acoustic events but also provides insight into what is not known.

This book will examine musical content in technical terms, and in so doing yield many new insights into how music may be considered. At the same time, technical terms will never do the job entirely. There is no technical explanation that can adequately address the emotional power of a Beethoven symphony or the sublime heights of a Louis Armstrong improvisation. Reducing music to technical terms, to the extent that it is possible to do so, only brings about a greater appreciation of the magic of musical genius. This appreciation is the result of knowing what can and what cannot be explained objectively.

CHAPTER 4

Introduction to Computers

During the last decades of the twentieth century, computers evolved from being massive, high-end research machines—viewed by the general public primarily through the lenses of science fiction books and movies—to small and inexpensive devices that are a ubiquitous part of everyday life. Computer technology is inherent in everything from wristwatches to calculators, microwave ovens, bank teller machines, and automobile parts. It is difficult to imagine anyone going through a normal day without having some kind of interaction with a computer. Musical instruments are no exception, and this book will focus primarily on how computers play a role in musical instruments and music production. Computer technology is advancing at rates that astonish even those who are at its cutting edge. The only thing that can be certain is that over time computers will continue to become smaller and faster and have increased capacity for storing information.

Despite the advancements, computers remain primarily what they have always been: fast idiots, capable of performing calculations much faster and more accurately than humans can. Computer data consist of numbers assigned to memory locations that are analogous to post office boxes. Memory refers to how many post office boxes are available. Computer programs are sequences of instructions that carry out arithmetical operations on data.

Peripherals are devices that allow the computer to interact with the outside world when manipulating data, either by sending directions to other devices—such as a printer or monitor—or by receiving directions from a human user—via devices such as a keyboard or mouse. Subsequent chapters will explore peripherals created by and for musicians.

Instructions used to be entered by typing text onto a command line displayed on a monitor. Now, *graphical user interfaces* (GUIs) are far more common, allowing users a more intuitive method of entering instructions by clicking the mouse, dragging objects on a virtual desktop, and selecting commands from a menu. Computers are now designed to have visual appeal and to present engaging work environments that incorporate sound and moving images.

Multimedia

Traditionally, this term has referred to performances that incorporated a variety of presentation formats. For example, a dance performance that also featured video, live music, and a laser light show might be described as a "multimedia performance."

The term could also refer to the different storage and delivery methods for different types of material. Music was stored on vinyl records or tape. Video was stored on another type of tape format. Animation was created by hand and stored on video or film.

All of these time-based media can now be stored digitally, in the form of numbers. Once they are in numeric form, they may be stored and manipulated in a computer. Thus, computer workstations are blurring traditional distinctions among media types. Music, video, animation, and graphics may be imported into a multimedia production program and combined in ways that were either impossible or extremely expensive before computers.

Multimedia learning tools now abound in all fields, music being no exception. Educational material can be presented in a manner akin to a computer game, with animated graphics and interactive environments in which users may click on an icon to be taken to a new setting or lesson. Music CD-ROMs can display simultaneous text, photos, audio, and notated music on a screen describing the work of a composer. Or they can offer introductions to instrument types, allowing students to click on a map of the world, go to a menu of instruments from the region selected, and see photographs and hear recordings of the instruments. Other multimedia programs may allow users to "produce" a multitrack piece of music via a software mixing board or to create a piece out of a selection of stored sound clips. Subsequent chapters will discuss in greater detail how music may be digitized and stored to a CD or CD-ROM.

The Internet

The World Wide Web

This historical period has been dubbed "The Information Age" due to the fact that more information is available more quickly than ever before. This observation is perhaps nowhere more evident than on the World Wide Web. The Web has revolutionized the way people conduct business, do research, shop, communicate, and invest (although perhaps it has not revolutionized commerce as much as many dot-commers anticipated). A Web site is now considered synonymous with a business's identity. Although some fear that large Web sites allow large companies to overshadow small ones, there are many examples of the opposite occurring. When a small bakery on the outskirts of London, for example, put together a Web page, it received an influx of orders from Japan, as Japanese business travelers, following meetings in London offices, ordered baked goods to be sent to their hosts as a goodwill gesture. Suddenly, this small, unassuming family bakery had become an international business.

Caveat Emptor

The availability of the Web gives computer users everywhere unprecedented access to information. With an Internet search engine, information on virtually any topic may be found—no matter how wonderful or disgusting it might be. The Internet is currently wide-open territory with few restrictions. Because anyone can put anything on the Web, material found on Web sites must be treated with an appropriate degree of caution. The source of any information must be considered, as editorial standards vary from stringent to nonexistent, depending on who posts the page.

The presence of the Web only serves to underline the point that computers are part of society and can no longer be ignored as the playthings of niche hobbyists. A recent Pennsylvania news story involved a young woman who was abducted by a stranger who locked her in his basement with every intention of molesting and abusing her. Luckily, she was found, physically unharmed. Her parents lamented that she had made contact with the man in an Internet chat room, and that since they were computer illiterates, they had no way to monitor her activities. Although the woman was found in time, the incident points up an essential lesson: no one can afford to remain ignorant about computers.

Streaming Media

The Internet was created to transmit text and images, which can be distributed fairly easily and quickly. The full nature of Internet networks is beyond the scope of this book, but in broad strokes, Web content resides on *servers*. By going to a Web site, a user requests information from the server that is then transmitted to the user's computer. Like a cook in a fast-food restaurant, the server fulfills these requests as quickly as possible.

Time-based media, such as music or video, are not transmitted effectively on the Internet. Files of this type are much larger than static text and image files and require inordinate transmission times. *Streaming* allows time-based material to be displayed as it loads. The material resides on an Internet server in a compressed format that reduces the size of the file (audio compression will be discussed in Chapter 10). A streaming media player (such as RealNetwork's RealPlayer™, Microsoft's Windows Media Player, or Apple's QuickTime) acts somewhat like a funnel. It receives content on one end, decompresses it, and dispenses it out the other. A *buffer* acts as the large end of the funnel, closing off the dispensing end until a set amount of material is downloaded. Ideally, the funnel never empties and playback is continuous.

The decompression method determines the quality of the material and is tied to the bit rate. The bit rate is selected by the user when the streaming media player is installed and depends on the type of Internet connection that is active on the computer. A bit rate of 128,000 bits per second (128 kbps) is standard for MP3 files, a common compression method for video and audio. This rate produces audio at about the same quality as FM radio. A bit rate of 64 kbps produces audio at about the quality of AM radio. A bit rate of 32 kbps is usually noticeably distorted, but may be the only option for people with slow Internet connections.

Streaming allows music, television, and radio content to be delivered via a Web browser. Rather than saving large files on the receiving computer, the streaming player discards its contents after they are displayed. This avoids having to store large files and also allows content providers to prevent their material from being pirated.

The Web and Music Research

Like all fields, music research has had essential resources placed on-line. Music scholars, like all scholars, must be proficient in basics such as e-mail and file transfers. They also owe it to themselves to become aware of what resources are available over the Web. Many universities make audio materials available to their students for Web delivery. Figure 4–1 is a page from Penn State University's Digital Music Library that is a component of a music theory class. Students may access the page for the course's listening materials, and the pieces are streamed to the student's computer. This allows many students to access the material simultaneously from different computers, at any time of the day or night. There are many such resources available on the Web. While any attempt at a comprehensive listing would likely become outdated before this book was even printed, the following are examples of resources that are likely to remain available indefinitely. They may serve as starting points that lead to additional materials.

The New Grove Dictionary of Music and Musicians
http://www.grovemusic.com/index.html

The Edna Loeb Music Library at Harvard University
Music Information Meta-Sites
http://hcl.harvard.edu/loebmusic/online-ir-musmeta.html

William and Gayle Cook Music Library
Indiana University School of Music
Worldwide Internet Music Resources
http://www.music.indiana.edu/music_resources/

International Index to Music Periodicals
http://iimpft.chadwyck.com/

Figure 4–1

Web Page Featuring Musical Examples Available as Streamed Audio

Printed courtesy of Penn State University Libraries.

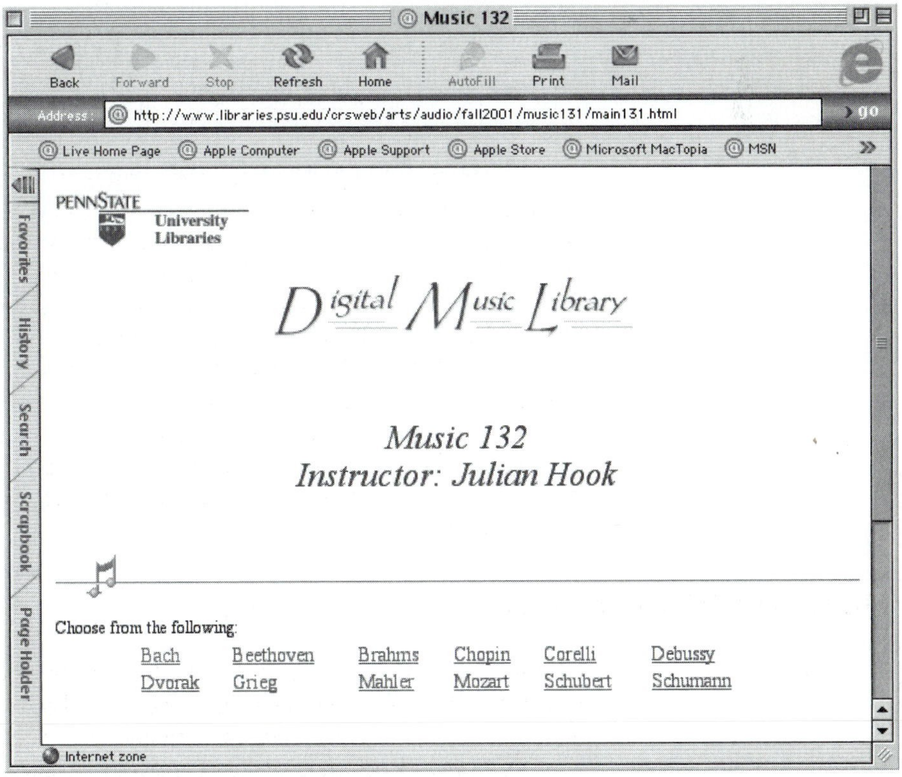

CHAPTER 5

Representing Numbers

Given the graphics-oriented nature of computing and the ability of computers to display a variety of multimedia types, it is easy to forget that they are essentially calculators. Everything they do involves information in the form of numbers, including the manipulation of musical information. Before proceeding to chapters that discuss computer music applications, an introduction to the methods by which computers represent numbers is in order.

Numbers Are Power

Numbers are represented as successive powers of a *base,* or *radix.* The powers increment upwards to the left, starting with zero to the far right. The number 1234 for any base *b* represents:

> one times *b* to the third power
>
> +
>
> two times *b* to the second power
>
> +
>
> three times *b* to the first power
>
> +
>
> four times *b* to the zeroth power
>
> (Note: Any number to the power of zero is 1.)

Any value may be expressed with any radix.

A base of 10, termed the *decimal* system, is most commonly used (this is probably due to the fact that humans have 10 fingers). Thus, the columns in base 10 are termed the ones' column, the tens' column, the hundreds' column, the thousands' column, and so on. A digit placed in each column is a multiplier for each successive power. Therefore, the value 1324 represents:

> one times 10 to the third power
>
> +
>
> three times 10 to the second power
>
> +

two times 10 to the first power

+

four times 10 to the zeroth power

Of What Value Power?

For any base b, there exist b distinct numerical symbols. For example, in base 10, there are 10 distinct symbols—0 through 9. In any base b, if there are n digits, the range of values that may be represented is b^n. For example, with two digits in base 10, $b = 10$ and $n = 2$. With two digits, the range of values that may be represented is 10^2 (100) values—0 through 99.

Numbers in Computers

Computers do not store values in decimal form—perhaps because they do not have 10 fingers. What they have instead are circuits. A circuit has two possible states: ON and OFF. Computers are therefore able to represent numbers in a system that has two symbols. Base 2, the *binary* system, fits this description.

The Binary Number System

The binary number system consists of only two digits: 0 and 1. That distinction aside, the system of representing numbers is exactly the same as in the decimal system. With only two digits, a sequence of binary numbers changes columns more quickly than a series of decimal numbers. The binary number fields are

$\ldots$	2^4	2^3	2^2	2^1	2^0
	sixteens' column	eights' column	fours' column	twos' column	ones' column

Compare the notation of a sequence of decimal numbers with a sequence of the same binary numbers:

Decimal	Binary
0	0
1	1
2	10
3	11
4	100
5	101
6	110
7	111
8	1000

and so on.

Some Essential Terminology

- A single digit of a binary number stored in a computer is called a *bit* (an abbreviation of BInary digiT) (Figure 5–1).
- Numbers, or computer *words,* are usually stored in sequences of 8 bits, called *bytes.*
- A sequence of 4 bits is called a *nibble.*
- The rightmost bit, which represents the lowest power, is called the *least significant bit* (or LSB).
- The leftmost bit, which represents the highest power, is called the *most significant bit* (or MSB).

Larger numbers need to be represented with two or more bytes (16 or more bits).

- The byte that represents the lower powers of the number is called the *least significant byte.*
- The byte that represents the higher powers of the number is called the *most significant byte.*

A computer system is often referred to as an "n-bit system," meaning it has n digits available to represent numbers. Recalling the preceding discussion of value ranges, in a binary system, $b = 2$, so an n-bit system is a statement that describes the resolution of the system. An 8-bit system can represent 2^8 (256) values. A 16-bit system can represent 2^{16} (65,536) values.

Figure 5–1

Essential Numeric Terminology

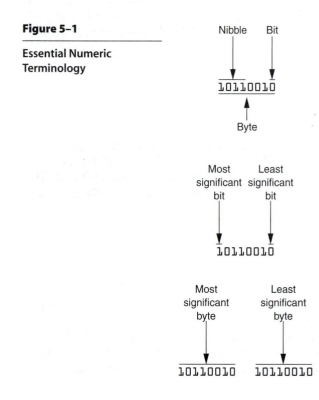

The Hexadecimal Number System

Base 16, the *hexadecimal* system, is often used in computer parlance. Because the Arabic number system does not have digits to represent values greater than 9, alphabetic characters are used:

Decimal	Hexadecimal	Binary
0	0	0
1	1	1
2	2	10
3	3	11
4	4	100
5	5	101
6	6	110
7	7	111
8	8	1000
9	9	1001
10	A	1010
11	B	1011
12	C	1100
13	D	1101
14	E	1110
15	F	1111
16	10	10000
17	11	10001

Hexadecimal notation is a convenience. Notice that a 4-bit nibble can be expressed as one hexadecimal bit, since a binary nibble can express 16 values—the range of one hexadecimal digit. Frequently, an 8-bit byte will be expressed as two hex bits:

Binary	1010	0110
Hexadecimal	A	6
Decimal	10	6

Hexadecimal notation can be helpful because it takes less space on a page to write a number. It can also be easier to read than a sequence of ones and zeroes.

To convert two hex bits to decimal, multiply the most significant nibble by 16, then add the least significant nibble. For the 8-bit number shown above the process is

$$(10 \times 16) + 6 = 166$$

Integers and Floating Points

Numbers within the set of positive whole numbers (1, 2, 3), negative whole numbers (-1, -2, -3), and zero (0) are called *integers*. Negative integers are often stored in a form known as *two's complement*. To represent negative numbers in computers, the values of bits are switched—zeroes to ones and ones to zeroes—and a value of 1 is added to the result:

$$6_{10} = 1010_2$$
$$-6_{10} = 0101_2 + 1 = 0110_2$$

The advantage of two's complement representation is that it allows subtraction to be performed as addition. To subtract B from A, A is added to the two's complement representation of B. If the result requires a 1 to be carried over to the leftmost bit, the sum is a positive number. If there is no carry bit, the answer is negative and is represented in two's complement form:

$7_{10} - 6_{10}$	$6_{10} - 7_{10}$
0111	0110
+ 1010	+ 1001
10001	1111
The leftmost carry bit indicates a positive result.	Since there is no carry bit, the result is the two's complement representation of a negative number: 0001_2, or -1_{10}.

Numbers that include a decimal point (for example, 3.14159) are called *floating-point numbers*. Floating-point representation in computers usually involves a base (sometimes called a *mantissa*) and an exponent. Typically, 3 bytes represent the mantissa and 1 byte represents the exponent. Floating-point numbers stored in computers are usually approximations. The fraction $\frac{1}{3}$, for example, cannot be represented accurately in decimal form (0.33333 . . .). To represent such numbers in a computer, rounding has to occur after some maximum number of available bits has been used up. For example, the number $\frac{1}{3}$ may need to be represented with only three decimal places, as 0.333. This can lead to a certain degree of error in arithmetic operations. The following illustrates a simple example:

$$\frac{1}{3} \times \frac{1}{3} = \frac{1}{9} = 0.11111 \, . \, . \, .$$
$$0.333 \times 0.333 = 0.110889$$

This degree of error may be insignificant or crucial, depending on the circumstances in which the number is used. A series of operations with floating-point numbers has the potential to accumulate error with each operation.

CHAPTER 6

Introduction to MIDI

The first level of digital musical information to be explored is the MIDI standard, an acronym for Musical Instrument Digital Interface. Simply put, MIDI is a digital communication protocol allowing devices to send and/or respond to instructions. MIDI information is to computers what sheet music is to humans: a series of instructions that, when properly carried out, produces a piece of music. This next series of chapters discusses the nature of these instructions.

A Brief Historical Background

Electronic (or electro-acoustic) music in its present form dates back to the end of World War II. After the war, many military communications devices were declassified, such as tape recorders and various oscillators, filters, and amplifiers that were used for radio communications. The first large-scale electronic music studios were components of government broadcast facilities. Smaller home studios typically consisted of equipment obtained through an informal network that originated with military officers who had happened to pick up some of these devices when stations were abandoned. In Paris, the Groupe de Recherche de Musique Concrète (GRM), led by Pierre Schaeffer, was established to create an aesthetic based on the use of recorded sounds as a new musical form. In Cologne, the Westdeutscher Rundfunk (WDR) set up a studio, eventually led by Karlheinz Stockhausen, that was dedicated to the creation of a musical aesthetic through the use of electronically produced sounds. In Milan, the Radio Audizioni Italiane (RAI) created the Studio di Fonologia Musicale, under artistic directors Luciano Berio and Bruno Maderna, to explore an aesthetic of performance works meant for radio broadcast that blended acoustic instruments, human voices, recorded sound, noise, and an extensive complement of oscillators. At the University of Illinois at Urbana, Lejaren Hiller created works composed by computer in which random numbers were generated and mapped to musical characteristics such as pitch, timbre, or rhythm. Each randomly generated number was tested according to specified principles (just as all possible notes in a species counterpoint exercise may be tested for their suitability according to voice leading principles), then the final set of numbers was translated by hand into musical notation.

The first dedicated music synthesizers also appeared in the 1950s. With oscillators to produce waveforms, they allowed the creation of new timbres. In addition to sound synthesis capabilities, computer technology also allowed precise timing of musical events. These synthesizers were large and expensive devices, costing on the order of a quarter of a million dollars. Clearly, machines of this magnitude were only suitable for well-funded research centers, not for home use. The most notable American facility was that owned by Columbia-Princeton, with a RCA Mark II Synthesizer. The first composers to produce works on this synthesizer included Milton Babbitt, Vladimir Ussachevsky, Otto Luening, and Charles Wuorinen.

In the 1960s, small, modular synthesizers were introduced. They were not computer based, but relied entirely on controlling electrical voltage to create an *analog* of a sound wave. The cost of these synthesizers was on the order of thousands, rather than hundreds of thousands, of dollars, and therefore they were accessible to musicians who had the inclination to master them. In America, Moog (pronounced to rhyme with "vogue") and Buchla were the first major brands. Among the first composers to work with these instruments were Morton Subotnick, who recorded pieces composed with the Buchla, and Wendy Carlos, who worked with the Moog.

Synthesizers gained widespread frame with Wendy Carlos's recording *Switched on Bach,* released in 1968. This electronic realization of classical pieces was enormously successful, outselling by far any previous classical music recordings. Synthesizers captured the popular imagination and began appearing with increasing frequency in popular music. Films such as *A Clockwork Orange* featured electronic music scores, and popular musicians such as Keith Emerson, Stevie Wonder, the Beatles, Herbie Hancock, and Pink Floyd began using them in recordings and onstage. By the 1980s, any self-respecting rock musician was expected to feature synthesizers in his or her ensemble of devices. Electronic instruments were now big business, with more and more companies competing to release the most innovative products. Standard features on synthesizers included two wheels to the left of the keyboard. A *pitch bend* wheel allowed a performer to change pitch dynamically for held notes. A *modulation wheel* allowed dynamic control of vibrato level. Dynamic volume control was often available by means of a pedal.

By this time, electronic music devices included instruments other than synthesizers. *Samplers* were keyboards that contained recordings of acoustic instruments. *Drum machines* allowed rhythm parts to be programmed. *Sequencers* contained instructions for a sequence of musical notes to be played back (an electronic version of the player piano). When a sequencer was connected to a synthesizer and/or drum machine, it could trigger an accompaniment part. Thus, an instrumentalist equipped with a sequencer, drum machine, and synthesizer could operate as a one-person band.

As soon as it became feasible, manufacturers began to incorporate digital technology into their instruments. Digital controls offered distinct advantages. Modular synthesizers relied on networks of modules connected by physical patchcords (the same way that telephone switchboard operators used to patch one caller to another). There was no way to store a particular sound internally. To recall a timbre (called a *patch,* due to the configuration of patch cables required), the spaghetti of patch cables and knob positions needed to be re-created. With digital controls, patch configurations could be stored internally, rather than by external cables, and could be recalled at the push of a button. Also, the tuning of analog instruments was inherently unstable, and pauses to retune oscillators were a fact of life for users. Some manufacturers began to introduce instruments that were completely digital, which produced signals by means of numbers and did not have such tuning instability (digital audio is the topic of upcoming chapters). It was rare that any tuning calibration was required once they were shipped from the factory.

In an effort to lure customers and establish brand loyalty, many companies made it possible to connect their devices, so that their drum machine could play rhythmic patterns in time with their synthesizer, or so that their sequencer could control both a drum machine and a synthesizer. This interconnectivity was useful, but not all musicians wanted to commit to purchasing devices from only one company. It became clear that a standard was needed so that machines from different companies could be interconnected. Such standards were already in place in the computer industry, where computers, printers, modems, and the like were able to work together in a manufacturer-independent fashion.

Music manufacturers began to discuss the idea among themselves, and the MIDI standard was created. It was first demonstrated at the National Association of Music Merchants convention in January 1983. A keyboard from the Prophet company was connected to a keyboard from the Roland company. Playing a note on one keyboard triggered the same note on the other, allowing their timbres to be combined. The industry collectively rose to its feet in amazement at this new level of compatibility and the possibilities it offered. Further refinements to the standard followed the convention, and MIDI specification 1.0 was formally introduced in August 1983. At about the same time, affordable digital synthesizers were introduced, with great commercial success. Musicians, who might have regarded computers as comprehensible only to strange introverts in lab coats, suddenly found themselves faced with an array of computer-related musical devices. The tools of the Information Age had reached the music studio.

What MIDI Is, and What It Is Not

The MIDI protocol allows devices to exchange various types of instructions. In the demonstration of 1983, a message to play a particular note was transmitted from a *master device* to a *slave device*. When the player lifted his or her finger from the key, a message to stop playing the note was also sent from master to slave. MIDI consists solely of instructions such as these. MIDI data is *not* an audio signal and contains no audio information. The production of audio is left to the device that receives the instruction.

As an analogy, consider a comparison between a CD and a printed page of music. The CD contains a description of the complex wave comprising an audio signal. (How a computer may store actual audio will be discussed in Chapter 9.) MIDI, in contrast, is analogous to a printed page of music. Sheet music does not contain audio information, but is rather a set of instructions that a (human) instrumentalist is trained to carry out in the realization of a piece of music. In a similar fashion, MIDI consists of a series of instructions that a (computer) instrumentalist may carry out with its audio components. Thus, a file of MIDI instructions is small and easily transmitted, since it contains instructions only and leaves the creation of the actual audio to the receiving device.

MIDI Compromises

The MIDI protocol was designed to be affordable. Thus, a number of compromises were made for efficiency. MIDI is transmitted through a 5-pin DIN connector, as shown in Figure 6–1. While MIDI jacks are a familiar feature on today's instruments,

Figure 6–1

Five-Pin DIN Connector

in 1983 many manufacturers were less than pleased at the idea of having to add a new type of cable jack to their designs. Their displeasure was more than doubled by the fact that a MIDI cable transmits information in one direction only. For an instrument to send and receive MIDI, two cables (and two jacks) are necessary (Figure 6–2).

Although these design hurdles have been solved, an issue that remains is the *serial* transmission (one bit at a time) of MIDI information. Serial transmission is significantly slower than *parallel* transmission (many bits simultaneously). The difference is shown in Figure 6–3. Imagine how slowly traffic would move if all highways had only one lane in each direction. MIDI is like a one-lane highway.

Figure 6–2

MIDI Cables

MIDI cables transmit in one direction only.

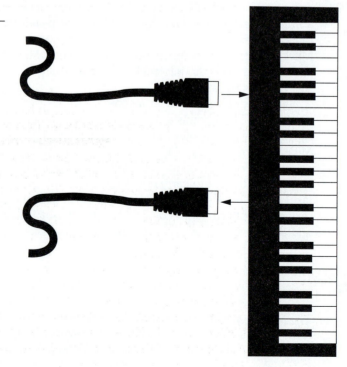

Figure 6–3

Serial vs. Parallel
Transmission

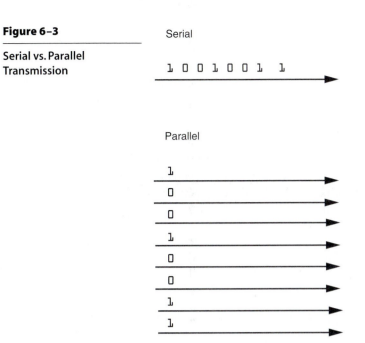

MIDI instructions are transmitted among devices at 31,250 bits per second (31.25 kilobaud). Each MIDI instruction is in the form of a 10-bit word, meaning that 3125 words may be transmitted per second. Most complete instructions require two to three words, so that 1042.6 three-word instructions may be transmitted per second. Although this may sound quite speedy, it will soon become clear that this can be noticeably slow for complex musical applications.

MIDI Channels

A great deal of MIDI information is transmitted in a multichannel format. For example, a MIDI message directing a given note to be played contains information about the note and also defines a receive channel for that note. The MIDI specification provides 16 channels. Different instruments may be configured to respond to information on different channels, just like televisions, which display broadcasts of only one channel at a time. Thus, MIDI instructions contain definitions of musical events as well as the channels on which those events are meant to be carried out. Specific examples of MIDI instructions and ways that they might be used will be discussed presently.

Computers and MIDI

MIDI came into being at the same time as the personal computer, and it did not take long for programmers to begin developing software meant to allow computers to interface with MIDI instruments. Computers soon became the heart of a MIDI studio via a variety of software applications.

Central Traffic Control

To physically connect a computer to MIDI instruments, a translator is needed to convert MIDI code to computer code. Such a translator is known as a *MIDI interface.* Some MIDI interfaces are dedicated pieces of hardware, while others are part and parcel of a sound card that gives a computer audio capabilities.

Typically, MIDI software comes with a utility that stores a diagram of the user's MIDI studio, with the type of interface, the number and type of instruments, and the channels on which each instrument is set to respond (Figure 6–4). It is possible to rename instruments within the configuration, so that a user may, for example, call an instrument "my vintage brown keyboard" if that should prove more mnemonic than having to remember "Yamaha DX7." With such a utility acting as a traffic director, users may direct MIDI messages from software programs to instruments in their studios, rather than having to remember what instruments correspond to what MIDI channels.

Sequencing Software

A sequencer stores a musical performance, which may be recalled, played back, or edited. Earlier forms of sequencers have existed for hundreds of years. Music boxes, which consisted of a revolving wooden drum with raised pins that plucked

Figure 6–4

The Open Music System (OMS) MIDI Utility

Source: Opcode Systems, Inc., a subsidiary of the Gibson Guitar Corporation. Reprinted with permission.

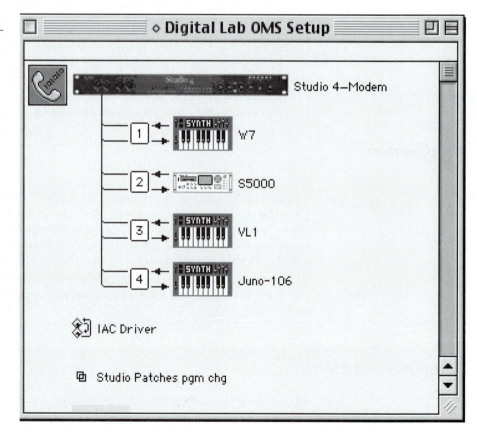

musical tines as they rolled past, were an early form of sequencer. Later, the player piano, which operated by means of a paper roll with holes punched in it, was used to activate the notes of a musical work. In electronic music, hardware sequencers had existed since the 1960s, allowing musicians to store sequences of notes to be played by synthesizers.

Software sequencers featured expanded capabilities and soon became the most comprehensive type of MIDI software. The sequencer's capabilities could be expanded via simple software upgrades, rather than by purchasing new hardware for every technological advance. Figure 6–5 shows features common to many sequencing programs.

The MIDI protocol does not include information about time. What a sequencer does is combine MIDI transmission with a clock and attach *timestamps* to each MIDI event that specify when it happens. With 16 MIDI channels, a typical sequence file may be considered an all-purpose broadcast to up to 16 instruments, with a specific set of instructions for each, allowing arrangements of up to 16 parts to be played.

Sequencers operate as a simulation of a multitrack tape recorder. Streams of MIDI information are organized in discrete *tracks.* The multitrack layout works in conjunction with MIDI data, which exists in 16 channels. Each instrument may be set up to receive information directed to a separate channel. The directions in each channel may be stored on separate sequencer tracks. Tracks may be copied, muted, or soloed. Alternative performances of the same part may be stored on different tracks, and these performances may be activated or deactivated on playback by muting these tracks selectively. Each track typically contains information on one MIDI channel only, but this is not a requirement. One track may contain information directed to a number of MIDI channels. By the same token, different tracks may contain information directed to the same channel, although arranging a sequence in this way may be an invitation for confusion. Instruments may be defined via the MIDI "traffic cop" utility just discussed, which informs the sequencer of the current studio environment. Working in conjunction with this utility, instruments to play back each track may be selected, and different instruments may be selected as the source of information when material is to be recorded.

There are typically a number of ways to record material in a sequencer. The most straightforward approach may be to use the sequencer like a tape recorder: click on the record button and play the material on a MIDI instrument. *Punch recording* allows a segment of an otherwise flawless recording to be replaced: if, out of a 20 measure recording, measures 12 through 15 contain mistakes, measure 12 beat 1 may be designated a *punch-in* point, and measure 16 beat 1 may be designated a *punch-out* point. Activating the record function results in simple playback until measure 12 is reached, at which point the sequencer records material for the next three measures. *Loop/overdub* mode allows a complicated part to be recorded in successive passes. This is often appropriate for recording percussion parts. A number of measures is set to loop. If the first eight measures are selected, then as soon as eight measures have elapsed recording jumps back to the beginning of measure 1, and anything played will be added to what was recorded previously. In this way, a complicated percussion part may be entered one instrument at a time and layered gradually.

Figure 6–5

Software Sequencing

Sample screens from the program Digital Performer.

Used with permission of Mark of the Unicorn Software, Inc.

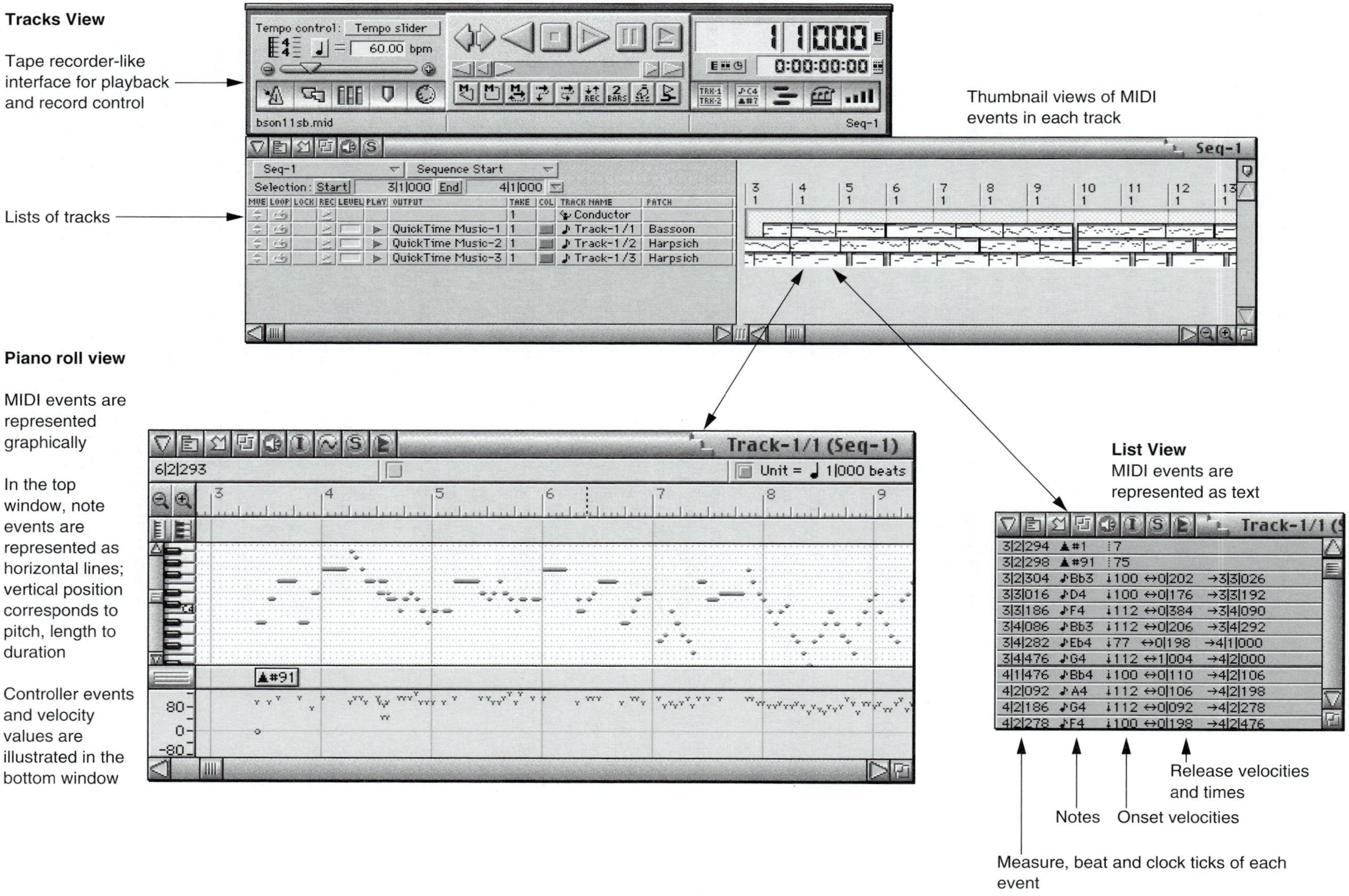
Tracks View
Tape recorder-like interface for playback and record control
Lists of tracks
Thumbnail views of MIDI events in each track
Piano roll view
MIDI events are represented graphically
In the top window, note events are represented as horizontal lines; vertical position corresponds to pitch, length to duration
Controller events and velocity values are illustrated in the bottom window
List View
MIDI events are represented as text
Measure, beat and clock ticks of each event
Notes
Onset velocities
Release velocities and times
Tempo control: Tempo slider
60.00 bpm
bson11sb.mid
Seq-1
Sequence Start
Selection: Start 3|1|000 End 4|1|000
Conductor
QuickTime Music-1 Track-1/1 Bassoon
QuickTime Music-2 Track-1/2 Harpsich
QuickTime Music-3 Track-1/3 Harpsich
Track-1/1 (Seq-1)
6|2|293
Unit = 1|000 beats
Track-1/1
3|2|294 #1 7
3|2|298 #91 75
3|2|304 Bb3 100 0|202 3|3|026
3|3|016 D4 100 0|176 3|3|192
3|3|186 F4 112 0|384 3|4|090
3|4|086 Bb3 112 0|206 3|4|292
3|4|282 Eb4 77 0|198 4|1|000
3|4|476 G4 112 1|004 4|2|000
4|1|476 Bb4 100 0|110 4|2|106
4|2|092 A4 112 0|106 4|2|198
4|2|186 G4 112 0|092 4|2|278
4|2|278 F4 100 0|198 4|2|476

The playback tempo of a sequence may be altered at any time. A complicated part may be played with the sequencer metronome set to a slow tempo. The tempo may then be sped up when the completed track is played back. Recorded material may be *quantized,* meaning that events may only occur at specified subdivisions of a measure—at 16th notes, 32nd notes, 8th notes, or whatever resolution the user finds appropriate. Depending on the music, quantizing material may ensure an appropriate level of precision or an overly mechanized recording.

For those who do not feel capable of playing a complicated part to be recorded, an alternative method is *step entry.* This allows notes to be entered one at a time, without the clock ticking. A note duration is selected, and a MIDI note entered from an instrument is recorded with the selected note value. Another note duration may be selected, another note entered, and so on. In this way, parts may be entered at the musician's own pace, and all MIDI note durations are automatically assigned by the program.

Many sequencers also feature a notation screen. Notes may be entered by clicking on a graphic of a staff. Many sequencers allow notation views to be printed, but professional-level music notation is more likely to be achieved with a dedicated notation program, which will be discussed shortly.

Typically, tracks may be edited in one of three views. In a *notation view,* notes may be viewed on a traditional staff and may be edited by dragging note symbols to other locations. This allows those most comfortable with standard notation to work with the established system of clefs, staves, and note values. An *event list* displays each event as text in an itemized list. An event list is sometimes the easiest way to determine the order of events in a sequence and may be the place to correct problems such as instrument changes not occurring at the right time. A *piano roll view* displays MIDI events as horizontal lines. The length of each line indicates the event's duration, and the vertical position of each line gives the value of the event. For instance, the note number corresponds to pitch. Just as in notated music, events that lie at higher vertical positions represent higher pitches. Controller information from devices such as a volume pedal, pitch bend wheel, or modulation wheel may usually be "drawn" in. Once material is entered, it may be cut, copied, and pasted in a manner typical to that of a word processor. A series of measures may be recorded, then copied and pasted elsewhere with modifications made, eliminating the necessity of recording the same material more than once. Playback can often be controlled with a *mixer* screen that allows the relative volume and stereo pan position of the various tracks to be adjusted.

Sequencers allow music to be arranged hierarchically. Many sequencers feature a song mode, which allows a number of sequences to be mixed and matched in a modular fashion, as though they were building blocks of a larger musical work. Song mode allows musicians to create "sequences of sequences." For example, a song's introduction might exist as one short sequence. A verse might be another, along with bridge and chorus sequences. When verses or choruses are repeated, their sequences may be copied and treated as another sequence, with changes such as the addition or deletion of an instrument to allow for variety.

Sequencer files may be saved in proprietary format, which describes them as originating from the sequencer software in which they were created. Alternatively, they may be exported as *Standard MIDI files,* which is a generic file format that may be opened in other sequencers or other types of MIDI software. Standard MIDI files allow, for example, a sequence to be imported into a notation program, where it can be edited to appear as professionally copied music.

Notation Software

Notation software may well be on a par with sequencers as the most commonly used type of MIDI software. Notators combine MIDI with the graphic capability necessary to create and print musical scores (Figure 6–6) by translating MIDI information into notated music. Notators have many things in common with sequencers. Both can import Standard MIDI files, record MIDI from an instrument, and play files back with variable tempo and instrument assignments. The difference between the two is that sequencers focus primarily on storing performance information, while notators focus on creating renditions of music in standard notation.

In addition to converting MIDI notes to notated pitches on a staff, notators allow musicians to create slurs, ties, tuplets, dynamics, and articulation markings. Lyrics may be attached to notes, and guitar tablature chords may be inserted above the staff. Special characters may be used by creating them within the notator or by creating them in a graphics program and importing them into the notation program and adding them to a library of special symbols. Text may be entered for titles and composer information, as well as nonstandard performance instructions.

Notators offer a variety of layout options. Users may choose the number of staves, their clefs, key, and meter. The spacing between staff systems and between individual notes may be adjusted with click-and-drag operations. The staff size is also variable, allowing ossia measures for information such as trill instructions to be placed above the main staff or for a solo part to be printed smaller in a part meant for a piano accompanist. The number of lines in a staff system may be variable in some programs, allowing, for example, percussion parts to be created with one staff line only. Some notators allow nonstandard key signatures to be produced or polymetric sections where different instruments are playing in different meters simultaneously.

As in a sequencer, once material is entered, it may be cut, copied, or pasted so that repetitions of similar material may be duplicated easily. The capability of playing back material allows musicians to check for errors. Once a score is complete, parts may be extracted, allowing composers to be secure in the knowledge that no measures have been inadvertently added or forgotten from a given part.

Figure 6–6

Example Screen from a Notator

Used with permission of Coda Music Technology, a division of Net4Music, Inc.

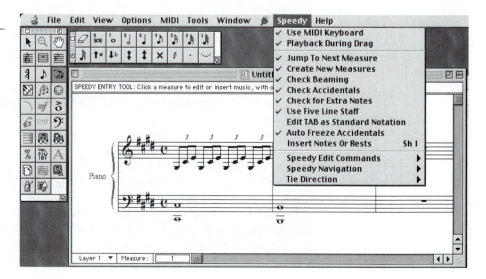

Notators have become virtually an essential skill for composers. Players are less and less tolerant of handwritten scores, particularly when special notation is required for expanded playing techniques. Anyone with a high-quality printer and the wherewithal to learn a notation program has the capability of producing professional-level music copy. Notators also offer advantages to theorists and musicologists who are willing to look beyond the capabilities intended for these programs. Music notation characters are created with a special font that comes bundled with the programs. Once the program is loaded into a computer, this font becomes available to any other program on the computer, such as a word processor or drawing program. In these programs, graphics may be created to illustrate concepts such as Schenkerian structural levels, using notes with different font sizes along with objects such as text and arrows placed anywhere on a page to create effective illustrations.

Many notators also have the capability of creating graphic files from a selected portion of the screen. An excerpt may be created in a notator, made into a graphic file, and then brought into another program such as a word processor, drawing program, or presentation program to be used as an example figure with text or other graphics incorporated.

It is now possible to purchase music created from notation files on CD-ROM as opposed to paper. Collections grouped by instrumental ensemble or composer can be stored en masse on a single CD and printed out by the purchaser.

Computer-Aided Instruction (CAI) Software

A sequencer works by combining a clock with MIDI data. To this capability notators add the association of MIDI events with graphic symbols. CAI programs add to these functions the computer's ability to store and update data, utilizing MIDI as an adjunct to teaching fundamentals of musicianship (Figure 6–7). Students may be prompted to play a given scale or interval on a MIDI keyboard, and the computer can spot errors and track a student's progress, keeping a record of the student's history.

Figure 6–7

Computer-Aided Instruction

Printed courtesy of Ars Nova.

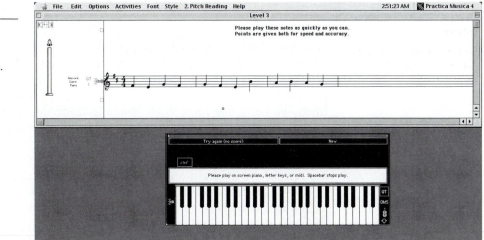

CAI software can typically be set to operate at beginner, intermediate, or advanced levels of difficulty. Students may enter information either by a MIDI device (identified to the program via the "traffic director" software utility) or by clicking on an on-screen graphic. CAI programs that offer practice drills attempt to make what used to be an arduous process of learning scales, key signatures, chords, and the like more like a computer game. Engaging graphics, or animated characters that appear to offer congratulations or supportive suggestions, may be employed to make learning rudiments a fun experience, rather than a chore.

Other types of programs may offer introduction to musical concepts for young beginners. Games may teach children listening skills or recognition of tonal direction. A melody may be played twice, and the child asked to determine whether it was repeated exactly or with changes. Or a melody may be played that simultaneously appears in notated form on the screen with errors that the student is to identify. Some programs allow children to use graphic tools to draw melodic shapes that the computer can play back. Others can play melodies and allow students to change timbres, notes, rhythms, or tempi, or to rearrange phrases or switch parts off and on again.

Accompaniment Software

Auto-accompaniment software generates accompaniments as an aid to students while they are practicing, thus adding a degree of enrichment to what might ordinarily be considered a sentence of solitary confinement (Figure 6–8). Set accompaniments may be played for classical pieces, or for jazz pieces a set of standard riffs may be programmed to play at random in a given style, allowing a student to improvise over an accompaniment. Standard chord progressions may be available, or students can enter their own progressions and choose from a menu of styles with which to realize them. Repeats may be indicated so that songs may be created out of repetitions of a phrase. Chord symbols may also be altered so that substitute chords may be entered into standard pieces. Songs may be saved or exported as standard MIDI files, so that arrangements generated by the program may be subsequently imported into a notation program to be printed.

Editor/Librarian Software

With the advent of digital synthesizers, the construction of patches became increasingly complex, with over 100 values specifying different aspects of a given patch. Paradoxically, it seemed that the greater the number of available parameters, the smaller the display screen manufacturers provided on the instrument. With only one value visible at a time, it was difficult to keep a sense of context of the patch as a whole. Some described it as "looking at the world through a keyhole." *Editor/Librarian* software allows complex synthesizer patches to be created more intuitively with the aid of a graphical user interface (Figure 6–9). Patches may be arranged and stored in *banks,* which are groups of 128 patches. Groups of banks may be stored in a computer and quickly transferred to the instrument.

Usually, editor/librarians come as a universal bundle, meaning that most major instrument brands are included. A studio configuration may be set up that coexists with the "traffic cop" utility, allowing edit parameters of any of a user's

Figure 6–8

MIDI Accompaniment Software

Printed courtesy of PG Music Inc.

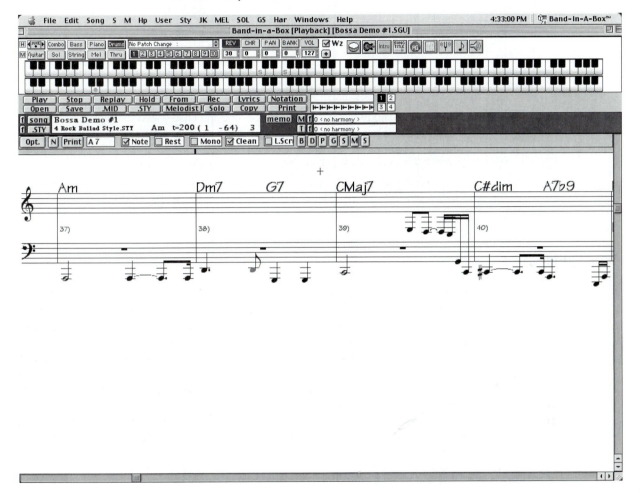

instruments to be changed at any time. Typically, a patch that is being edited is transmitted to an edit buffer within the instrument, allowing changes to be auditioned with any adjustment, without the user having to take the extra step of downloading a patch to the instrument.

Connecting MIDI Instruments

Basic Configurations

Typically, a MIDI instrument has three MIDI jacks, or ports: IN, OUT, and THRU (Figure 6–10). In a simple configuration, one main instrument acts as the master to a number of slave instruments. The sound of the master may be enhanced by

Figure 6-9

Example Screens from an Editor/Librarian

Source: Opcode Systems, Inc., a subsidiary of the Gibson Guitar Corporation. Reprinted with permission.

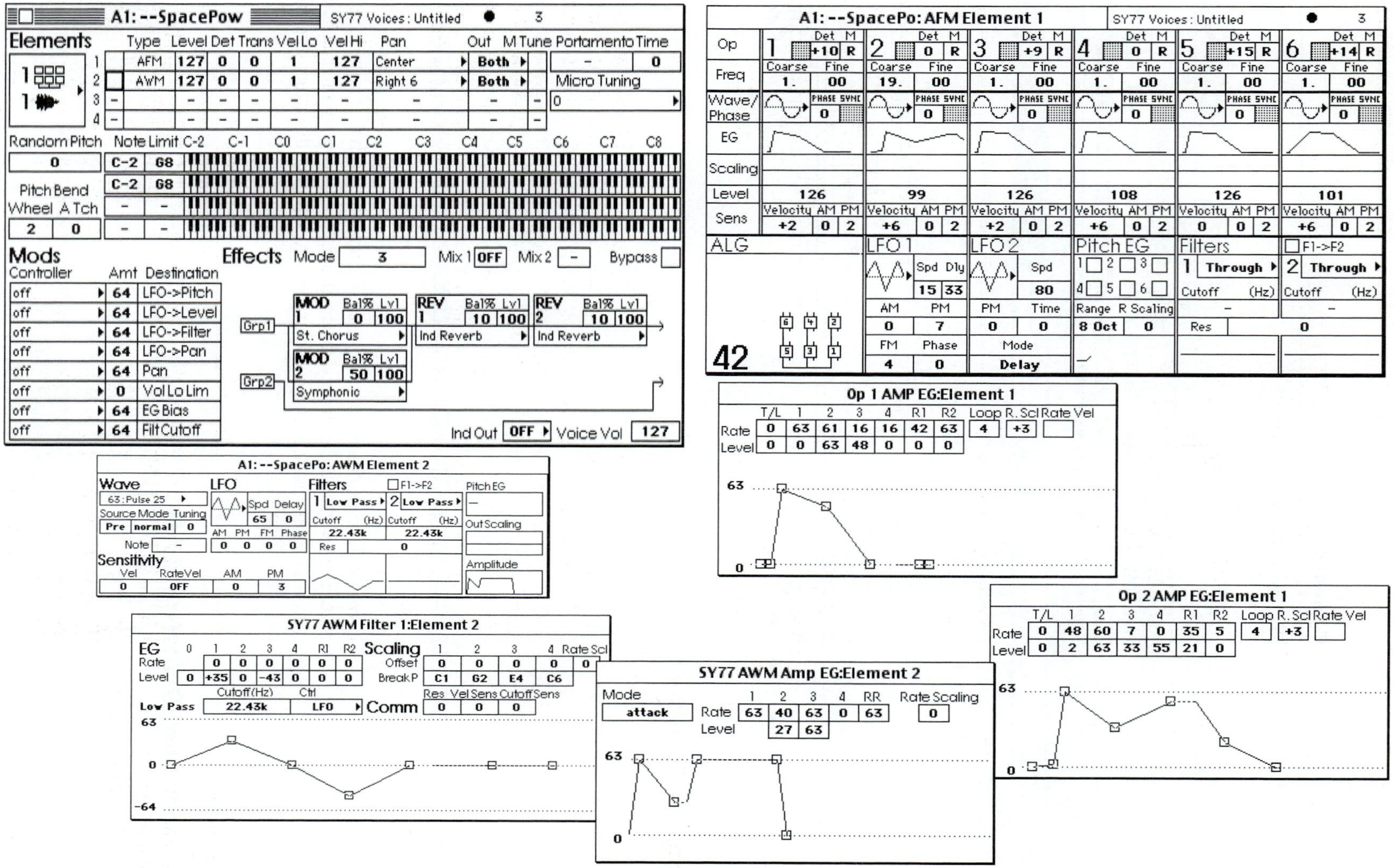

Figure 6–10

The Three Types of MIDI
Jacks

Used with permission of Yamaha
Corporation of America.

doubling its sound with the sound of a slave instrument that is set to play a different type of sound. This is accomplished by connecting a MIDI cable from the MIDI OUT of the master to the MIDI IN of the slave (Figure 6–11).

To enhance the sound still further, more slave devices may be added by "daisy chaining" more instruments together via the MIDI THRU port (Figure 6–12). The MIDI THRU port simply passes on what comes to the instrument via the IN port. In some situations, daisy chains can lead to delays at the end of the chain. A tidier configuration is to use a *MIDI Thru Box* (Figure 6–13). Moving beyond simple doubling, MIDI may also be used to play a multipart arrangement. A *MIDI sequencer* can send instructions to a group of instruments (Figure 6–14).

Computer Configurations

A simple configuration that includes a computer, a MIDI interface, and a number of instruments is shown in Figure 6–15. The master keyboard is able to both send MIDI information to the computer and also receive MIDI information from it. This instrument is used to enter information for each musical part into a software sequencer. The slave instruments are only configured to receive MIDI on playback, when they and the master instrument each play different musical parts. The MIDI sequence is analogous to the broadcast spectrum that contains many television channels, and each instrument is analogous to a single television that picks up one channel at a time.

Figure 6–16 shows a more complex configuration that, over time, has become more typical. By the early 1990s, manufacturers began to introduce instruments that could respond to information on multiple channels, operating in *Multi Mode* (channel mode messages will be covered in the next chapter). Different patches

Figure 6–11

Simple Master-Slave
Configuration

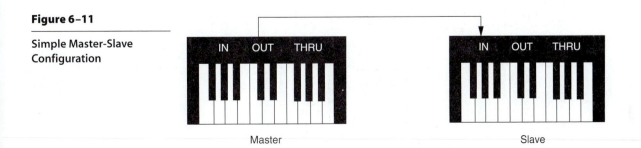

Master   Slave

Figure 6–12

Daisy-Chain Configuration of MIDI Instruments

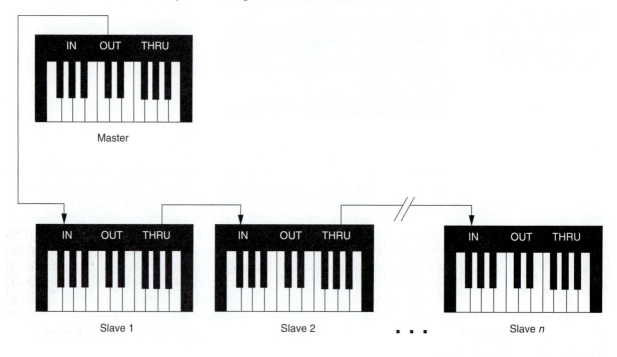

Master

Slave 1   Slave 2   . . .   Slave *n*

Figure 6–13

Multiple Instruments Connected via a MIDI Thru Box

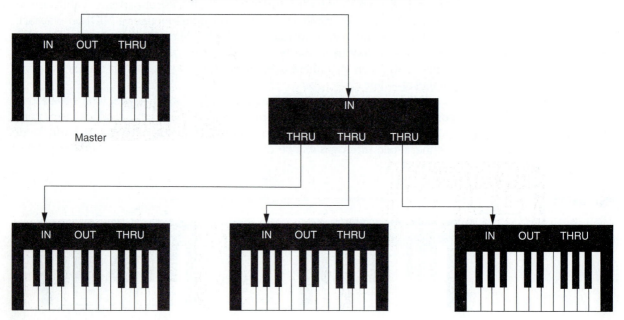

Master

Figure 6–14

Multipart Arrangement Realized with a MIDI Sequencer

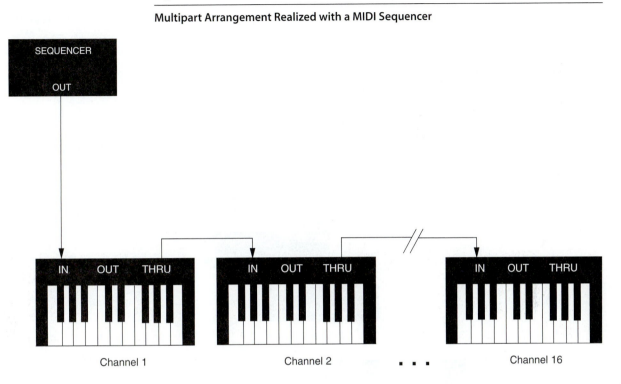

Figure 6–15

Simple Configuration of Computer and MIDI Instruments

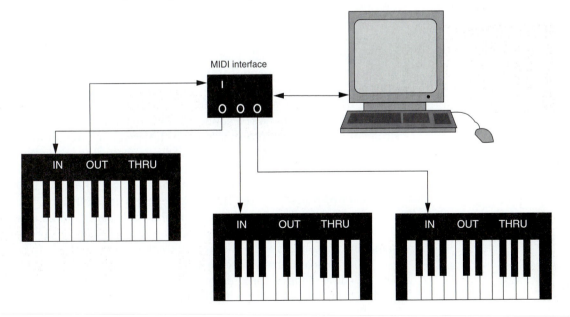

Figure 6–16

MIDI Configuration with Instruments Operating in Multi Mode (able to play multiple parts)

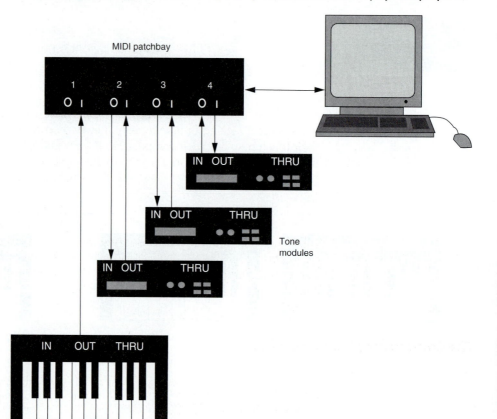

could be assigned to different channels, allowing one instrument to play multipart arrangements. This is analogous to a television being able to display 16 channels simultaneously. With many instruments operating in Multi Mode, a *multiport interface,* also called a *patchbay,* is necessary. On a multiport interface, there are pairs of IN and OUT ports, each of which may transmit information on 16 channels. Each instrument may be connected to such a pair of ports, allowing each instrument to exchange information with the computer. When the "traffic cop" software is set up for a studio with a MIDI patchbay, it adds a level of bookkeeping to the address of each MIDI message, directing each to a given channel on a given port. Therefore, the number of available channels is increased to <number of ports> × 16. This bookkeeping is usually invisible to the musician, as the software utility does this work in the background. Musicians using a sequencer, for example, simply have to select an instrument and channel number within that instrument to specify where they want a sequencer track to be directed.

With each instrument sending and receiving information to and from a patchbay, an editor/librarian program may receive changes made to an instrument's patches from its controls, or changes made at the computer may be sent to each instrument. In a concert situation, complex configurations may be programmed where a master controller keyboard sends information to different combinations of slaves. Different instruments may be deactivated for different songs, or a program change to the patchbay may change an instrument's receive channel so that sometimes it responds to the same information as another instrument, while at other times it operates independently.

Figure 16–6 also illustrates two variants on the design of a MIDI keyboard. One is a *master controller keyboard.* Such a controller does not contain any sound-generating circuitry, but simply acts as a source of MIDI information that is sent to slave instruments. For the most part, MIDI instruments are constructed so that the priority is given to audio circuitry. To keep costs down, the keyboard hardware is often lacking in functionality. Fewer than 88 keys may be provided, and their touch may be crude compared to the sensitivity of a piano keyboard. With a master controller, the priority is given to the physical playing interface. There is likely to be a full complement of keys, and the weight and feel is designed to match as closely as possible that of an acoustic instrument.

With master controller keyboards generating MIDI messages, it becomes unnecessary, and even cumbersome, to have keyboards on all slave instruments. It is often more desirable to purchase *tone modules,* which contain only the sound-generating circuitry of a synthesizer, but no keyboard. With tone modules, it becomes easier to construct flexible studio configurations by mixing and matching tone modules as necessary, maintaining one's favorite controller as the master keyboard.

The Computer as Sound Generator

Since the mid-1990s, with the introduction of the advanced multimedia capabilities of Pentium and PowerPC personal computers, it has become increasingly common for musicians to use computers themselves as sound-generating instruments. Computer sound cards often contain banks of MIDI instruments. Various timbres are stored onto chips within the sound card, just as they are stored onto chips within commercial instruments. Information from a MIDI sequence may thus be sent to the sound card, which produces the audio.

Some sound cards support a format known as Sound Fonts. This allows the sounds on the sound card to be replaced with recordings of acoustic instruments, which often results in greatly improved quality of sound. The nature of digital recordings will be discussed further in Chapters 9 and 13.

Multimedia software programs, such as Apple's QuickTime, often come bundled with a set of instrument sounds, also allowing a computer to play MIDI files. Media handlers such as these also function as Internet browser plug-ins. Web pages may contain embedded MIDI sequence files that the browser may direct to the appropriate MIDI plug-in, allowing Web pages to play music. MIDI files may also be used as components of multimedia slide presentations so that selected slides may have sound tracks.

Therefore, the simplest configuration of a MIDI studio is simply a computer, equipped with audio capability and MIDI software, acting as a stand-alone music player and editor.

CHAPTER 7

The MIDI Language

This chapter will cover specifics of the MIDI language, with an explanation of what types of messages may be communicated among instruments. MIDI messages fall into five categories:

Channel Messages (Pertaining to Information on a Particular Channel)

1. Voice
2. Mode

System Messages (Pertaining to the System as a Whole)

3. Real-time
4. Common
5. System Exclusive (SysEx)

MIDI instructions are transmitted in the form of binary numbers. These binary numbers are transmitted by *pulse code modulation* (PCM), the alternation of voltage between high and low levels. A 1 indicates the high level; a 0 indicates the low level. MIDI messages are transmitted in 10-bit words. The first and last bits are start and stop bits, used to identify the beginnings and ends of words. The actual MIDI information is in the middle 8 bits. (Figure 7–1).

The MIDI Language, 1: Channel Voice Messages

Channel Voice messages are those used most commonly in musical performance. These are the messages that correspond to musical notation.

Structure of Channel Voice Messages

Channel Voice messages are transmitted with two types of bytes: *status* bytes and *data* bytes. A status byte determines the type of message and the channel number (*what?* and *where?*). The MSB of a status byte is 1:

```
1nnnnnnn
```

Figure 7–1

Bit Structure of a MIDI Message

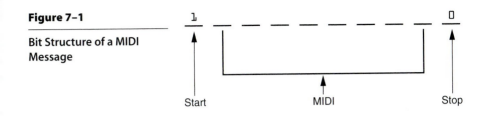

(The letter "n" is used to denote a binary bit having a value of one or zero.) A data byte gives a value (*how much?*) The MSB of a data byte is 0:

0nnnnnnn

With 7 bits following the MSB, a data byte's range of expressible values is 2^7, 0–127. A complete Channel Voice message consists of 1 status byte followed 1 or 2 data bytes, depending on the message type.

The status byte is divided into nibbles (Figure 7–2). Following the defining "1" of the most significant bit, the remaining 3 bits of the most significant nibble serve to define the message type. Thus, 3 bits in the most significant nibble define the message type, allowing a maximum of eight possible categories of messages (although only seven are defined). The 4 bits of the least significant nibble serve to define the channel number of the message.

Channel Voice Message Types

In the "Hex" (Hexadecimal) column, n is a digit from 0–F. In the "Binary" column, n is a digit of 0 or 1.

Note Off
(2 data bytes)

Hex	Binary	
8n	1000nnnn	*<status>*
	0nnnnnnn	*<note number>*
	0nnnnnnn	*<status>*

Note number: Each chromatic pitch is assigned a note number. Middle C is note number 60; middle C# is note 61, middle D is note 62, B below middle C is note 59, and so on.

Velocity: How quickly a note is released. A higher number denotes a quicker release, corresponding to a note fading quickly. A lower number denotes a slower release, corresponding to a note fading slowly.

Figure 7–2

Structure of a Channel Voice Message Status Byte

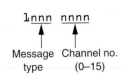

Note On
(2 data bytes)

Hex	*Binary*	
ꟼn	1001nnnn	*<status>*
	0nnnnnnn	*<note number>*
	0nnnnnnn	*<velocity>*

Note number: Same value as that used with Note Off.

Velocity: How quickly a note is depressed. A higher number results in a louder tone. A Note On velocity value of 0 is another way of specifying a Note Off.

Polyphonic Key Pressure (Poly Aftertouch)
(2 data bytes)

Hex	*Binary*	
An	1010nnnn	*<status>*
	0nnnnnnn	*<note number>*
	0nnnnnnn	*<pressure>*

Note number: Same value as that used with Note Off, Note On.

Pressure: Physical pressure applied to the keys after they are depressed. Pressure messages represent an attempt to expand the expressive capability of MIDI instruments in ways that are not possible on acoustic instruments. Pressure applied to the keys is mapped to some modulation parameter (specified for the particular instrument). Thus, each key can generate its own degree of modulation. This is a feature found mainly in higher-end instruments, as separate sensors must be installed for each key.

Channel Key Pressure (Channel Aftertouch)
(1 data byte)

Hex	*Binary*	
Dn	1101nnnn	*<status>*
	0nnnnnnn	*<pressure>*

This is a "poor person's" Aftertouch—less costly to implement and thus found on more instruments than Poly Aftertouch. One pressure value is applied to all notes on a given channel. The value is derived from the key that has the most pressure applied to it.

Program Change
(1 data byte)

Hex	*Binary*	
Cn	1100nnnn	*<status>*
	0nnnnnnn	*<program number>*

Change to a specified patch number on an instrument. With one data byte, up to 128 patch numbers may be specified. A separate message type (to be covered shortly) can allow specification of more than 128 patches.

Pitch Bend
(2 data bytes)

Hex	*Binary*	
En	1110nnnn	*<status>*
	0nnnnnnn	*<value, least significant byte>*
	0nnnnnnn	*<value, most significant byte>*

Like Aftertouch, Pitch Bend is a method of modifying the sound of a held note.

The Pitch Bend wheel on a MIDI instrument is *bidirectional*, meaning that its default position is at the center position of its range of motion. This quality allows the pitch to be bent up or down. When the wheel is released, it returns to this middle position, corresponding to no bend in pitch. By moving the wheel, the held pitches may be bent either up or down to a range that is programmable within the instrument. The range is typically from 1 semitone to 1 octave above and below the note being bent (12 semitones). The use of two data bytes to represent a single value allows a value range with 14 bits of resolution once the defining MSBs of zero are discounted. Pitch Bend messages thus have a value range from 0 to 16,383—8192 values above and 8191 values below the held pitch.

The combination of 2 bytes assigned to one value makes Pitch Bend events a unique Channel Voice structure. The reason is the need for increased resolution. One value byte assigned to the Pitch Bend value would give a range from 0 to 127—64 values above and 63 values below the held pitch. Recall that the range of Pitch Bend may be as much as one octave. While 64 Pitch Bend increments within the range of a semitone would be acceptable, the subdivision of an octave into 64 steps would result in audible discontinuities ("zipper noise").

Musically, Pitch Bend is a special class of Control Change (the next message type). The designers of MIDI assumed that this would be a commonly used form of modulation (just as bending notes is a common expressive technique of guitarists) and assigned it to its own message type with 2 data bytes combined into one value.

Control Change
(2 data bytes)

Hex	*Binary*	
Bn	1011nnnn	*<status>*
	0nnnnnnn	*<controller number>*
	0nnnnnnn	*<value>*

Controllers modify the sound of a sounding note, as do Aftertouch and Pitch Bend. This, however, is a generic category, meant to allow the invention of new performer interfaces that may modulate held notes.

The *controller number* specifies a stream of information. Depending on the type of stream, controller information may described in terms of either what type of device is originating the stream (e.g., a pedal, wheel, slider, etc.) or what type of sound parameter is being controlled (e.g., volume, tremolo, pan position, etc.). The first data byte specifies the control stream. Devices may be configured to respond to or originate MIDI messages on a certain controller number. The second data byte determines the value (or position) of the performance controller.

Controller numbers 120–127 are reserved for a special message type (Channel Mode messages, to be covered presently), leaving 120 definable controllers (0 to 119). The sound parameter affected by a physical controller may vary from instrument to instrument, or may be mappable within a particular instrument. Many controller numbers remain undefined, while certain conventions have become commonplace. Controllers 0–31 are typically *continuous* controllers, generating values within the range 0–127. Some examples are shown in Table 7–1. Controllers 64–69 are typically ON/OFF controllers, such that a value of 0 corresponds to an OFF position, and a value of 127 corresponds to an ON position.

Controllers 32–64 are used as extensions to controllers 0–31. There are times when more resolution than 0–127 is needed, similar to the example of the Pitch Bend message. These controllers allow a way to define a 14-bit number in a controller's value byte.

Controller numbers 32–63 correspond to controller numbers 0–31, respectively. It is expected that they will follow the corresponding lower controller number. The two message's value bytes are combined to form a 14-bit value that is assigned to the particular controller. For example, to get more resolution from a modulation wheel, a message on controller 1 may be followed by a message on controller 33. In this case, the value byte from controller 1 will form the most significant byte of the 14-bit number, and the value byte of controller 33 will form the least significant byte. More generally, if controller n within the range 32–63 is used, it must be used immediately following a message from controller $n - 32$. The value byte from controller $n - 32$ then forms the most significant byte of the combined controller value, and the value byte from controller n forms the combined controller value's least significant byte.

Another example addresses the problem of instruments that have more than 128 patches. Such instruments have their patches arranged in *banks,* each of which contains 128 patches. By convention, controller 0 is used as a bank selector, with the value byte specifying the bank number. Thus, a bank select message (controller 0) followed by a program change message allows selection of [128 $\times$ 128] total patches. If an instrument has more than 128 banks, controller 32 may be used to define a bank

Table 7–1
Standard Controller Number Assignments

	Controller Type	Controller Number	Description
Continuous	Modulation wheel	1	A wheel typically lying next to the pitch bend wheel on a synthesizer. It typically controls effects such as tremolo amount. In contrast to the pitch bend wheel, the modulation wheel is unidirectional, meaning that its default position is at the bottom end of its value range, but it will not "snap" back to this position automatically when the wheel is released.
	Breath controller	2	Controls similar effects to a modulation wheel but is a device that is blown into, with values taken from breath pressure.
	Foot controller	4	A continuous foot pedal, often (but not necessarily) used to control volume.
	Master volume	7	
	Pan	10	Stereo position: (value byte of 64 = CENTER) (value byte of 0 = HARD LEFT) (value byte of 127 = HARD RIGHT)
ON/OFF	Damper pedal	64	
	Soft pedal	67	

number's least significant byte. Thus, program 12 in bank 130 on channel 1 may be chosen with the following sequence of bytes:

Hex	Binary	
B0	10110000	*<status—Control Change, channel 1>*
00	00000000	*<controller number 0—bank select, most significant byte>*
01	00000001	*<value—bank number, most significant byte>*
B0	10110000	*<status—Control Change, channel 1>*
20	00100000	*<controller number 32—bank select, least significant byte>*
02	00000010	*<value—bank number, least significant byte>*
C0	11000000	*<status—Program Change, channel 1>*
0C	00001100	*<program number—12>*

Removing the most significant bit of the two value bytes in the two Control Change messages, the remaining bits are concatenated, producing a fourteen-bit value of 00000010000010, or 130 in decimal notation. This method of selection allows 2^{14} × 128, or 2,097,152 patches. While this amount is more than ample for performance situations, it allows for large databases of patches that may be chosen instantaneously.

Controller information can be extremely useful in both musical and nonmusical applications. Some MIDI instruments consist simply of a bank of physical sliders (or *faders*), each of which may be set to transmit Control Change messages to a different controller number. Therefore, anything that is set to respond to Control Change messages may be "played" with a fader box. Some types of puppets, for example, are configured to respond to Control Change messages, so that one controller number may control the height of an arm, another controller the horizontal position of the arm, another controller pair might control the other arm, and so on. In this way, a puppet's performance may be saved as a sequencer file, and its movements may be edited by modifying controller data within the sequence file.　∎

The MIDI Language, 2: MIDI Modes

Channel Mode Messages

Mode, in this context, refers to the way a device is set to respond to MIDI messages. The MIDI Specification defines four modes of operation.

MIDI Mode Change messages are a special class of Control Change message (controller numbers 120–127). This may be confusing, but the reason is entirely pragmatic. With all the message types that needed to be defined with MIDI's 7 bits, there simply wasn't room in the standard to create a separate message type for mode changes. But since the specification allowed for 128 controller types, far more than existed in 1983, Control Change messages became, in some instances, a miscellaneous repository for other message types.

MIDI Channel Mode messages involve defining two possible states of two parameters: Omni On/Off and Poly/Mono. Four controller numbers determine the four combinations possible with these two parameters:

Omni

1. Off: The device responds to messages on one channel only (controller 124).
2. On: The device responds to messages on any channel (controller 125).

Mono

3. The device can only play one note at a time (controller 126).

Poly

4. The device can play polyphonically (multiple notes simultaneously) (controller 127).

Because each parameter is addressed by a Control Change message, two Control Change messages are required to define a complete change of mode. The four modes are listed next.

Mode 1: Omni On/Poly

Hex	*Binary*	
Bn	1011nnnn	*<Status: Control Change/channel number>*
7D	01111101	*<Controller 125: Omni On>*
00	00000000	*<Value: the value byte has no meaning with controllers 124 and 125>*
Bn	1011nnnn	*<Status: Control Change/channel number>*
7F	01111111	*<Controller 127: Poly On>*
00	00000000	*<Value: the value byte for controller 127 has no meaning when it follows controller 125>*

In Mode 1, an instrument responds polyphonically to MIDI messages on any channel. This mode is meant for troubleshooting to make sure a device is responding to MIDI messages. It has little use in musical applications.

Mode 2: Omni On/Mono

Hex	*Binary*	
Bn	1011nnnn	*<Status: Control Change/channel number>*
7D	01111101	*<Controller 125: Omni On>*
00	00000000	*<Value: the value byte has no meaning with controllers 124 and 125>*
Bn	1011nnnn	*<Status: Control Change/channel number>*
7E	01111110	*<Controller 126: Mono On>*
00	00000000	*<Value: the value byte for controller 126 has no meaning when it follows controller 125>*

In Mode 2, an instrument responds monophonically to messages on any channel. This mode has limited (if any) usefulness and is rarely (if ever) used. It is often not even implemented on instruments. This combination of mode parameters exists more by definition than out of any practicality.

Mode 3: Omni Off/Poly

Hex	*Binary*	
Bn	1011nnnn	*<Status: Control Change/channel number>*
7C	01111100	*<Controller 124: Omni Off>*
00	00000000	*<Value: the value byte has no meaning with controllers 124 and 125>*
Bn	1011nnnn	*<Status: Control Change/channel number>*
7F	01111111	*<Controller 127: Poly On>*
00	00000000	*<Value: the value byte for controller 127 has no meaning when it follows controller 124>*

In Mode 3, an instrument responds polyphonically to messages on one channel only. In the 1980s, this was the standard mode for studio configurations in which each instrument was set to respond messages on one base channel.

Mode 4: Omni Off/Mono

Hex	Binary	
Bn	1011nnnn	*<Status: Control Change/channel number>*
7C	01111100	*<Controller 124: Omni Off>*
00	00000000	*<Value: the value byte has no meaning with controllers 124 and 125>*
Bn	1011nnnn	*<Status: Control Change/channel number>*
7E	01111110	*<Controller 126: Mono On>*
0n	0000nnnn	*<Number of channels to receive; SEE EXPLANATION BELOW>*

In Mode 4, an instrument responds monophonically to messages on one channel only.

In the 1980s, many instruments featured a portamento effect, in which one pitch would slide to the next during legato playing when Mode 4 was activated. As MIDI instruments expanded beyond keyboard types, Mode 4 became the standard mode for instruments that were being triggered by a wind or string controller. Since the early 1990s, this mode has taken on a special implementation in many polyphonic devices. As MIDI instrument design developed, manufacturers began to create instruments that could respond to messages on more than one channel.

This was not a case of Omni On, which implies that an instrument is insensitive to the channel portion of a MIDI message. This new feature signified, rather, a new type of mode in which an instrument had a number of "subinstruments," or parts, each of which was set to play messages on one particular channel polyphonically. These multitimbral devices respond differently to Mode 4: when Mode 4 is activated, they operate in *Multi Mode,* which is not monophonic. For such instruments, the last byte of the Mono On message determines how many channels the instrument may respond to. If the third byte's value is 0, then the instrument responds to as many channels as it has parts (typically 16). However, it may be desirable for a Multi Mode instrument to respond to fewer than 16 channels. If the second nibble of the value byte is some number from 1 to 15, the instrument will respond to the number of channels that corresponds to the value of this nibble, starting with channel 1. For example, if the value of the nibble is 5, the instrument will respond to messages on channels 1 through 5.

Other Types of Mode Messages

All Notes Off (controller 123)

Hex	Binary	
Bn	1011nnnn	*<Status: Control Change/channel number>*
7B	01111011	*<Controller 123: All Notes Off>*
00	00000000	*<The value byte has no meaning with controller 123>*

Sends a Note Off to all notes on the specified channel (except those notes currently being played). Eliminates "stuck notes" on an instrument, a condition that sometimes occurs following a large amount of MIDI activity: sometimes a Note Off gets lost, resulting in a note continuing to sound.

All Sound Off (controller 120)

Hex	*Binary*	
Bn	1011nnnn	*<Status: Control Change/channel number>*
78	01111000	*<Controller 120: All Sound Off>*
00	00000000	*<The value byte has no meaning with controller 120>*

Immediately mutes all notes, regardless of any envelope release times that would normally follow a Note Off message. This is more immediate and global than an All Notes Off message. It is a useful command to send when the "Stop" button is hit in a sequencer program.

Reset All Controllers (controller 121)

Hex	*Binary*	
Bn	1011nnnn	*<Status: Control Change/channel number>*
79	01111001	*<Controller 121: Reset All Controllers>*
00	00000000	*<The value byte has no meaning with controller 121>*

Returns all controllers to their default state (Mod Wheel to 0, Pan to 64, and so on).

Local Control (controller 122)

Hex	*Binary*	
Bn	1011nnnn	*<Status: Control Change/channel number>*
7A	01111010	*<Controller 122 Local Control>*
00–7F	0nnnnnnn	*<Value byte: 0–63 = Off; 64–127 = On>*

Disables the sound-generating circuitry of a device, so that it only functions to send MIDI information to other devices. In many cases, a Volume setting of zero would have the same auditory effect. Turning Local Control off, however, is more efficient computationally. Even when a device has its volume lowered, it still constantly scans its status for held notes, Aftertouch, wheel settings, etc. This command stops it from doing this extra work. Also, there could be complicated multi-instrument performance configurations in which a device might be able to receive information that it is also sending. Turning Local Control to Off alleviates any MIDI feedback problems from such a configuration. ∎

The MIDI Language, 3: System-Level Messages

System messages are meant to address not just one device, but all devices on a MIDI network. System messages are in the form:

Hex	*Binary*
Fn	1111nnnn

The first nibble identifies it as a System message, with the second nibble defining message type. (*Note:* this explains why there are only seven out of a possible eight Channel Voice messages. The most significant nibble, 1111, is reserved for System Level messages.) Some System messages require more bytes, others are a single byte in length.

System Common Messages

System Common messages address certain housekeeping issues in preparing instruments for an appropriate playing state. These messages fall into the range

Hex	*Binary*
F1-F7	11110001-11110111

MIDI Time Code Quarter Frame

Hex	*Binary*	
F1	11110001	*<MTC Quarter Frame>*
	0nnnnnnn	*<timestamp>*

Used for synchronizing MIDI with SMPTE timecode used in video. The first byte is a MTC Quarter Frame identifier, signifying that the next byte will be a component of the SMPTE `hour:minute:second:frame` timecode specification. Two MTC byte pairs are required to specify a value for each of the four time fields (hence the name, as each set of pairs specifies one quarter of the total specification). Thus 16 bytes are needed to transmit the time coordinates of a given frame. This and the next message type will be covered in more detail in the section "MIDI and Time."

Song Position Pointer

Hex	*Binary*	
F2	11110010	*<Song Position Pointer>*
	0nnnnnnn	*<beat position, least significant byte>*
	0nnnnnnn	*<beat position, most significant byte>*

Used to set a sequencer or drum machine to start at a point other than the beginning of a sequence, some specified number of MIDI beats from the sequence's first beat. MIDI beats will be covered in more detail in the section "MIDI and Time."

Song Select

Hex	*Binary*	
F3	11110011	*<Song Select>*
	0nnnnnnn	*<song number>*

Used to choose a particular sequence number from memory; the equivalent of a Program Change message, directed to a sequencer or drum machine file.

Tune Request

Hex	*Binary*
F6	11110110

Sends a command for analog synthesizers to tune themselves; largely obsolete, because analog synthesizers are rarely produced today.

End System Exclusive

Hex	*Binary*
F7	11110111

System Exclusive is another message class (to be covered shortly). Because of extra available bits in the System Common range, this command is defined with a System Common message number.

System Real-Time Messages

This message class is for controlling clock-based operations during playback. They are all 1 byte, and their range is 11111nnn.

Timing Clock

Hex   *Binary*
F8   11111000

When active, a Timing Clock byte is transmitted 24 times per quarter note as a metronome pulse to keep slave instruments in synchronization with the timing master. In the 1980s, a complex performance setup might involve a number of dedicated sequencers and drum machines, all running in tandem. The need for Timing Clock messages in theory could be used today, as on-board sequencers are a feature of many instruments. All such devices may act as slave sequencers under the control of a master sequencer. With all slave instruments configured to receive time information from Timing Clock messages, the master clock device can keep them all in tempo by means of Timing Clock synchronizing pulses.

Sequence Start

Hex   *Binary*
F A   11111010

Begins playback of a sequence from its beginning.

Sequence Continue

Hex   *Binary*
F B   11111011

Resumes playback of a paused sequence from the current position.

Stop

Hex   *Binary*
F C   11111100

Halts playing a sequence immediately.

Active Sensing

Hex   *Binary*
F E   11111110

This byte, an announcement of "I am still here," may be sent at least every 300 msec when a device is sending no other information. Its purpose is to allow a sequencer to verify that all devices remain connected. Active sensing is often not implemented because the added bytes can slow down transmission of other information.

System Reset

Hex   *Binary*
F F   11111111

Returns all an instrument's values to factory presets. This command is only likely to be useful in extreme emergency situations.

System Exclusive Messages

System Exclusive (SysEx) allows a device to be addressed in ways that are not covered by the MIDI standard. It was a compromise meant to reassure manufacturers who feared that a standard would prohibit them from implementing unique features. SysEx allows manufacturers to include proprietary features in their products and still have the features addressable by MIDI commands. Messages to change these proprietary elements are sandwiched between SysEx Start and Stop bytes, as described next.

Start System Exclusive

Hex	Binary
F0	11110000

This command takes the system out of normal MIDI operating mode. It is followed by a manufacturer's identification byte. Unique identification bytes are assigned by the MIDI Manufacturers' Association to each manufacturer. Different devices by the same company may be identified by subsequent identification bytes. Following the identification bytes, any number of bytes may follow. The device is now in a state to receive proprietary, nonstandardized instructions as outlined by the manufacturer.

End System Exclusive (EOX)

Hex	Binary
F7	11110111

Returns the system to normal MIDI operating mode. SysEx messages may be used to address programmable elements of a particular instrument. Voice Editor/Librarians rely on System Exclusive messages to modify the patches of an instrument. Some early writers criticized System Exclusive as an "escape hatch," defeating the purpose of a standard by allowing manufacturers to deviate from it at their whim. However, contrary to these warnings, no manufacturer has relied on SysEx to replace any message types covered by the MIDI standard. It remains a means for proprietary features of an instrument to be addressed, as per its original intention. ∎

MIDI and Time

The MIDI specification provides for a variety of event types, but it contains no information about time or duration. A sequencer allows a certain degree of time control by adding timestamps to MIDI events. But an added level of time control is necessary for multiple time-based devices to work together. To address this need, MIDI does contain specifications by which multiple clock-based devices may operate in synchronization.

MIDI Synchronization

There are two types of MIDI synchronization. Before they are discussed in detail, consider two examples in which synchronization is necessary:

Example 1: A live performance may involve multiple sequencers and drum machines. All devices must have a common clock source if they are to play together.

Example 2: A studio project may involve work with a multitrack tape deck and a sequencer. Each tape track may record a multitrack (MIDI) sequence. The tape deck and the sequencer must have a common clock source so that successive recordings on separate tape tracks are in synchronization.

Relative synchronization uses clicks—in the form of voltage changes—to act as a common metronome pulse among devices. Relative synchronization is simple and economical to implement, but it lacks flexibility. All pulses are the same, based on the piece's tempo. Therefore, the piece must always be run from the beginning to ensure that all devices are playing at the same place in the piece.

Absolute synchronization involves the use of distinct pulses, each containing a time address. Although this is a more complicated method of transmission, it is much more flexible than relative synchronization. Playback or recording may begin from any point in a piece. This is much more convenient when creating material that is to be placed several minutes into the piece.

MIDI Clock

MIDI Clock is a MIDI form of relative synchronization. A Timing Clock message, described earlier, is used as a "conductor track," a common pulse that governs all devices. It is based on a resolution of 24 pulses per quarter note (ppqn). This is a useful value, as 24 can be divided by 2 or 3, allowing resolution to 64th-note triplets. Many sequencers now use finer resolution, such as 240 or 480 ppqn. But when MIDI Clock is being used to synchronize devices, pulses are generated at 24 ppqn.

Song Position Pointer

Synchronization of devices by pulses existed prior to the creation of MIDI. But one of MIDI's innovations was to allow sequences to play from a point other than the beginning of a piece. Song Position Pointer messages allow an offset of a specified number of MIDI Clock pulses as a playback starting point.

Frequency Shift Keying (FSK)

MIDI Clock messages allow devices to be synchronized via MIDI, as in the first synchronization example. For MIDI devices to be synchronized with tape decks, as in the second synchronization example, MIDI Clock pulses must be converted to an audio signal that may be recorded to tape. Pulses are converted to a tone that alternates regularly in frequency, an FSK signal. This audio signal may then act as the pulse source to drive other devices.

FSK allows MIDI to be recorded on multiple tape tracks by the following steps (Figure 7–3):

- The sequencer is set to run from its internal clock.
- The FSK pulse is sent to an input of the tape deck to be recorded on one track of the tape.
- The sequence is run, but no instruments are recorded. Only the FSK signal is recorded to tape. Recording the synchronization signal on one track is termed "striping" the tape.
- The tape is rewound.

Figure 7–3

Recording an FSK
Synchronization Track to
Tape

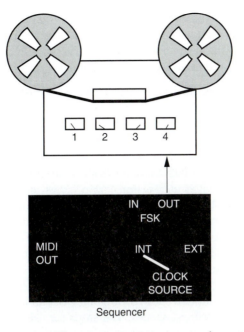

Sequencer

- The sequencer is set to run by external clock (Figure 7–4).
- Audio out is connected from the striped tape track to the sequencer's clock source.
- The instrument's audio out is directed to another tape track.
- PLAY is activated on the sequencer. With the sequencer set to external clock mode, playback will not start until OVERDUB/RECORD is activated on the tape deck. At that point the master clock signal is sent to the sequencer and playback commences.
- At the end of the piece, the tape is rewound.

Figure 7–4

Recording Audio with FSK
as the Clock Source

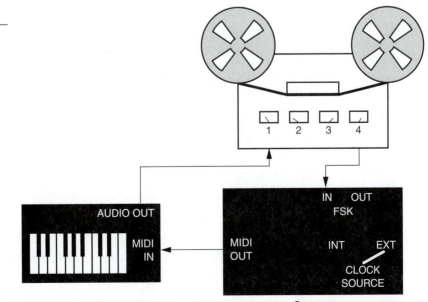

Sequencer

- Appropriate adjustments are made to the MIDI instrument (such as patch changes). Its audio output is sent to another tape track. The sequence is run again, OVERDUB/RECORD is activated on the tape deck, and the next track is recorded.

This process is repeated until all MIDI tracks are recorded onto all necessary tape tracks.

MIDI Time Code (MTC)

MTC represents absolute time synchronization, in which pulses are not generic, but rather are associated with a timestamp. Thus, each pulse contains information about where in the piece it occurs. MTC is a MIDI translation of SMPTE timecode, the standard used for synchronizing video in the film and television industry. (SMPTE is an acronym for Society of Motion Picture and Television Engineers.)

In SMPTE timecode, timestamps are defined by four fields: `hour:minute:second:frame`. Thus, a MIDI sequencer, set to run by an external SMPTE signal, may be used to score a video meant for film or TV. A sequencer slaved to a SMPTE synchronization signal allows music or sound effects to be placed at the correct frame to match visual cues. The steps for using a sequencer and a tape deck striped with SMPTE code are the same as those in FSK synching. But in this configuration, there is the added element of a VCR. A VCR with a SMPTE-striped video acts as the master for both a tape deck and a sequencer.

A more recent alternative to film scoring has become possible now that video material may be digitized fairly easily and computers typically are equipped with enough memory to store video files. Many sequencing programs are now able to work with video files, allowing composers to create scores for videos without having to configure multiple tape decks to run together. A video file may act as a component of a sequence file so that activating PLAY, either from the video file or from the sequencer, causes both to run in tandem.

The function of MIDI Time Code Quarter Frame messages is to translate between SMPTE and MIDI. `hour:minute:second:frame` are each defined by 4 bytes, two pairs of 2 bytes. The first byte of a pair is an MTC identifier, and the second gives information about one of the four time coordinate fields. Each SMPTE field is defined by an 8-bit byte. The second byte of each pair contributes one nibble to this 8-bit byte. Figures 7–5, 7–6, and 7–7 illustrate how 16 bytes are used to define the four fields that define a given video frame.

MIDI Implementation Charts

Typically, MIDI devices cannot send and/or receive every message type. A MIDI implementation chart details which messages a device is capable of sending and receiving. The implementation chart is part of the MIDI documentation, along with information about what parameters may be addressed via SysEx. Shoppers who are uncertain of whether a particular device is fully featured in MIDI may check the implementation chart prior to purchase. The MIDI implementation chart shown in Figure 7–8 lists MIDI functions in the leftmost column, with two columns to indicate whether messages are transmitted or received. An "o" indicates that the instrument is capable of sending or receiving the function, and an "x" indicates that the instrument does not have this capability.

Figure 7–5

MTC Message Structure, 1

MTC Quarter Frame messages translate SMPTE `hour:minute:second:frame` definitions. Eight pairs of bytes define a single frame.

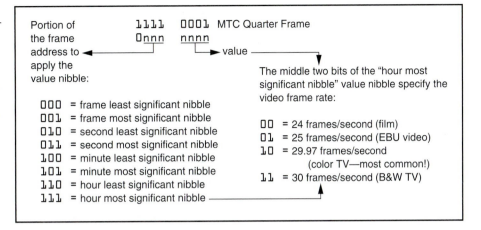

Portion of the frame address to apply the value nibble:

`1111` `0001` MTC Quarter Frame
`0nnn` `nnnn`

value

The middle two bits of the "hour most significant nibble" value nibble specify the video frame rate:

`000` = frame least significant nibble
`001` = frame most significant nibble
`010` = second least significant nibble
`011` = second most significant nibble
`100` = minute least significant nibble
`101` = minute most significant nibble
`110` = hour least significant nibble
`111` = hour most significant nibble

`00` = 24 frames/second (film)
`01` = 25 frames/second (EBU video)
`10` = 29.97 frames/second (color TV—most common!)
`11` = 30 frames/second (B&W TV)

Figure 7–6

MTC Message Structure, 2

Message sequence defining a video frame n = 0 or 1, read as a value; U = undefined, transmitted as 0 but containing no numeric information; F = frame rate definer.

Frame least significant nibble
`1111` `0001` MTC Quarter Frame
`0000` `nnnn`

Frame most significant nibble
`1111` `0001` MTC Quarter Frame
`0001` `UUUn`

5 bits define frame number, range of 0–30

Second least significant nibble
`1111` `0001` MTC Quarter Frame
`0010` `nnnn`

Second most significant nibble
`1111` `0001` MTC Quarter Frame
`0011` `UUnn`

6 bits define frame number, range of 0–60

Minute least significant nibble
`1111` `0001` MTC Quarter Frame
`0100` `nnnn`

Minute most significant nibble
`1111` `0001` MTC Quarter Frame
`0101` `UUnn`

6 bits define second number, range of 0–60

Hour least significant nibble
`1111` `0001` MTC Quarter Frame
`0110` `nnnn`

Hour most significant nibble
`1111` `0001` MTC Quarter Frame
`0111` `UFFn`

5 bits define hour number, range of 0–24

Figure 7–7

MTC Message Structure, 3

Message sequence defining 1:57:13:17 at 29.97 frames/sec

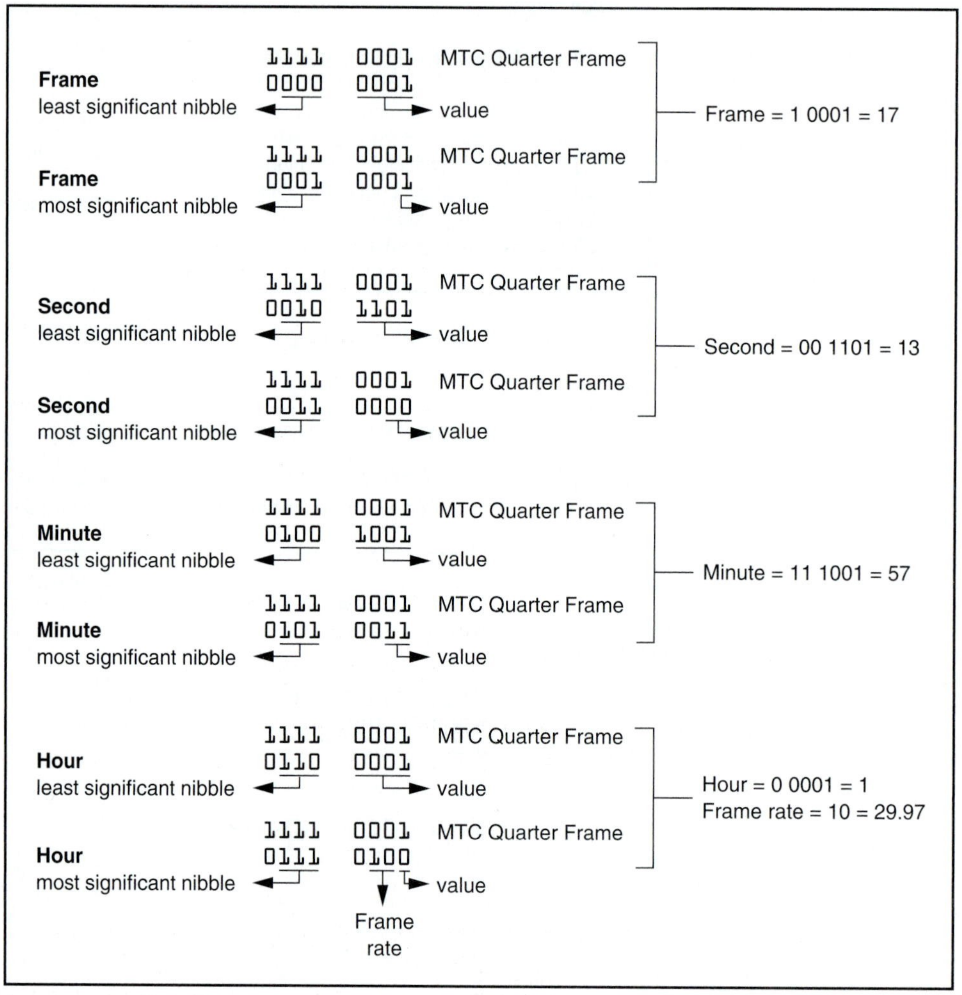

```
                    1111  0001   MTC Quarter Frame
Frame               0000  0001
least significant nibble  ◄───┘   └──► value              Frame = 1 0001 = 17

                    1111  0001   MTC Quarter Frame
Frame               0001  0001
most significant nibble  ◄───┘   └► value


                    1111  0001   MTC Quarter Frame
Second              0010  1101
least significant nibble  ◄───┘   └──► value              Second = 00 1101 = 13

                    1111  0001   MTC Quarter Frame
Second              0011  0000
most significant nibble  ◄───┘   └► value


                    1111  0001   MTC Quarter Frame
Minute              0100  1001
least significant nibble  ◄───┘   └──► value              Minute = 11 1001 = 57

                    1111  0001   MTC Quarter Frame
Minute              0101  0011
most significant nibble  ◄───┘   └──► value


                    1111  0001   MTC Quarter Frame
Hour                0110  0001
least significant nibble  ◄───┘   └──► value              Hour = 0 0001 = 1
                                                          Frame rate = 10 = 29.97
                    1111  0001   MTC Quarter Frame
Hour                0111  0100
most significant nibble  ◄───┘  ▼ └──► value
                                Frame
                                rate
```

From Figure 7–8, the instrument appears incapable of transmitting most MIDI message types. This is because the particular instrument is a tone generator and not a keyboard, so it not meant to create MIDI data, but mainly to receive it. The instrument does not transmit a velocity value for Note Off messages, so presumably the instrument transmits Note Offs with Note On messages with velocity values of zero. The instrument is also not capable of recognizing Polyphonic Aftertouch. Furthermore, its Pitch Bend range is only 7 bits, although the assignable range is 12 semitones. Presumably, this was a compromise to allow faster processing of incoming MIDI Pitch Bend messages, at the expense of the added resolution provided by the MIDI specification. It would be up to a prospective purchaser to determine whether Polyphonic Aftertouch was needed, and whether the 7 bits of Pitch Bend resolution created noticeable discontinuities.

Figure 7–8

MIDI Implementation Chart

Used with permission of Yamaha Corporation of America.

```
YAMAHA  [ Tone Generator ]                    Date :07-MAY-1990
        Model  TG77    MIDI Implementation Chart  Version : 1.0
+----------------------------------------------------------------------+
:                    : Transmitted  :  Recognized  :    Remarks        :
:          Function ... :           :              :                   :
:------------------------+-------------+--------------+-----------------:
:Basic     Default  : x            : 1 - 16       : memorized         :
:Channel   Changed  : x            : 1 - 16       :                   :
:------------------------+-------------+--------------+-----------------:
:          Default  : x            : 1,2,3,4      : memorized         :
:Mode      Messages : x            : x            :                   :
:          Altered  : ************* : x            :                   :
:------------------------+-------------+--------------+-----------------:
:Note               : x            : 0 - 127      :                   :
:Number : True voice: ************* : 1 - 127      :                   :
:------------------------+-------------+--------------+-----------------:
:Velocity Note ON   : x            : o  v=1-127   :                   :
:         Note OFF  : x            : x            :                   :
:------------------------+-------------+--------------+-----------------:
:After    Key's     : x            : x            :                   :
:Touch    Ch's      : x            : o            :                   :
:------------------------+-------------+--------------+-----------------:
:Pitch Bender       : x            : o  0-12 semi :7 bit resolution:  :
:------------------------+-------------+--------------+-----------------:
:                 1 : x            : o            :Modulation wheel:  :
:                 2 : x            : o            :Breath control     :
:                 4 : x            : o            :Foot control       :
: Control         6 : x            : o            :Data entry knob    :
:                 7 : x            : o            :Volume             :
: Change         64 : x            : o            :Sustain            :
:                65 : x            : o            :Portamento         :
:                96 : x            : o            :Data entry +1      :
:                97 : x            : o            :Data entry -1      :
:        0 -      6 : x            : o            :Assignable         :
:        8 -    120 : x            : o            :Assignable         :
:                   :              :              :                   :
:                   :              :              :                   :
:------------------------+-------------+--------------+-----------------:
:Prog               : x            : o 0-127  *1  :assignable         :
:Change : True #    : ************* : *2           :                   :
:------------------------+-------------+--------------+-----------------:
:System Exclusive   : o       *3   : o       *3   :voice etc.         :
:------------------------+-------------+--------------+-----------------:
:System : Song Pos  : x            : x            :                   :
:       : Song Sel  : x            : x            :                   :
:Common : Tune      : x            : x            :                   :
:------------------------+-------------+--------------+-----------------:
:System   :Clock    : x            : x            :                   :
:Real Time :Commands: x            : x            :                   :
:------------------------+-------------+--------------+-----------------:
:Aux  :Local ON/OFF : x            : x            :                   :
:     :All Notes OFF: x            : x            :                   :
:Mes- :Active Sense : o            : o            :                   :
:sages:Reset        : x            : x            :                   :
:------------------------+-------------+--------------+-----------------:
:Notes: *1 ; receive if program change sw is not off.              :
:      *2 ; voice  : 0 - 63 , multi : 0 - 15                       :
:                  ( if program change sw is not "table" )         :
:      *3 ; transmit/receive if device No. is not off.             :
:                                                                  :
+----------------------------------------------------------------------+
    Mode 1 : OMNI ON,  POLY   Mode 2 : OMNI ON,  MONO   o : Yes
    Mode 3 : OMNI OFF, POLY   Mode 4 : OMNI OFF, MONO   x : No
```

CHAPTER 8

MIDI and More

Nonkeyboard MIDI Instruments

The Challenge Imposed by MIDI

MIDI is most compatible with keyboard and percussion-type instruments. A MIDI message may be thought of as corresponding to each written note in a piece of notated music. However, a "note" or "musical event" means something different when played by a keyboard or percussion instrument than it does when played by a wind or string instrument. With percussive/keyboard instruments, the sound is triggered and then released, with little possibility for alteration by the performer during the note's duration. Granted, Aftertouch, Pitch Bend, and Control Change messages are meant to add a level of performer expressiveness during a note's duration. Still, keyboard instruments are in an entirely different expressive class from wind and string instruments, for which the concept of a "note" is not a static event at all. Instruments such as the flute or the violin produce constant sonic variations in the hands of a skilled performer. Each event from a page of music notation is subject to an uncountable number of subtle and unwritten "micromodulations." In the case of a violin, these modulations may be due to changes in finger position and pressure. In the case of a flute, breath pressure, embouchure shape, and position of the instrument in relation to the mouth keep the instrument's sound in a constant state of evolution. These subtle adjustments are the result of years of training and are likely to be unconscious when carried out by a virtuoso performer. MIDI versions of wind and string instruments will be discussed following a discussion of the problem of equipping these instruments with sufficient expressive capability.

Micromodulations on a MIDI instrument are likely to take the form of Control Change messages. It was noted in the section "MIDI Compromises" (Chapter 6) that at the MIDI transmission rate, approximately 1 millisecond is required to transmit a 3-byte message. The capability of transmitting 1000 Control Change messages per second may seem ample until consideration is given to the degree of nuance in the performance of these instruments. Each of these variation types—pressure, vibrato, embouchure, and so on—may conceivably be mapped to a different controller stream and set to affect different aspects of an instrument's timbre. These changes are likely to be complex, simultaneous, and interacting. Yet MIDI, with its serial transmission, is in reality incapable of transmitting simultaneous events. With many Control Change events occurring close together in time, the intended rate of modulation may surpass the MIDI event rate. "MIDI choke" refers to a condition where instruments are not able to keep up with the activity generated by a performer. It may have a number of unfortunate results. The response time of instruments may suffer from an audible delay between the time a performer activates it and the time its effects are heard. Thus, the instrument will lack effective responsiveness necessary for virtuosic playing. Alternatively, some events may simply be lost in the transmission shuffle and never received by the instrument. A common example of this is the "stuck note." After a flurry of MIDI activity is brought to a halt, occasionally one note continues sounding after all the others have stopped. This is the result of a Note Off message being lost in the event stream.

Another problem particularly challenging for string instruments is that of creating a note number value as a result of sensing the motion of a vibrating string. Typically, two to three complete cycles are necessary before an estimation of the string's fundamental frequency may be made. This estimation is not possible until the steady-state portion of the string's vibration has established itself following the initial transient. Thus, there is necessarily some delay between the time a string is activated and when its frequency may be estimated. The delay is most noticeable with low tones, particularly those from a bass. A frequency of A at 110 Hz requires 27 milliseconds to complete three cycles. This interval following a transient can result in an audible delay between the string's activation and the transmission of the Note On message.

Although manufacturers of nonkeyboard MIDI instruments have ways to reduce the possibility of MIDI choke, musicians are advised to take instruments for a "road test" before purchasing them. It would be a mistake to expect these instruments to function as substitutes for their analog counterparts. They should be evaluated in terms of what new capabilities they can offer, rather than how well they imitate orchestral instruments.

MIDI String Instruments

Manufacturers of MIDI guitars have addressed the problem of pitch-to-MIDI conversion in two ways. One is to use filters to "see through" the noise of the transient, thus reducing the time necessary to sense a string's vibration frequency (filters will be covered in Chapter 9). The other is an early-detection technology whereby the initial transient wave pattern reaching the bridge of the instrument is compared to patterns that were "learned" at the factory. This learning is achieved by a *neural net,* a computer technology by which computers estimate interpretations of data and the errors are fed back to the "estimator" and identified as such. The result is that with repeated estimations, the computer "learns" how to interpret input correctly. Due to this factory "training," with these instruments the MIDI note number is determined quickly and is not based on analyzing the motion of a string once it has reached its steady state of vibration. Furthermore, the neural net can allow the instrument to sound differently depending on the location of the pluck, allowing the musician added expressivity.

MIDI string instruments include guitars, mandolins, banjos, violins, violas, cellos, basses, and some specialized designs that do not resemble any acoustic instrument. They are typically configured so that each string transmits on a different MIDI channel. This allows note bending on a single string to be translated into Pitch Bend messages on one channel only, so that the bending of each string is a discrete MIDI stream. This also allows each string to trigger different patches for polytimbral effects.

A string instrument is meant to send MIDI to a device operating in Omni Off/Mono Mode, which means that the receiving instrument is configured to receive instructions only on certain channels and is capable of playing single-line melodies only. (The particulars of MIDI Channel Modes were described in the last chapter.) Monophonic transmission is necessary for two reasons. One is so that each string may transmit on a separate channel so that its expressiveness is directed to only one voice on the receiving synthesizer. Another is so that notes from one string do not overlap and clog the MIDI event stream with simultaneous note events; rather, each new note activated from a string releases the currently sounding note.

MIDI string instruments may be classified into three construction types, with ascending levels of expressive capability:

1. Pitch-to-MIDI conversion may occur within an instrument, which is equipped with a MIDI OUT jack.

2. Others leave the MIDI conversion to an external device. A 13-pin MIDI guitar cable connects to a guitar-to-MIDI converter.

3. A special pickup may be attached to any guitar (even an acoustic one) that connects to a converter box. Guitar players may thus retain the sound of their instruments and add the sound of a MIDI instrument to it, provided they are willing to alter their instrument by attaching a pickup to it. In this construction type, each string has its own pickup, making this the most flexible type of string MIDI instrument.

Some MIDI string instruments have onboard buttons or switches with capabilities that include sending Program Change messages to receiving instruments or controlling various synthesis parameters. Although the instruments that perform pitch-to-MIDI conversion are the easiest to set up, converter boxes typically contain greater levels of expressive capability. They need to be calibrated, however, to match the expressiveness of the player. Pitch Bend range, for example, has to be tweaked so that a player's bent strings produce the desired change in pitch from the receiving MIDI device.

Some converter boxes include a built-in synthesizer, while others simply generate MIDI information that is then sent on to another MIDI instrument. The pitch sensing from converter boxes is typically faster than that achieved by converters built into an instrument, meaning that the timing of quick passages and strums will be maintained more accurately and that bending strings will result in smoother Pitch Bend values. Converter boxes may also contain jacks for MIDI foot pedals, allowing additional control of parameters such as volume, pan position, balance among synthesizer patches, and timbral elements. Some are able to transmit information about the position of the pick between the pickup and neck of the instrument and translate pick position into MIDI Control Change messages that may be addressed to timbral controls on the receiving MIDI instrument. More advanced converters on MIDI violins, violas, cellos, and basses may have algorithms to track bow movements.

MIDI Wind Instruments

MIDI wind instruments may be classified into two types: reed instruments and brass-like valve instruments. However, these instruments are not as direct an analog to their acoustic counterparts as are MIDI string instruments. Although there are definite similarities, MIDI winds are really different instruments, and wind players should expect a certain retraining time to master them. Like master controller keyboards, wind controllers do not produce sound, but only MIDI events. The fingering of MIDI wind instruments is sometimes different from that of acoustic wind instruments. Another difference is that extra buttons may be included to send Control Change and Program Change events.

Reed instruments send Pitch Bend events generated from bite pressure on the reed. Breath pressure may be used to transmit a variety of expressive messages, including Aftertouch and controller types such as Modulation and Volume. A note's initial breath pressure translates into a Note On event's velocity value.

Some wind controllers allow polyphonic playing with settings that generate additional Note On events at fixed intervals in relation to each note produced by the player, thus forming chords. A variation on this capability is a function that can hold a sounding note as a pedal point while new notes are played over it.

A problem with MIDI wind instruments may arise when a change of note requires more than one finger to change position. In reality, human performers rarely have all fingers in position simultaneously, an inaccuracy that is not noticeable on acoustic instruments because a certain amount of time is necessary for a note to sound following breath pressure. With a MIDI instrument, each change in fingering may produce a new Note On event, so these inaccuracies become audible. Many wind instruments have a *lag* setting that slows the response of the sound, thus shadowing the unwanted extra note events.

MIDI Percussion Instruments

Percussion, being triggered like a keyboard instrument, is more naturally inclined toward the event-based structure of MIDI transmission. Hence, MIDI percussion instruments do not need to address the level of performance-related issues that is necessary for expressive wind and string instruments. Still, manufacturers of percussion instruments have been no less diligent in addressing the performance issues of their products.

MIDI percussion instruments have the ability to continue to play when dampened, allowing effects such as that achieved by many vibraphone players when they lightly touch a key with a mallet after it has been struck. Similarly, MIDI cymbals may respond to being choked by grabbing them after they are struck, emulating another common acoustic effect. MIDI drums may also sense velocity, with separate sensors on the edges for rim shots. Special instruments for mallets may be able to respond to a player dragging the mallet across the key, be capable of transmitting Aftertouch messages from mallet pressure, or even have a sensor that generates MIDI data based on the mallet's position on the striking surface. MIDI percussion instruments often contain jacks for extra controllers that do not require the use of the hands, such as breath controllers, or pedals for messages such as Control Change, Program Change, or sustain.

The level of timbral flexibility that exists with any MIDI instrument extends to drums: a signal triggered by a drum pad may trigger any type of sound. Thus, a single drum set may be made to sound like any number of instruments (percussion or nonpercussion), limited only by the capabilities of the receiving MIDI instrument.

A significant pragmatic issue with MIDI drums and percussion concerns amplification and balance. Drums create particular challenges in small auditoriums and clubs, where microphones are often necessary on smaller drums to avoid their being drowned out by a bass drum. This situation then creates a slippery slope in which every other instrument must then be amplified in order to balance properly with the drum set. A MIDI drum set, having no acoustic sound, is entirely controllable by amplification and thus alleviates the balance problems created by acoustic drum sets. Ironically, MIDI percussion is on the expensive end of the MIDI spectrum and may not be easily affordable for musicians who play small venues.

Additions to the MIDI Protocol

Since MIDI was introduced, its widespread adoption has virtually locked the music industry into the standard as it was originally laid out. Any upgrades would involve rendering such a large number of devices obsolete that it seems that MIDI will most likely remain in its initial form. Practical issues, however, have led to numerous expansions of MIDI functionality meant either to improve compatibility among devices or to refine what may be done with certain message types.

Standard MIDI Files

The proliferation of MIDI software on the market created a need for a file standard so that information could be exchanged among software made by different man-ufacturers or so that musicians could switch or upgrade software programs with-out having to discard their earlier work. Definition of the Standard MIDI file (SMF) was added to the MIDI standard in 1988. Standard MIDI files are to sequencers what plain text files are to word processors—a generic file format that may be opened in a variety of applications (typically sequencers and notation programs). They have the extension ".mid." Most sequencers and notators can export their con-tents to Standard MIDI files.

SMFs begin with a *header,* which is an information segment that precedes the MIDI data. The header indicates

1. The file type (the three SMF file types will be discussed below)
2. The number of tracks in the file
3. A *division* value that determines whether the time values stored in the file are relative or absolute (see the section "MIDI and Time" in Chapter 7 for a discussion of relative and absolute time measurements)

Standard MIDI files come in three flavors:

Type 0: All information is contained in one sequencer track. When Type 0 files are imported into a sequencer, some programs prompt the user to decide whether the file should be "exploded" into 16 tracks, with each track containing information from the corresponding channel number.

Type 1: Track information is maintained. Note that sequencer tracks and MIDI channels are two different things. A single sequencer track may con-tain information on more than one channel (though this is probably not advisable); likewise, multiple tracks may contain information on the same channel.

Type 2: Track information is maintained, and each track has its own tempo.

Standard MIDI files interleave MIDI events with time values, so each MIDI event is preceded by a *delta time* value that indicates the number of elapsed clock ticks since the last MIDI event. Depending on the division value in the file's header, the delta time values may refer to relative time (clock ticks per quarter note) or absolute time (hour, minute, and second). The delta time is a variable-length value, expressed in 8-bit bytes that are combined to form as large a value as is needed (just as two value bytes are combined to form one value with Pitch Bend messages). Seven bits of each byte indicate its value; the MSB of each byte indicates whether further delta time bytes will follow or not. An MSB of 1 indicates that further delta time bytes are to come, and an MSB of 0 indicates that this is the last delta time byte, and the next value contained in the file describes a MIDI event.

Standard MIDI files also allow *meta-events* to be stored. Meta-events refer to other information that is not related to timing or MIDI events, but may provide added information about the file. Examples of meta-events include tempo changes, track names, key signatures, lyrics, and instrument names. Meta-event types are registered with the International MIDI Association, and each has a unique number that allows it to be specified within a Standard MIDI file. A meta-event follows a delta time event and precedes a MIDI event. A unique byte of **11111111** indicates that a meta-event is to follow. Following this byte is the identification number of the meta-event. The next byte indicates the number of data bytes that are necessary to describe the event. Then the actual bytes describing the event follow. The meta-event is considered complete when the specified number of bytes has been read.

Finally, SMFs allow SysEx data to be stored. SysEx events also are placed between a delta time event and a MIDI event. As per the specification described earlier, a SysEx instruction starts with a value of $F0_{16}$ and ends with a value of $F7_{16}$. Immediately following the Start SysEx byte is a byte defining the number of bytes in the SysEx message (including the End SysEx byte). If the total number of bytes in a SysEx message is greater than can be expressed with one byte (greater than 127), the same variable-length encoding used for delta times may be employed.

General MIDI

This "standard within a standard" was adopted in 1991 to allow Standard MIDI files to be played on different instruments. Prior to General MIDI, before a MIDI file could be played on a new instrument it was necessary to check a MIDI file for Program Change patch numbers before it was played. The instrument types used in the file had to be noted and the patches on the receiving instrument had to be assigned to appropriate patch numbers so that the file's Program Change messages called up the appropriate instrument types.

General MIDI creates a standardized set of patch assignments so that instrument types correspond to patch numbers. For example, General MIDI instruments have a piano patch assigned to patch 0, an organ assigned to patch 19, a trumpet assigned to patch 57, and so on. The quality of patches differs from instrument to instrument, and no promises can be made as to how a timbre may sound on the "cheesy to excellent" scale. But standardized patch numbers at least ensure that a MIDI file sounds intelligible on any instrument that plays it. Table 8–1 shows the set of instrument types that are mapped to patch ranges, and Table 8–2 shows the list of standardized patch assignments for all 128 patches.

Table 8–1
General MIDI Instrument Families

Patch Nos.	Instrument Family
1–8	Piano
9–16	Chromatic percussion
17–24	Organ
25–32	Guitar
33–40	Bass
41–48	Strings
49–56	Ensemble
57–64	Brass
65–72	Reed
73–80	Pipe
81–88	Synth lead
89–96	Synth pad
97–104	Synth effects
105–112	Ethnic
113–120	Percussive
121–128	Sound effects

Drum parts are a special case that is also addressed by General MIDI. On a MIDI instrument, drum patches differ from instrumental patches in that drum sounds are not pitched. Therefore, each note number produces the sound of a different type of percussion instrument. With General MIDI, note numbers are standardized for drum patches, as shown in Table 8–3. Furthermore, MIDI channel 10 is reserved for drum tracks only. Thus, comprehensibility of drum parts can be achieved through standardized key mappings on channel 10. The adoption of Multi Mode (to be discussed presently) and General MIDI drum protocols has to some extent eclipsed the presence of dedicated drum machines. (Drum machines have evolved into *groove boxes,* which are combination percussion and synthesis devices that are popular in dance venues.)

Although some musicians in 1991 claimed that General MIDI was a "dumbing down" of MIDI instruments, its adoption has allowed MIDI to become a standard multimedia element. For example, games are generally focused more on graphics than sound, and game producers would rather use the available memory on a CD for high-resolution graphics than for high-quality audio sound tracks. General MIDI allows game producers to enhance sound tracks with MIDI files, knowing that the files will be functional with any General MIDI sound card. MIDI files may also be added to Web pages, to be realized by an appropriate General MIDI plug-in on the receiving computer. Today, the early objections to General MIDI are all but forgotten. Virtually all synthesizers have a General MIDI bank of patches available for users who need to ensure portability of their files.

Table 8–2
General MIDI Patch Assignments

Patch No.	Instrument	Patch No.	Instrument	Patch No.	Instrument	Patch No.	Instrument
1	Acoustic grand piano	33	Acoustic bass	65	Soprano sax	97	FX 1 (rain)
2	Bright acoustic piano	34	Electric bass (finger)	66	Alto sax	98	FX 2 (soundtrack)
3	Electric grand piano	35	Electric bass (pick)	67	Tenor sax	99	FX 3 (crystal)
4	Honky-tonk piano	36	Fretless bass	68	Baritone sax	100	FX 4 (atmosphere)
5	Electric piano 1	37	Slap bass 1	69	Oboe	101	FX 5 (brightness)
6	Electric piano 2	38	Slap bass 2	70	English horn	102	FX 6 (goblins)
7	Harpsichord	39	Synth bass 1	71	Bassoon	103	FX 7 (echoes)
8	Clavi	40	Synth bass 2	72	Clarinet	104	FX 8 (sci-fi)
9	Celesta	41	Violin	73	Piccolo	105	Sitar
10	Glockenspiel	42	Viola	74	Flute	106	Banjo
11	Music box	43	Cello	75	Recorder	107	Shamisen
12	Vibraphone	44	Contrabass	76	Pan flute	108	Koto
13	Marimba	45	Tremolo strings	77	Blown bottle	109	Kalimba
14	Xylophone	46	Pizzicato strings	78	Shakuhachi	110	Bag pipe
15	Tubular bells	47	Orchestral harp	79	Whistle	111	Fiddle
16	Dulcimer	48	Timpani	80	Ocarina	112	Shanai
17	Drawbar organ	49	String ensemble 1	81	Lead 1 (square)	113	Tinkle bell
18	Percussive organ	50	String ensemble 2	82	Lead 2 (sawtooth)	114	Agogo
19	Rock organ	51	SynthStrings 1	83	Lead 3 (calliope)	115	Steel drums
20	Church organ	52	SynthStrings 2	84	Lead 4 (chiff)	116	Woodblock
21	Reed organ	53	Choir aahs	85	Lead 5 (charang)	117	Taiko drum
22	Accordion	54	Voice oohs	86	Lead 6 (voice)	118	Melodic tom
23	Harmonica	55	Synth voice	87	Lead 7 (fifths)	119	Synth drum
24	Tango accordion	56	Orchestra hit	88	Lead 8 (bass + lead)	120	Reverse cymbal
25	Acoustic guitar (nylon)	57	Trumpet	89	Pad 1 (new age)	121	Guitar fret noise
26	Acoustic guitar (steel)	58	Trombone	90	Pad 2 (warm)	122	Breath noise
27	Electric guitar (jazz)	59	Tuba	91	Pad 3 (polysynth)	123	Seashore
28	Electric guitar (clean)	60	Muted trumpet	92	Pad 4 (choir)	124	Bird tweet
29	Electric guitar (muted)	61	French horn	93	Pad 5 (bowed)	125	Telephone ring
30	Overdriven guitar	62	Brass section	94	Pad 6 (metallic)	126	Helicopter
31	Distortion guitar	63	SynthBrass 1	95	Pad 7 (halo)	127	Applause
32	Guitar harmonics	64	SynthBrass 2	96	Pad 8 (sweep)	128	Gunshot

Table 8–3
General MIDI Percussion Key Mappings

Note No.	Instrument	Note No.	Instrument
35	Acoustic bass drum	59	Ride cymbal 2
36	Bass drum 1	60	Hi bongo
37	Side stick	61	Low bongo
38	Acoustic snare	62	Mute hi conga
39	Hand clap	63	Open hi conga
40	Electric snare	64	Low conga
41	Low floor tom	65	High timbale
42	Closed hi-hat	66	Low timbale
43	High floor tom	67	High agogo
44	Pedal hi-hat	68	Low agogo
45	Low tom	69	Cabasa
46	Open hi-hat	70	Maracas
47	Low-mid tom	71	Short whistle
48	Hi-mid tom	72	Long whistle
49	Crash cymbal 1	73	Short guiro
50	High tom	74	Long guiro
51	Ride cymbal 1	75	Claves
52	Chinese cymbal	76	Hi wood block
53	Ride bell	77	Low wood block
54	Tambourine	78	Mute cuica
55	Splash cymbal	79	Open cuica
56	Cowbell	80	Mute triangle
57	Crash cymbal 2	81	Open triangle
58	Vibraslap		

Multi Mode

Channel Mode messages were discussed earlier, but the nature of one mode type was altered starting in the early 1990s. In Multi Mode, an instrument is able to respond polyphonically to all 16 MIDI channels and to assign a patch to each channel. A single instrument may thereby consist of up to 16 "subinstruments," or parts.

Just as virtually all MIDI instruments now have General MIDI banks, virtually all MIDI instruments may be set to operate in Multi Mode. When an instrument is in Multi Mode and it has a General MIDI bank, it can play 16-channel Standard MIDI files. Older instruments may not have Multi Mode implemented, and some newer instruments may have the option to disable Multi Mode.

With Multi Mode instruments, a critical specification is degree of polyphony. An instrument with 32-note polyphony that is playing all 16 channels simultaneously is limited to 2 notes per channel at a time. While *dynamic voice allocation* can redistribute the notes available to each channel on an as-needed basis, it is clear that higher degrees of polyphony are more desirable for complex arrangements. Thus, the degree of polyphony plays a large part in determining the price tag of instruments.

Karaoke Files

This file type was specified in 1998 to allow creation of sing-along arrangements, a recreational activity extremely popular in Asian countries. A karaoke file is a Standard MIDI file with lyrics as meta-information and typically has the extension ".kar." A karaoke machine is able to play back MIDI tracks and project lyrics.

GS MIDI and XG MIDI

GS MIDI, an expansion of General MIDI, was created by Roland for its Sound-Canvas® module. GS MIDI features multiple drum kit banks and standardizes more controllers to include effects such as reverberation and brightness. It was GS MIDI that introduced the convention of controllers 0 and 32 as Bank Select messages, thus allowing more than 128 patches to be specified.

XG MIDI was created by Yamaha for its MU80 module. This protocol also adds conventions to the list of standardized controllers that address additional expressiveness (chorus, attack time, release time, etc.). In addition, XG MIDI includes the definition of special SysEx messages to allow processing of an input signal, such as a karaoke vocalist.

Many Web sites with downloadable MIDI files specify that the files are GS MIDI or XG MIDI, meaning that such files take advantage of the special features on these types of devices.

MIDI Machine Control (MMC) and MIDI Show Control (MSC)

These are two standardized sets of SysEx messages that allow additional levels of control via MIDI. MIDI Machine Control addresses recording and playback devices. It allows sequencers to send commands to tape decks, such as play, record, stop, fast forward, rewind, or pause. MIDI Show Control specifies messages to control nonmusical theatrical devices such as lighting, scenery, pyrotechnics, or sound effects. Thus, MSC allows an entire production to be controlled by a sequencer.

CHAPTER 9

Digital Audio

Introduction

By the mid-1990s, personal computers had advanced to the point that the capability to handle digital audio had become a standard feature. Digital audio recorders and editors that once required expensive extra hardware peripherals could now operate entirely within software.

Virtually all software types discussed in Chapter 6 have been enhanced by the addition of digital audio features alongside MIDI capabilities. Sequencers are no longer meant primarily for MIDI data, but include the capability of placing digital audio tracks alongside MIDI tracks. This allows musicians to make a recording of a vocal part or an electric guitar solo and add it as an audio track that plays with MIDI tracks. A comparison of Figure 9–1 with Figure 6–5 illustrates the expanded capabilities of combined audio and MIDI sequencers. Notation software now allows musicians to enter material from their instruments via a microphone as well as from a MIDI instrument. Accompaniment software has become "smarter" in that some programs can track a student's playing of a piece via a microphone and make tempo adjustments to match those of the student.

This and the following chapters will discuss the mechanics of how audio information may be stored and edited in computer music systems.

Digitizing Audio—The Big Picture

The Central Problem

Waves in nature, including sound waves (amplitude as a function of time), are *continuous*. The mathematical definition of this term means that between any two points in time, even two points representing a virtually instantaneous interval, an infinite number of amplitude points may be identified (Figure 9–2).

Analog audio (vinyl, tape, analog synthesizers, etc.) involves the creation or imitation of a continuous wave. But analog waves are incompatible with computers, which do not have the capacity to represent continuity (or infinity). Computers can only deal with *discrete* values. Digital technology is based on converting continuous values to discrete values.

Figure 9–1

Audio and MIDI

Sample screens from the program Digital Performer. Used with permission of Mark of the Unicom Software, Inc.

Figure 9–2

Points on a Continuous
Wave

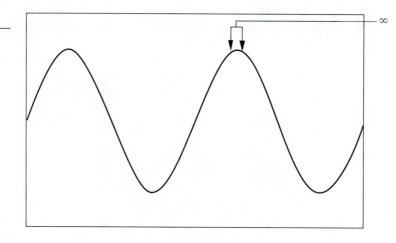

Digital Conversion

To digitize a continuous wave, it is measured (*sampled*) regularly. The discrete measurement values, *samples,* may be stored in a digital system (Figure 9–3). In the case of digital audio, it is the instantaneous amplitude measurements of a sound signal that are sampled regularly.

Digital representation of audio is analogous to cinematic representation of motion. It is common knowledge that "moving pictures" do not really move and that cinema is simply a series of still pictures. That is, motion is created by sampled images of an object's position; the images are then projected fast enough that the effect has the appearance of continuous motion. It is the same with digital audio: a sound is sampled often enough, and the samples are played back fast enough that the effect is apparent auditory continuity.

The theory underlying digital representation has existed since the 1920s. But it was not until the 1950s that technology caught up to the theory and it became possible to build the necessary hardware to create, record, and process digital audio. Max Mathews at Bell Labs produced the first digital audio synthesis systems in the 1950s by creating a type of program called an *acoustic compiler.* The workings of acoustic compilers remain fundamental to the production of digital audio. For computer synthesis, a waveform is calculated in the form of a series of samples that are stored in a *wavetable.* Reading through the wavetable at different rates (skipping every *n* samples, the *sampling increment*) allows different pitches to be created. Audio is produced by audifying the samples by sending them through a *digital-to-analog converter* (DAC). This is the process that is still used for commercial instruments. Wavetables are stored on memory chips within the instrument. Wavetables will be discussed further in Chapter 13.

Contemporary computer sound cards typically have a set of wavetable sounds. This is a library of stored sounds to be triggered by MIDI commands. A Note On message, for example, is translated into a given sampling increment that causes the wavetable to be read at a rate that produces the desired pitch. A Program Change message activates a different wavetable. Wavetable libraries are what enable computers to act as instruments, as described in Chapter 6.

Figure 9–3

Digitizing a Continuous Wave

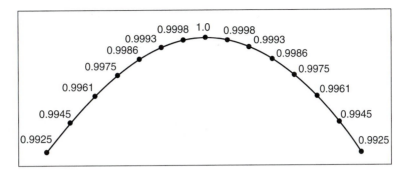

[0.9925, 0.9945, 0.9961, 0.9975, 0.9986, 0.9993, 0.9998, 1.0, 0.9998, 0.9993, 0.9986, 0.9975, 0.9961, 0.9945, 0.9925]

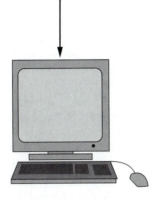

Digital recording also became possible in the 1950s. To record a sound and convert it to a series of samples, voltage input from a microphone is fed to an *analog-to-digital converter* (ADC), which converts the signal to a series of samples and stores them. The samples can later be sent through a DAC for playback.

Does Digital Sound as Good as Analog?

Audiophiles have argued this question since the widespread release of compact discs in the 1980s, and there is no sign of the argument abating. The following are some key points.

Con

Digital is, at best, only an approximation of the audio signal. Of course, the same can be said of analog recordings. It is also argued that analog has a "richer" or "warmer" sound. This is currently a pressing issue within the audio industry, and it is complicated by the fact that it is difficult to find concrete definitions of these two words. The differences between analog and digital recordings may be attributable to differences in frequency response and distortion, both of which can affect subjective responses to timbre. *Frequency response* refers to how fully different frequencies are represented in a digital audio system, which will be discussed further in the section on filters. *Distortion* refers to a reshaping of an audio wave.

Although the term might imply a less-than-ideal characteristic, it describes any system in which the output is not exactly equivalent to the input. Many analog components offer a degree of distortion that listeners find pleasing. *Symmetrical distortion* refers to an equivalent alteration of the extreme high and low ends of a wave. Symmetrical distortion may tend to flatten a wave, adding odd harmonics to it as the wave shape approaches a square wave (see Figure 2–8). *Asymmetrical distortion* produces different changes on the high and low ends of a wave and tends to add even harmonics. Many analog tapes add asymmetrical distortion. Other sources of analog distortion arise from vintage microphones or amplifiers or from slight variations in the motor speed (*wow*) of vinyl turntables. Specifying the precise differences between high-end digital and analog systems and creating digital simulations of analog characteristics are currently high priorities for audio systems manufacturers.

Pro

Digital recordings contain significantly lower background noise levels than analog recordings. In the early days of CDs, it was common for people to be surprised the first time they played a CD because they did not hear the usual hiss and crackle that had always been produced as a turntable needle made contact with a vinyl disc. In addition, the discrete numbers that are the basis of digital recordings are more reliably stored and duplicated than analog simulations, and digital audio is easier to manipulate. Rather than concern themselves with how to change the shape of a continuous wave, engineers need only perform appropriate numerical operations. The nature of these operations will be discussed in the section on filtering. Finally, the principal digital medium, the optical disc (examples of which include audio CDs, computer CD-ROMs, and MiniDiscs), does not degrade with multiple playings as do the earlier analog vinyl and tape media.

Ultimately, these practical advantages of digital audio have outweighed any objections. Despite the fact that in some circumstances the quality of analog audio may be superior, the pragmatic advantages of digital audio have rendered it the dominant means of storing audio signals.

Characteristics of Digital Audio

Digital audio signals are described by two measurements:

1. Sampling rate/sampling frequency
2. Quantization (also called *bit depth* or *word size*)

These measurements provide concrete descriptions of how well digitized audio represents the analog original.

Sampling Rate

This number describes how often an audio signal is sampled—the number of samples per second. The more often an audio signal is sampled, the better it is represented in discrete form (Figure 9–4). The question regarding optimal sampling rates is: "How often is often enough?"

Harry Nyquist of Bell Labs addressed this question in a 1925 paper concerning telegraph signals. Given that a wave is eventually to be smoothed by a

Figure 9–4

Sampling Rates of a Continuous Wave

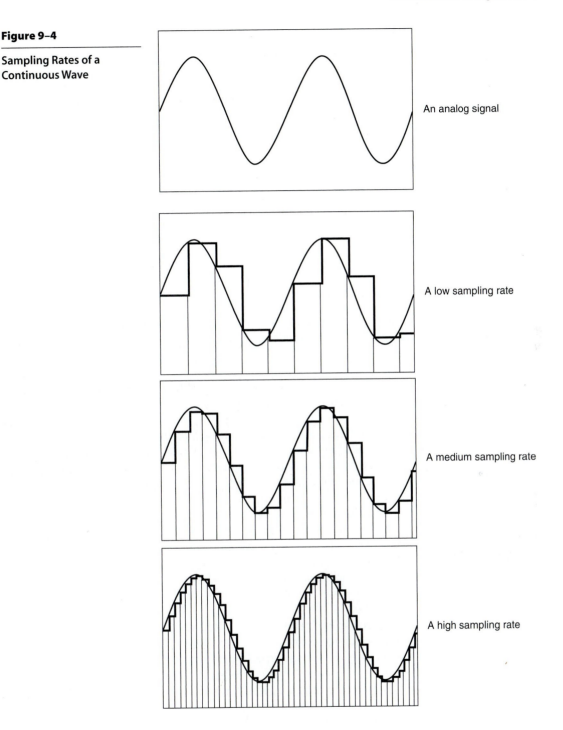

An analog signal

A low sampling rate

A medium sampling rate

A high sampling rate

subsequent filtering process (a topic that will be discussed presently), it is sufficient to sample both its peak and its trough (Figure 9–5). Thus arose the *sampling theorem* (also called the *Nyquist theorem*):

> To represent digitally a signal containing frequency components up to X Hz, it is necessary to use a sampling rate of at least $2X$ Hz.

Figure 9–5

Sampling the Peak and
Trough of a Digitized Wave

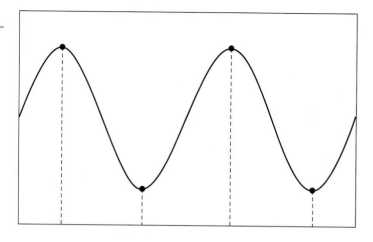

Conversely,

> The maximum frequency contained in a signal sampled at a rate of *SR* Hz is *SR*/2 Hz. The frequency *SR*/2 Hz is also termed the *Nyquist frequency.*

Therefore, in theory, since the maximum audible frequency is 20 kHz, a sampling rate of 40 kHz would be sufficient to re-create a signal containing all audible frequencies.

Most audible frequencies are *oversampled,* meaning that the audio frequency is below the Nyquist frequency, as shown in Figure 9–4. A signal sampled at precisely the Nyquist frequency is said to be *critically sampled.* Sampling at exactly the Nyquist frequency runs the risk of missing peaks and troughs and only sampling the zero crossings (Figure 9–6). The solution to this problem will also be covered in the section on filtering. A far more significant problem is that of *undersampling,* recording a frequency greater than the Nyquist frequency (Figure 9–7). Misrepresented frequencies such as those shown in Figure 9–7 are termed *aliases.* In general, if a frequency *F* sampled at a sampling rate of *SR* exceeds the Nyquist frequency, that frequency will alias to a frequency of

$$-(SR - F)$$

where the minus sign indicates that the frequency phase inverted. Digital audio frequencies are often illustrated on a polar diagram, as shown in Figure 9–8.

Aliasing has a visual counterpart often seen in cinema and television scenes that involve moving automobiles or covered wagons. When these vehicles are moving slowly, the wheels advance by less than one-half of a complete revolution per frame; the motion is recorded accurately and the wheels appear to be moving forward. As they increase in speed, the wheels may reach a point at which they make exactly one or one-half revolution per frame. The motion of the wheel is thus critically sampled, and the spokes of the wheel appear motionless. If the wheel turns between one-half and one full revolution per frame, the spokes appear to move backwards, in the direction opposite to the vehicle's direction.

Although wheels in apparent reversed motion may be part of the charm of cinema, the auditory correlate of misdirected wheels is far less tolerable. In the

Figure 9–6

Critical Sampling

Critical sampling runs the risk of sampling only at zero-crossing points.

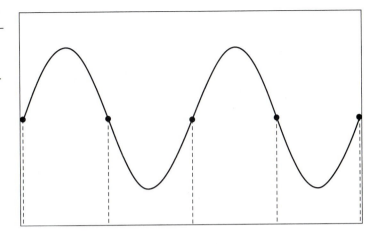

Figure 9–7

Undersampling

(a) Audio signal of 30 kHz, sampled at 40 kHz. (b) Result: The frequency is misrepresented at 10 kHz, at reverse phase.

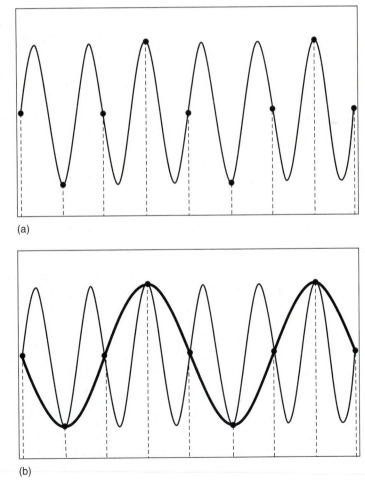

(a)

(b)

Figure 9–8

Polar Diagram of the Range of Frequencies in a Digital System

The upper half of the circle represents frequencies from 0 Hz to the Nyquist frequency (NF). The lower half of the circle represents *negative* frequencies from 0 Hz to the Nyquist frequency (there is no distinction in a digital audio system between ±NF). Any audio frequency above the Nyquist frequency will alias to a frequency shown on the bottom half of the circle, a negative frequency between 0 Hz and the Nyquist frequency. *Frequencies above the Nyquist frequency cannot exist in a digital audio recording.*

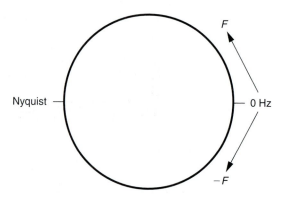

recording process, filters are used to remove all frequencies above the Nyquist frequency *before* the audio signal is sampled. This step is essential because any recorded aliases cannot be removed later. However, provided these frequencies are not in the sampled signal, the signal may be sampled and later reconverted to audio *with no loss of frequency information.*

The Sampling Rate of CD Audio and Its Origin

The sampling rate for audio CDs is 44.1 kHz. Occasionally, other rates may be encountered. A sampling rate of 32 kHz has been defined for digital radio broadcasts, and many digital audio tape (DAT) decks offer a sampling rate of 48 kHz. The CD rate of 44.1 kHz, however, is the most common. The origin of the CD rate dates back to video tape storage formats.

When digital audio recording began, audio tape was not capable of storing the density of digital signals (this will be discussed further in the section on DAT tape). The first digital masters were stored on video tape as a pseudo video signal in which sample values, represented as binary numbers with digits of 1 and 0, were stored as video levels of black and white. The sampling rate was determined by the format of video tape (Figure 9–9). Video pixels are drawn left to right in horizontal lines starting from the top of the screen and moving down. First the odd-numbered lines are drawn, then the even-numbered lines. Thus, each frame of video has two subsets: the odd field and the even field. The fields lie adjacent to each other on the video tape in a diagonal orientation (the reason for the angle will be discussed in the section on DAT tape). There are two video broadcast formats:

1. *USA (NTSC):* 525 lines, 30 frames per second, minus 35 blank lines, leaving 490 lines per frame, equals 60 fields per second, 245 lines per field.

Figure 9–9

Figure 9–9

The Format of Video Tape

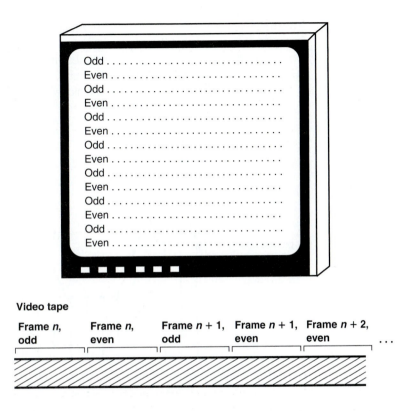

2. *European (PAL):* 625 lines, 25 frames per second, minus 37 blank lines, leaving 588 lines per frame, equals 50 fields per second, 294 lines per field.

With the pseudo format of black and white pixels, three samples could be stored on each line, allowing:

NTSC: $60 \times 245 \times 3 = 44{,}100$ samples per second

or

PAL: $50 \times 294 \times 3 = 44{,}100$ samples per second

Although video tapes are no longer necessary for storing digital audio, 44.1 kHz remains the standard sampling rate for CD audio.

Quantization

The discussion of sampling rate considered only how *often* the amplitude of the wave was measured. Discussion of how *accurate* these measurements actually were has been postponed—until now.

The effectiveness of any measurement depends on the precision of the ruler in use. If a fairly small object, such as a book, is measured with a ruler that only marks measuring increments in feet, the only option will be to make an estimate based on the nearest foot mark on the ruler. Just as there are practical limits to how often audio signals may be sampled, there are practical limits to the level of precision of the amplitude measurements. Like all numbers stored in computers, the amplitude values are stored as binary numbers. The accuracy of the measurement depends on how many bits are available to represent these values. Clearly, with more bits, the ruler's resolution becomes finer (Figure 9–10). For CD audio, 16 quantization bits (2-byte words) are used.

Although aliasing is eliminated if a signal contains no frequencies above the Nyquist frequency, *quantization error can never be completely eliminated.*

Figure 9–10

Quantization Level (Bit Depth)

Recall that the acoustic pressure wave is transduced into an electrical signal, from which these measurements are taken. Each change of bit represents a change in voltage level.

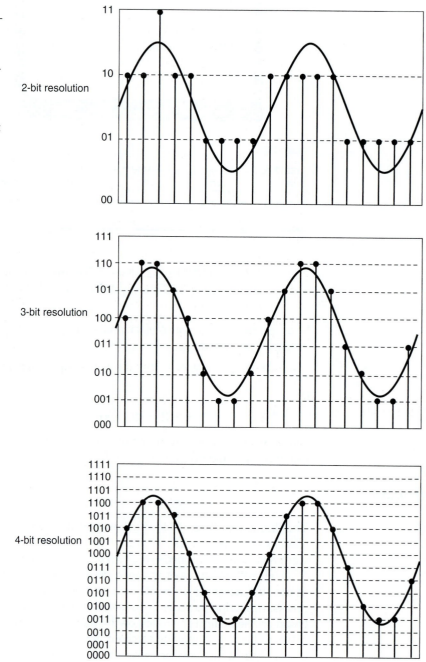

Every sample is within a margin of error that is half the quantization level (the voltage change represented by the least significant bit). The signal-to-error ratio for a given signal varies depending on the nature of the audio contents. As a base case example, for a full-level sine wave signal represented by n bits, the signal-to-error ratio is

$$S/E \text{ (dB)} = 6.02n + 1.76 \qquad\qquad 9-1$$

The derivation of this value is shown in Figure 9–11.

This error ratio may be acceptable for high signal levels. However, low-level signals do not use all available bits, and therefore the signal-to-error ratio is greater. Thus, while quantization error may not be audible at high audio levels, it can become audible at low levels. Figure 9–12 illustrates a worst-case scenario, where a low-level sine wave is interpreted as a square wave. The spectrum of a square wave was shown in Figure 2–8. Unlike the constant hissing noise of analog recordings, quantization error is correlated with the digital signal, varying with the signal level, and is thus a type of *distortion,* rather than noise.

The problem of quantization distortion is addressed by *dither.* Dither is low-level noise added to the audio signal before it is sampled (Figure 9–13). Dither adds a level of *random* error to the signal, thus transforming the quantization distortion into added noise. The noise is a constant factor, not correlated with the signal as is quantization error distortion. The result is a noisy signal, rather than a signal broken up by distortion.

Although this may not seem like much of an improvement, dither capitalizes on the characteristics of the auditory system, trading one problem for a lesser problem. Recall from Chapter 2 that loudness is correlated with the average power of sound. The auditory system averages auditory information at all times; listeners never hear individual samples. With dither, this averaging allows low-level segments of the musical signal to coexist with the noise, rather than be temporarily eliminated due to distortion. Due to this averaging, dither allows resolution below the least significant quantization bit. Without dither, digital recordings would be far less satisfactory than analog recordings. And even with dither added, there is still significantly less noise in digital recordings than in analog recordings.

Quantization vs. Sampling Rate

In summary,

- The sampling rate determines the signal's frequency content.
- The number of quantization bits determines the level of noise in the signal (fewer bits require a higher level of dither to span the plus and minus halves of a quantization bit).

Many programs allow both of these factors to be either increased or reduced. This may be necessary for a variety of reasons. If memory is tight, it may be necessary to reduce a file's size by eliminating some of its information (see the following section, "The Size of Audio Files"). Or a given software program may work only with files having a given sampling rate and bit depth, so audio files need to be converted to these specifications to be edited in these programs. In the case of "upsampling" or increasing the bit depth, no information is added by the conversion. These processes simply increase the size of a file. To increase the sampling

Figure 9–11

Signal-to-Error Ratio in Digital Recording (Assuming a Steady-State, Peak-Valued Sine Wave)

rms of the Audio Signal

For a signal with quantizing interval Q, with 2^n bits, half the bits will describe the positive and negative regions of the wave. Thus, the peak amplitude will be $Q2^{n-1}$. As discussed in Chapter 2, the rms of a sine wave signal is its peak amplitude times 0.707. For our digital signal, the rms is

$$\frac{Q2^{n-1}}{2^{0.5}}$$

rms of the Error

Unlike the sine wave signal, which is completely deterministic from sample to sample, the error signal is assumed to be random. The error may be described for any sample as having an instantaneous amplitude of e, and thus its instantaneous power is e^2. The probability of this signal being at a given amplitude for any sample is defined by the probability curve of the error signal. The mean of all possible values (which translates into the amplitude of the error signal) over a continuous area (the probability curve) is mathematically defined as the integral of the product of the signal and its probability curve. In the case of this digital audio signal, the probability curve is uniform over the length of one quantization interval, since there is an equal probability of the analog signal being measured at its actual value ±$Q/2$. This means that the integration is only an integration of the signal itself, scaled by the probability curve.

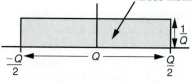

What is the mean of all possible values within this area?

The weights of all possible values must equal 1, implying 100% of the range of possible values. Since this probability curve is uniform, it may be described as a rectangle, with a length of Q and a height of $1/Q$, giving it an area of 1.

Calculation of the rms of the Error:

$$E_{rms} = \left[\int_{-\infty}^{\infty} e^2 p(e)\, de \right]^{1/2}$$

$$= \left[\frac{1}{Q} \int_{-Q/2}^{Q/2} e^2\, de \right]^{1/2} \quad \text{since } p(e) \text{ is } 1/Q \text{ within the interval } \pm Q/2$$

$$= \left[\frac{1}{Q} \left(\frac{1}{3} e^3\, de \right) \right]^{1/2}$$

$$= \left[\frac{1}{Q} \left(\frac{1}{3} \left(\frac{Q}{2} \right)^3 - \frac{1}{3} \left(\frac{-Q}{2} \right)^3 \right) \right]^{1/2}$$

$$= \left[\frac{1}{Q} \left(\frac{1}{3} \left(\frac{Q}{2} \right)^3 - \frac{1}{3} \left(\frac{-Q}{2} \right)^3 \right) \right]^{1/2}$$

$$= \left[\frac{1}{Q} \left(\frac{Q^3}{24} + \frac{Q^3}{24} \right) \right]^{1/2} = \left[\frac{1}{Q} \left(\frac{2Q^3}{24} \right) \right]^{1/2}$$

$$= \left[\frac{1}{Q} \left(\frac{Q^3}{12} \right) \right]^{1/2} = \left[\left(\frac{Q^2}{12} \right) \right]^{1/2} = \frac{Q}{\sqrt{12}}$$

Thus, the amount of error is dependent on the voltage range of Q. The smaller the range of one quantization increment, the less the rms of the error.

Calculation of the Signal-to-Error Ratio:

$$\frac{S}{E} = \left[\frac{S_{rms}}{E_{rms}} \right] = \frac{\left(\dfrac{Q2^{n-1}}{\sqrt{2}} \right)^2}{\left(\dfrac{Q}{\sqrt{12}} \right)^2} = \left(\frac{Q2^{n-1}}{\sqrt{2}} \times \frac{2\sqrt{3}}{Q} \right)^2 = \left(\frac{2^n \sqrt{3}}{\sqrt{2}} \right)^2 = \frac{3}{2} (2^{2n})$$

$$\frac{S}{E}(\text{dB}) = 10 \log_{10} \left[\frac{3}{2} (2^{2n}) \right] \quad \text{(power)}$$

$$= 20 \log_{10} \left[\sqrt{\frac{3}{2} (2^{2n})} \right] = 20 \log_{10} \left[\frac{\sqrt{3}}{\sqrt{2}} (2^n) \right] \quad \text{(amplitude)}$$

$$= 20 \log_{10} \left(\frac{3}{2} \right)^{1/2} + 20 \log_{10}(2^n)$$

$$= 20 \log_{10} \left(\frac{3}{2} \right)^{1/2} + 20n \log_{10}(2)$$

$$= 20 \log_{10}(1.2247) + 20n \log_{10}(2)$$

$$= 1.76 + 6.02n$$

Thus, more quantization bits produce a higher ratio, meaning that there is more signal and less quantization noise.

Figure 9–12

Quantization Error

Worst case: a sine wave fluctuating within one quantization increment is stored as a square wave.

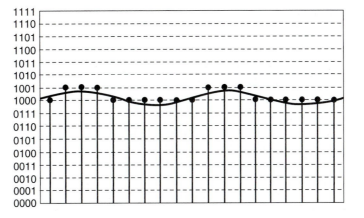

rate, samples are added between existing samples. Either the values of existing samples are duplicated for the new samples, or the new samples are assigned values that are interpolations between the preceding and succeeding sample. Increasing the bit depth simply adds more bits with a value of zero to each quantization value.

There are likely to be audible results from either "downsampling" or decreasing bit depth. It usually is preferable to decrease the sampling rate, which simply lowers the frequency range of the file since a lower sampling rate has a lower Nyquist frequency. Reducing the bit depth can have one of two results. A lower bit depth requires a higher level of dither in the file to remove quantization error distortion. If the converter adds the appropriate level of dither, then the noise floor of the signal is increased. If the converter does not add dither, then the conversion adds quantization error distortion to the converted file. (There is often no easy way to predict whether a particular converter adds dither or not when it reduces a file's bit depth. To test the process with a certain converter, a sine wave file may be used as a test file. If the converted file sounds buzzy, it is likely that dither was not added; if it sounds noisy, with a "sh" or hissing sound in the background, it is likely that dither was added.)

Figure 9–13

Dither

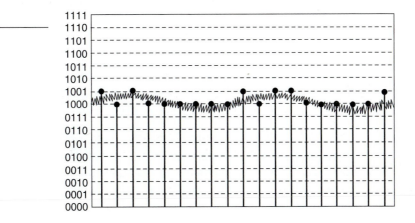

The Size of Audio Files

The following arithmetic derives the size of audio files:

$$44{,}100 \quad \times \quad 2 \quad \times \quad 2 \quad \times \quad 60 \quad \approx 10 \text{ MB/min}$$

samples	bytes per	channels	seconds
per	sample	(for stereo	per
second	(16 bits)	audio)	minute

There are occasions where the size of audio files is far larger than is practical, particularly in contexts involving transmission. Data reduction techniques will be discussed in Chapter 10 in the section "Perceptual Coding."

Filtering

What Is Filtering?

The purpose of any filter—be it a water filter, coffee filter, color filter on a camera, or any other type of filter you can think of—is to allow some things to pass through it and to stop other things from passing through it. In the case of audio, filtering is spectral shaping. A filter modifies the spectrum of a signal by emphasizing or deemphasizing certain frequency ranges. Filtering is a critical aspect of audio production. With filtering, the practical advantages of digital over analog signals become clear, as simple arithmetic can have large-scale effects, as the next section, "The Digital Filtering Process," will demonstrate.

Filter Types

There are four basic filter types, shown in Figure 9–14. Each filter's spectral shaping is shown by means of an input signal that is flat spectrally, a *white noise* signal. White noise was introduced in Figure 2–1 as a random waveshape. Digital white noise consists of random values only, with no correlation from one sample to the next. The spectrum of a signal created from pure randomness is flat—the average amplitude of all frequencies is equal. (The term *white noise* is a comparison to white light, in which the proportion of all spectral light frequencies is equal.)

Lowpass

A lowpass filter reduces or eliminates higher frequencies (it "lets the lows pass"). A lowpass filter is described by its *cutoff frequency*. This is the spectral component for which the amplitude on output is 0.707 of its amplitude on input. The value of 0.707 is significant because of the equivalent power value of this amplitude. Recall that power is proportional to amplitude squared:

$$0.707^2 = 0.5$$

Therefore, the cutoff frequency represents the half-power level, -3 dB. As was discussed earlier, lowpass filters are an essential component in the design of digital recorders. The audio signal must be lowpass filtered before it is sampled to eliminate frequencies above the Nyquist frequency.

Figure 9–14

Four Basic Filter Types

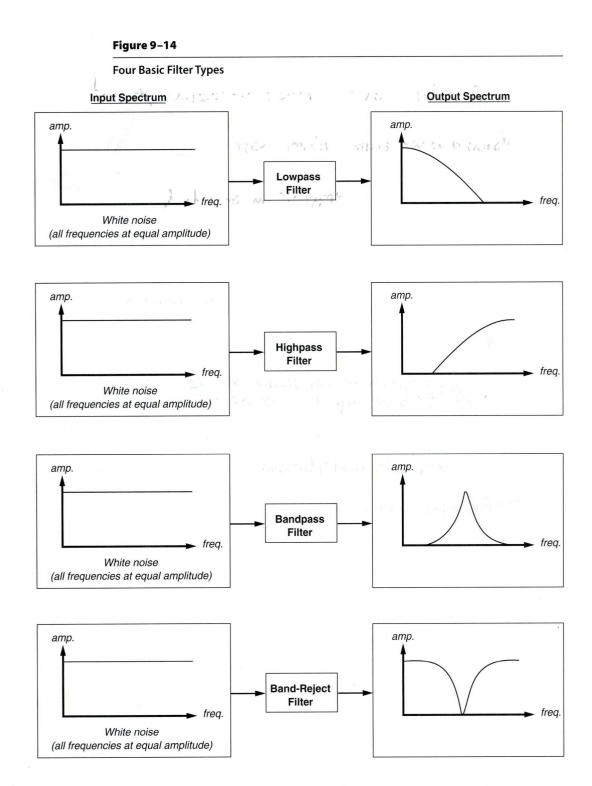

A lowpass frequency response such as that shown in Figure 9–14 is created by a *feedforward* filter, which creates dips ("zeroes") in the spectrum of its input. Another lowpass filter type is a *feedback filter* (or *resonant filter* or *recursive filter*). A feedback filter adds a spectral "hump" near the cutoff frequency. The filter is said to resonate at this spectral peak, just as natural materials have resonant frequencies (as discussed in Chapter 2). The filter's resonance adds a distinct coloration to the input that is often useful in musical applications.

Figure 9–15 compares the frequency responses of a feedforward and a feedback lowpass filter. Notice the resonant peak in the feedback filter near the cutoff frequency. This resonance adds a pronounced ringing effect to feedback filters. Figure 9–16 shows spectrograms of feedforward and feedback lowpass filters. A wah-wah pedal, a characteristic effect of Jimi Hendrix and other rock guitarists, is a resonant lowpass filter, with the cutoff frequency determined by the pedal position.

Highpass

A highpass filter is the opposite of a lowpass filter. It reduces or eliminates lower frequencies (it "lets the highs pass"). Like the lowpass filter, a highpass filter is characterized by its cutoff frequency, at which the amplitude on output is 0.707 of its amplitude when input. Also like the lowpass filter, a highpass filter may be feedforward

Figure 9–15

Frequency Responses of Feedforward and Feedback Lowpass Filters

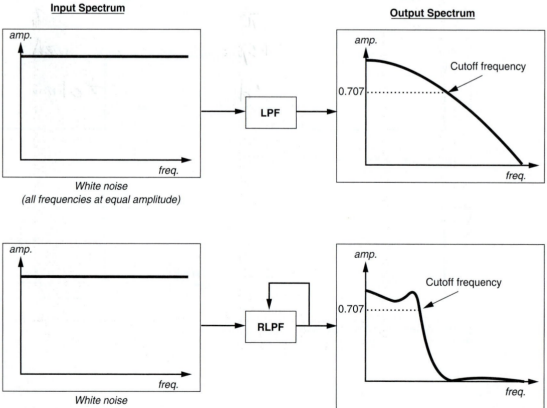

Figure 9–16

Spectrograms of Lowpass-Filtered Signals: (Oscillating Cutoff Frequencies, 400–4000 Hz)

Feedforward

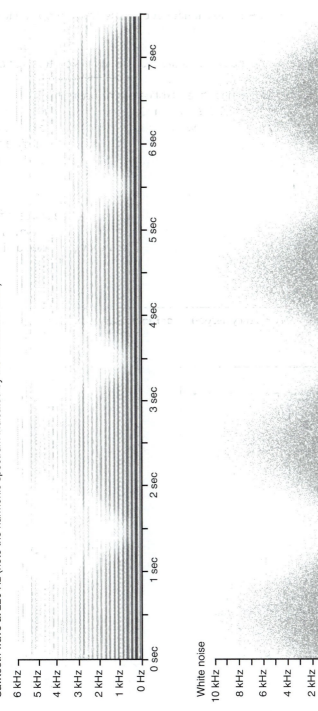

Sawtooth wave at 220 Hz (note the harmonic spectrum indicated by the horizontal lines)

White noise

Figure 9–16, cont'd

Feedback

(Note the spectral resonance at the cutoff frequency)

Sawtooth wave at 220 Hz (note the harmonic spectrum indicated by the horizontal lines)

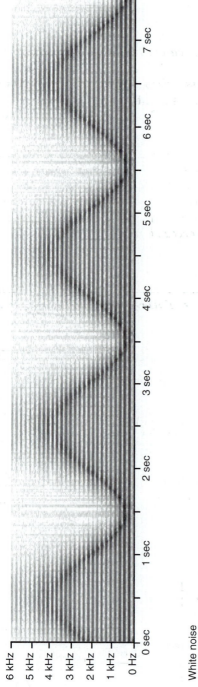

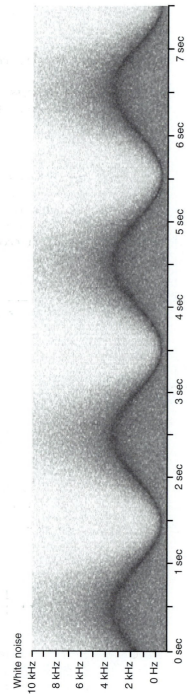

White noise

or feedback. Figure 9–17 compares the frequency responses of a feedforward and a feedback highpass filter. Figure 9–18 shows spectrograms of feedforward and feedback highpass filters.

Bandpass

A bandpass filter reduces or eliminates frequencies above and below a specified band of frequencies (it "lets a band of frequencies pass"). A bandpass filter is characterized by two values: *center frequency* and *bandwidth*, as illustrated in Figure 9–19. The center frequency is the frequency that is at the midpoint of the band of frequencies that passes through the filter. The bandwidth is the difference between spectral components on either side of the center frequency that the filter lowers in power by 3 dB. Figure 9–20 shows spectrograms of bandpass filters.

Band-Reject

A band-reject filter is the opposite of a bandpass filter. It reduces or eliminates frequencies within a specified band of the spectrum. Like the bandpass filter, a band-reject filter is characterized by *center frequency* and *bandwidth,* as shown in Figure 9–21. Band-reject filters are more specialized than the other three types and are not as common a musical effect. One possible use would be to remove a narrow band of noise from a recording. Figure 9–22 shows spectrograms of band-reject filters.

Figure 9–17

Frequency Responses of Feedforward and Feedback Highpass Filters

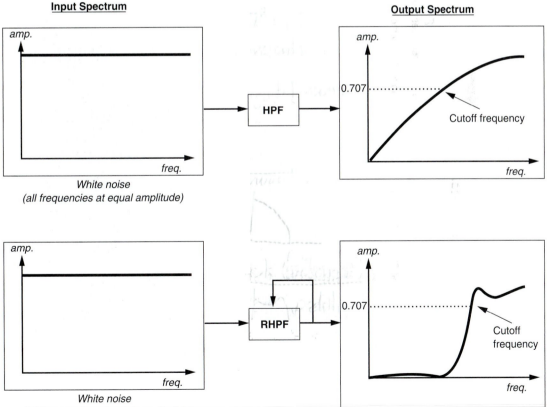

Figure 9–18

Spectrograms of Highpass-Filtered Signals: (Oscillating Cutoff Frequencies, 400–4000 Hz)

Feedforward

Sawtooth wave at 220 Hz (note the harmonic spectrum indicated by the horizontal lines)

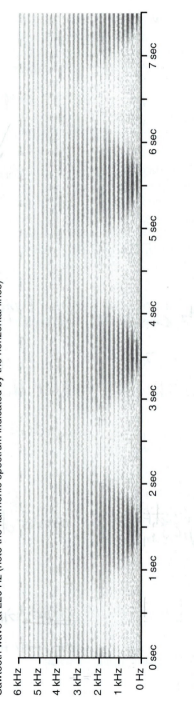

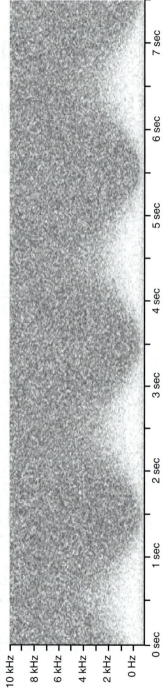

Figure 9–18, cont'd

Feedback

(Note the spectral resonance at the cutoff frequency)

Sawtooth wave at 220 Hz (note the harmonic spectrum indicated by the horizontal lines)

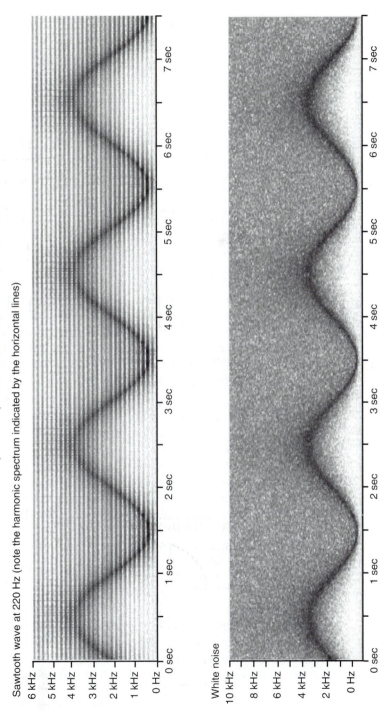

White noise

Figure 9–19

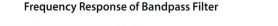

Frequency Response of Bandpass Filter

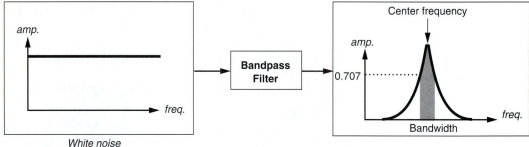

White noise
(all frequencies at equal amplitude)

Everything Is a Filter! This assertion, made by Julius Smith of Stanford University's Center for Computer Research in Music and Acoustics (CCRMA), underlines the central importance of filters in audio systems. Anything that transmits sound filters it in some way. Audio speakers filter their signals, and serious audiophiles look at the frequency response of speakers before buying them. When a person speaks and puts a hand in front of his or her mouth, the sound of the voice is lowpass filtered, as the higher frequencies reflect off the hand and back toward the mouth—this is the effect obtained by brass players who use hat mutes. The size and shape of a room filter the sound propagating within it. Thus, filters underlie audio at every stage of recording, processing, transmission, and production.

The Digital Filtering Process

An audio signal x is termed $x[n]$ when digitized, where n represents a series of discrete sample values (Figure 9–23); n may be thought of as the position (also termed *index* or *address*) of any given sample in signal x. The output of a filter is termed $y[n]$ (Figure 9–24). The digital filter combines the present sample with multiples of past samples to compute each output sample:

$$y[n] = a \times x[n] + b \times x[n-1] + c \times x[n-2] \\ + d \times x[n-3] + \cdots$$

9–2

This general description is called the *filter difference equation.* The symbol n may be interpreted to mean "now," or "the current sample value." $x[n-1]$ may be interpreted as "the value of the sample just previous to the present sample," $x[n-2]$ as "the value of the sample two samples previous to the present sample," and so on. The values multiplied by the series of samples, $[a, b, c, d, . . .]$ are termed *coefficients.*

Although the connection is not intuitive from the filter difference equation, the number of coefficients and their values make it possible to calculate a filter's *frequency response* and thus come up with specific spectral shapes such as those shown in Figure 9–14. The reverse, taking a desired frequency response and

Figure 9–20

Spectrograms of Bandpass-Filtered Signals

Oscillating Center Frequencies; 400–4000 Hz; Fixed *Q*

Sawtooth wave at 220 Hz (note the harmonic spectrum indicated by the horizontal lines)

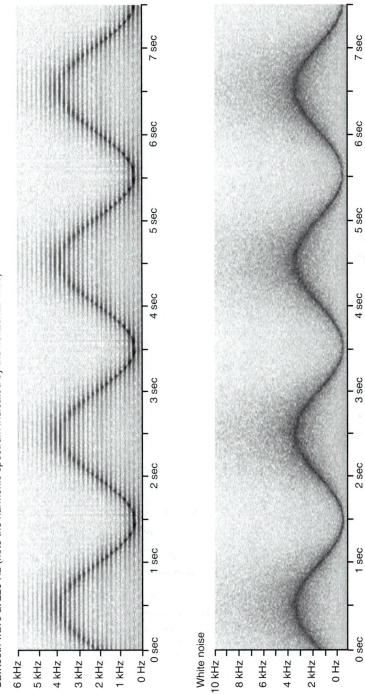

Figure 9–20, cont'd

Fixed Center Frequencies at 1000 Hz; Oscillating *Q*

Sawtooth wave at 220 Hz (note the harmonic spectrum indicated by the horizontal lines)

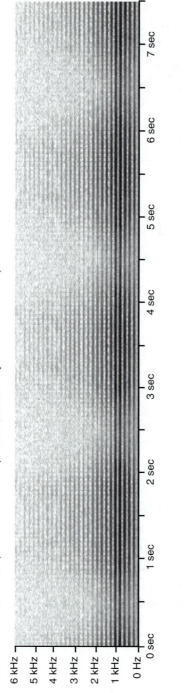

White noise

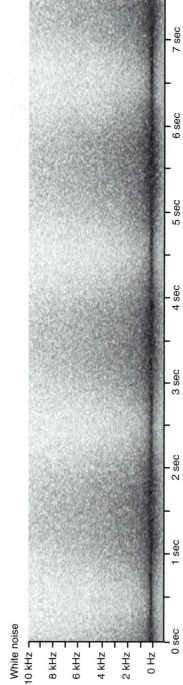

Figure 9–21

Frequency Response of a Band-Reject Filter

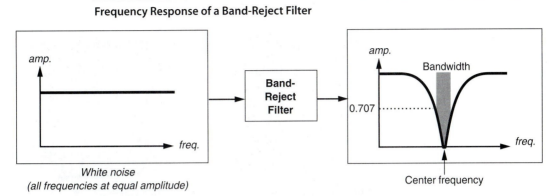

White noise
(all frequencies at equal amplitude)

Center frequency

determining the coefficients that will achieve it, is more complicated (people get degrees in electrical engineering to become experts in how to design filters).

This chapter's references provide excellent descriptions of how the filter difference equation translates into the frequency response. The general overview provided here is meant to demonstrate a practical value of digital audio: all that is necessary to alter the spectrum of an audio signal is hardware that is able to delay samples for a certain number of sample periods and to perform basic arithmetic on the samples held in memory.

Feedforward vs. Feedback Filters

A filter difference equation such as Equation 9–2 combines the present input sample with past input samples and is called a *feedforward* filter. Feedforward filters create dips (*zeroes*) in the spectrum of their output. Table 9–1 illustrates the mechanics of taking a simple "dummy" signal of [0.4, 0.5, 0.6, 0.7] and filtering it with a difference equation with the coefficients [0.3, 0.15, 0.3].

A feedback filter performs multiplications on past output samples as well as past input samples. Thus the difference equation of a resonant filter has two sets of coefficients, the feedback coefficients and the feedforward coefficients:

$$y[n] = a \times y[n-1] + b \times y[n-2] + c \times y[n-3] + \cdots \qquad \text{9–3}$$
$$+ \, d \times x[n] + e \times x[n-1] + \cdots$$

As shown in the last section, feedback filters create peaks (*poles* or *resonances*) in the spectrum of their output. Table 9–2 performs the same processing on a dummy signal as Table 9–1, with the addition of a feedback coefficient of [0.5]. Feedback filters are able to perform fine degrees of spectral shaping with fewer coefficients than would be possible with a feedforward filter.

Lowpass Filters

A simple feedforward lowpass filter may be created by taking the average of the current and preceding sample:

$$y[n] = 0.5x[n] + 0.5x[n-1] \qquad \text{Coefficients: [0.5, 0.5]} \qquad \text{9–4}$$

Figure 9–22

Spectrograms of Band-Reject-Filtered Signals

Oscillating Center Frequencies; 400–4000 Hz; Fixed Q

Sawtooth wave at 220 Hz (note the harmonic spectrum indicated by the horizontal lines)

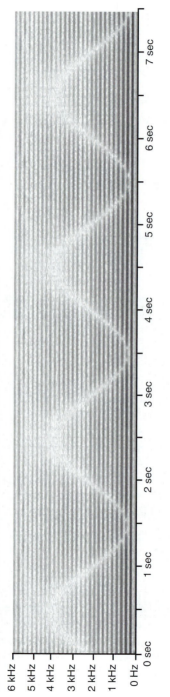

White noise

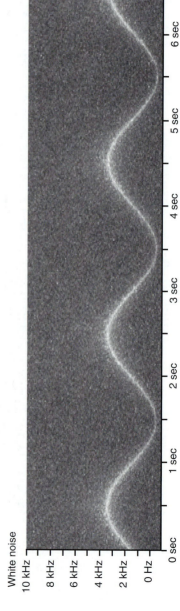

Figure 9–22, cont'd

Fixed Center Frequencies at 1000 Hz; Oscillating *Q*

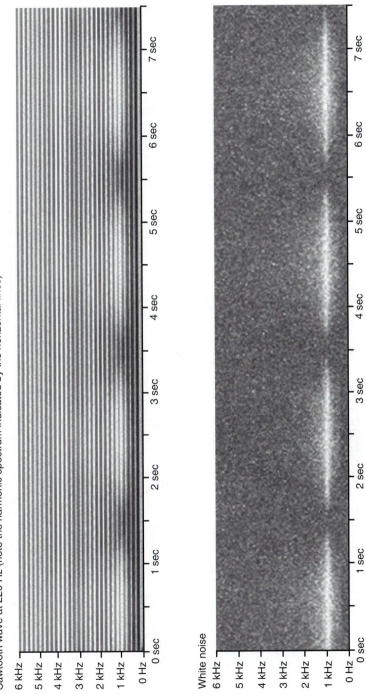

Sawtooth wave at 220 Hz (note the harmonic spectrum indicated by the horizontal lines)

White noise

Figure 9–23

A Digital Signal, $x[n]$

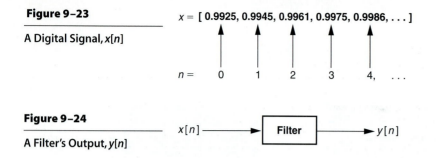

$x = [\ 0.9925, 0.9945, 0.9961, 0.9975, 0.9986, \ldots \ ]$

$n = \quad 0 \quad 1 \quad 2 \quad 3 \quad 4, \quad \ldots$

Figure 9–24

A Filter's Output, $y[n]$

$x[n] \longrightarrow \boxed{\text{Filter}} \longrightarrow y[n]$

Table 9–1
Mechanics of a Feedforward Filter

Input signal: $\quad\quad\quad\quad x[n] = [0.4, 0.5, 0.6, 0.7]$
Coefficients: $\quad\quad\quad\quad$ **[0.3, 0.15, 0.3]**
Filter difference equation: $y[n] = 0.3x[n] + 0.15x[n - 1] + 0.3x[n - 2]$

Now n	Previous Sample $n - 1$	Two Samples Previous $n - 2$	Output Now $y[n]$
0.4 $\times$ **0.3** $\downarrow$ 0.12 $+$	— $\times$ **0.15** $\downarrow$ — $+$	— $\times$ **0.3** $\downarrow$ — $=$	0.12
0.5 $\times$ **0.3** $\downarrow$ 0.15 $+$	0.4 $\times$ **0.15** $\downarrow$ 0.06 $+$	— $\times$ **0.3** $\downarrow$ — $=$	0.21
0.6 $\times$ **0.3** $\downarrow$ 0.18 $+$	0.5 $\times$ **0.15** $\downarrow$ 0.075 $+$	0.4 $\times$ **0.3** $\downarrow$ 0.12 $=$	0.375
0.7 $\times$ **0.3** $\downarrow$ 0.21 $+$	0.6 $\times$ **0.15** $\downarrow$ 0.09 $+$	0.5 $\times$ **0.3** $\downarrow$ 0.15 $=$	0.45
— $\times$ **0.3** $\downarrow$ — $+$	0.7 $\times$ **0.15** $\downarrow$ 0.105 $+$	0.6 $\times$ **0.3** $\downarrow$ 0.18 $=$	0.285
— $\times$ — $\downarrow$ 0 $+$	— $\times$ — $\downarrow$ 0 $+$	0.7 $\times$ **0.3** $\downarrow$ 0.21 $=$	0.21

$y[n] = [0.12, 0.21, 0.375, 0.45, 0.285, 0.21]$

Table 9–2
Mechanics of a Feedback Filter

Input signal: $x[n] = [0.4, 0.5, 0.6, 0.7]$
Feedforward Coefficients: [0.3, 0.15, 0.3]
Feedback Coefficient: [0.5]
Filter difference equation: $y[n] = 0.5y[n-1] + 0.3x[n] + 0.15x[n-1] + 0.3x[n-2]$

Previous Output $y[n-1]$	Now $x[n]$	Previous Sample $x[n-1]$	Two Samples Previous $x[n-2]$	Output Now $y[n]$
—	0.4	—	—	
×	×	×	×	
0.5	0.3	0.15	0.3	
↓	↓	↓	↓	
— +	0.12 +	— +	— =	0.12
0.12	0.5	0.4	—	
×	×	×	×	
0.5	0.3	0.15	0.3	
↓	↓	↓	↓	
0.06 +	0.15 +	0.06 +	— =	0.27
0.27	0.6	0.5	0.4	
×	×	×	×	
0.5	0.3	0.15	0.3	
↓	↓	↓	↓	
0.135 +	0.18 +	0.075 +	0.12 =	0.51
0.51	0.7	0.6	0.5	
×	×	×	×	
0.5	0.3	0.15	0.3	
↓	↓	↓	↓	
0.255 +	0.21 +	0.09 +	0.15 =	0.705
0.705	—	0.7	0.6	
×	×	×	×	
0.5	0.3	0.15	0.3	
↓	↓	↓	↓	
0.3525 +	— +	0.105 +	0.18 =	0.6375
0.6375	—	—	0.7	
×	×	×	×	
0.5	0.3	0.15	0.3	
↓	↓	↓	↓	
0.31875 +	— +	— +	0.21 =	0.52875
0.52875	—	—	—	
×	×	×	×	
0.5	0.3	0.15	0.3	
↓	↓	↓	↓	
0.264375 +	— +	— +	— =	0.264375

Continued

Table 9–2
Mechanics of a Feedback Filter   (continued)

Previous Output y[n − 1]	Now x[n]	Previous Sample x[n − 1]	Two Samples Previous x[n − 2]	Output Now y[n]
0.264375	—	—	—	
×	×	×	×	
0.5	0.3	0.15	0.3	
↓	↓	↓	↓	
0.1321875 +	— +	— +	— =	0.1321875
0.1321875	—	—	—	
×	×	×	×	
0.5	0.3	0.15	0.3	
↓	↓	↓	↓	
0.06609375 +	— +	— +	— =	0.06609375
0.06609375	—	—	—	
×	×	×	×	
0.5	0.3	0.15	0.3	
↓	↓	↓	↓	
0.033046875 +	— +	— +	— =	0.033046875
0.033046875	—	—	—	
×	×	×	×	
0.5	0.3	0.15	0.3	
↓	↓	↓	↓	
0.016523438 +	— +	— +	— =	0.016523438

$y[n]$=[0.12, 0.27, 0.51, 0.705, 0.6375, 0.52875, 0.264375, 0.1321875, 0.06609375, 0.033046875, 0.016523438 . . .]

An intuitive way of understanding the effect of Equation 9–4 is to bear in mind that a waveform with sharp edges contains many high frequencies. The sawtooth and square wave illustrations shown in Chapter 2 (Figure 2–8) were idealized. In a digital system the harmonics do not extend to infinity, but only to the Nyquist frequency. As more harmonics are added, the wave shape approaches the angular shape of the idealized waveform, but the ripples never disappear entirely. Thus, the sharper the edges of a waveform, the more high frequencies it contains. The averaging effect of Equation 9–4 serves to smooth the edges of the output, thus lessening the high-frequency content of a complex wave.

Highpass Filters

A simple feedforward highpass filter may be created by taking the average of the difference between the current and the preceding sample:

$$y[n] = 0.5x[n] - 0.5x[n - 1] \qquad \text{Coefficients: } [0.5, -0.5] \qquad 9\text{–}5$$

Recalling the explanation of the lowpass filter's equation, Equation 9–5 has the opposite effect. The minus sign in the equation results in edges that are made sharper, accentuating high frequency content.

Bandpass and Band-Reject Filters

These filter types are typically feedback filters. It is difficult to do this degree of spectral shaping with feedforward filters. Music synthesis software often terms bandpass filters *resonz,* since they resonate at a center frequency.

Center frequency and bandwidth are often combined to create a descriptor termed *Q* (*quality*), which is the ratio of the center frequency to the bandwidth (CF/BW). Q is often a more useful description than simple bandwidth. Very few bandpass filters maintain a consistent bandwidth when their center frequency is changed. *Constant Q* filters maintain a set ratio of CF/BW, thus maintaining a band that represents a constant musical interval, with a narrower bandwidth for low center frequencies than for high center frequencies.

Other Filter Characteristics

A filter's *transient response* describes the filter's initial output when there is a sudden change in the input (such as the attack of a new note). The transient response is critical to the way a filter's effect is perceived. Figure 9–25 illustrates the output of the same filter illustrated in Table 9–1. The input signal is more characteristic of an actual audio example in that it is periodic, consisting of a sinusoidal wave. The output of the filter is calculated in the same way that it was calculated in Tables 9–1 and 9–2. Notice that there is an initial transient of five irregular samples from the filter output before it settles into a periodic output.

Other useful observations may also be drawn from this figure. The *steady-state response* is what follows the transient response. A filter's initial transient output eventually settles to a steady state that corresponds to one of the four basic filter types shown in Figure 9–14. Notice that in Figure 9–25 the steady-state output is a periodic signal with the same frequency as the input. However, its peak amplitude is lower than that of the input signal. The filter in Figure 9–25 attenuates this frequency. Notice also that once the steady-state response is reached, the phase of the output is offset by one quarter of a cycle from that of the input. The amount of delay varies for different frequency components. A filter's *phase response* describes how much it delays the spectral components of its input.

Filter design is a weighing of compromises. An ideal "brick wall" filter, such as that shown in Figure 9–26, cannot be implemented. In practice, sharp cutoffs result in resonance as well as phase distortion near the cutoff frequency. Practical filter design involves consideration of ripple in the passband and stopband and the slope of the cutoff (expressed in dB/octave). A more realistic frequency response is shown in Figure 9–27.

The Digital Recording and Playback Process

Recording

An understanding of filters allows the steps of the digital recording process to be examined in more detail. Figure 9–28 illustrates the process for a two-channel stereo recording. The various components are discussed next.

Figure 9–25

Filter Transient Response

A periodic input signal causes an initial transient response before the output settles to a periodic pattern.

Filter difference equation: $y[n] = 0.3x[n] + 0.15x[n-1] + 0.3x[n-2]$

$x[n] = [1, 0.707, 0, -0.707, -1, -0.707, 0, 0.707, 1, 0.707, 0, \ldots]$

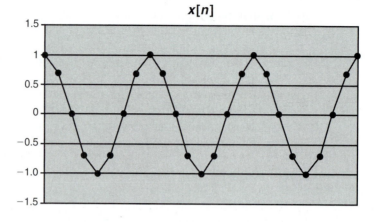

$x[n]$

$y[n] = [0.09, 0.362, 0.406, 0, -0.406, -0.406, -0.574, -0.406, 0, 0.406, 0.574, 0.406, 0, -0.406, -0.574, -0.406, 0, 0.406, \ldots]$

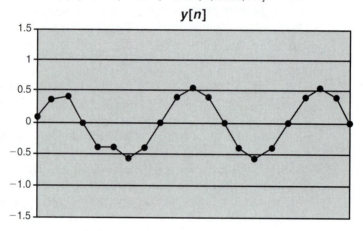

$y[n]$

Figure 9–26

An Ideal Lowpass Frequency Response

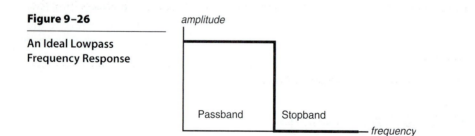

Figure 9–27

A More Realistic Frequency
Response

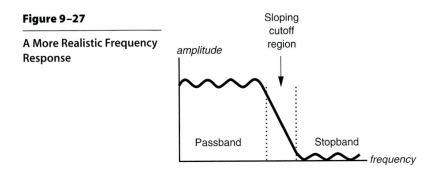

Dither

Low-level noise is added to the signal prior to sampling to reduce quantization error distortion, as discussed earlier.

Lowpass (Antialiasing) Filter

As stated earlier, the filtering step is essential to remove frequencies above the Nyquist frequency. Given the practical limitations of filters just discussed, extra caution is taken. Because an ideal brick wall filter is impossible, the cutoff starts a few thousand hertz below the Nyquist frequency. To ensure that no aliasing occurs, the filter's stopband may begin at a frequency lower than the Nyquist frequency. Thus, the problem of critical sampling, shown in Figure 9–6, is avoided as there are always more than two samples per period of any signal.

Sample and Hold

This is the step at which analog voltage levels are measured. The measurement values must then be held long enough to be read by the analog-to-digital converter.

Analog-to-Digital Converter

This is where the information is prepared for storage. The ADC reads values from the sample and hold circuit, determines the quantization level nearest to the actual value, and outputs it as a binary number for storage. The binary values are transmitted through pulse code modulation (PCM), which, as described in Chapter 7, represents an alternation between two voltage levels to transmit binary ones and zeroes.

Multiplexer

The purpose of the multiplexer is to take the parallel data streams from each stereo channel and transform them into a serial bit stream for storage. Samples from the

Figure 9–28

Components in the Digital Recording Process

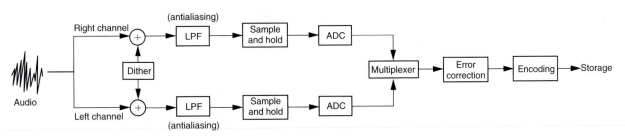

two channels are alternated in the serial stream, and extra bits are added to each sample to indicate which stereo channel it belongs to.

Error Correction

Digital audio would not be economically feasible without effective error correction. The density of the data stored on compact discs and digital audio tape is such that these media would be prohibitively expensive if they had to be robust enough to ensure perfect storage and reproduction. Therefore, effective error correction is required. This is an entire subfield of digital audio engineering, involving various forms of encryption.

A variety of bookkeeping measures are taken at this stage. Samples are stored in groups known as *frames*. Each sample is accompanied by bits that identify its frame number and stereo channel. In addition to information accompanying each sample, the beginning of each frame is marked by a unique series of bits that allow unambiguous identification of a frame's beginning. This *subcode* information allows listeners to fast-forward or reverse a CD and have playback begin at the beginning of the chosen frame. A variety of measures may also be taken to reduce errors. For example, the sum of all sample values in a frame is stored in a few bytes reserved for such bookkeeping. On playback, if the sum of samples in a frame does not match the stored sum value, an error is present. A variety of algorithms may be employed to try to correct it. Another approach involves scrambling the order of the samples, a process known as *interleaving*. The samples are reordered on playback. Interleaving ensures that if an area of the storage medium undergoes damage, the samples affected will not be contiguous. Noncontiguous errors may be remedied by correction algorithms, whereas a series of damaged samples may be irreparable.

Encoding

Before being transferred to the storage medium, the data must be encoded to ensure that it can be read accurately on playback. The nature of the encoding will be discussed in Chapter 10 in the section on storage media.

Playback

The process of playing digital audio is essentially the reverse process of recording it, as shown in Figure 9–29.

Buffer

The creation of audio from a series of stored numbers is a precisely timed operation. To ensure that samples are processed at a constant rate, they are initially held in a buffer from which they may be regularly dispensed. In *Principles of Digital Audio,* Ken Pohlmann compares the buffer to a pail of water. Although a spigot may pour water into a bucket irregularly, a small hole in the bottom of the bucket ensures that a consistent stream of water flows out.

Error Correction

Stored bits are deinterleaved and checked for accuracy in the error correction module. Depending on the degree of error present, a number of steps may be taken. Errors may be eliminated up to a certain point. Should absolute correction be impossible, a variety of concealment techniques may be employed. In some cases, a sample may be interpolated by assigning it a value based on the mean of samples

Figure 9–29

Components of the Digital Playback Process

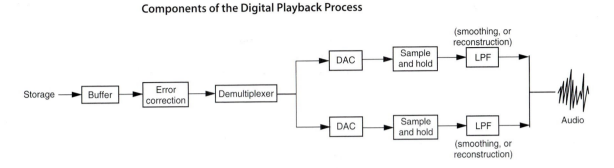

that precede and follow it. Given the deterministic, periodic nature of musical signals, interpolation is often a workable alternative. If even this approach proves impossible, a worst-case scenario is simply to mute the signal temporarily until samples become verifiable again.

DAC and Sample and Hold

The digital-to-analog converter reads binary sample values and translates them into voltage values. This is not an instantaneous process, however, and *glitching errors* may result from the fact that some bits may be translated before others. For example, if one digital word is

01111111 11111111

and the next is

10000000 00000000

the most significant bit may register in the DAC before the other bits, thus creating a short voltage spike resulting from the value of

11111111 11111111

before the intended value is reached.

To remove these voltage glitches, a sample and hold circuit acts as an intermediary between the DAC and the actual voltage output. The sample and hold circuit reads values from the DAC when the DAC has reached a stable state during each sampling period. This value is held until the DAC's next stable state during the next sampling period. Thus, glitches are eliminated, but the result is a staircase waveform, such as those shown in Figure 9–4. The sharp edges necessarily lead to extra high-frequency content that has to be smoothed by a lowpass filter.

Output Lowpass Filter

As a final step before the realization of audio, the staircase wave produced by the sample and hold circuit is smoothed by a lowpass filter. Output lowpass filters often employ a three-step process of *oversampling:*

1. Samples are inserted between the original samples, and the output sampling rate is correspondingly multiplied. For example, at 4× oversampling, three samples at a value of zero are inserted between each sample, and the sampling rate is multiplied by 4. At 8× oversampling, seven samples at a value of zero are inserted between each sample, and

the sampling rate is multiplied by 8. The audio is thus produced at this higher sampling rate.

2. These added samples are calculated to an interpolated value between the original samples so that they fit the curve of the signal. The staircase wave from the sample and hold unit is thus smoothed.

3. The smoothing process may then be completed by a filter that has a more gradual and smooth cutoff slope. The resulting signal is cleaner than conversion at the original sampling rate.

Oversampling is often complemented by *noiseshaping,* a process that high-pass filters quantization error so that the distortion is pushed to frequencies above the audible range. The process of oversampling and noiseshaping will be covered in more detail in Chapter 10.

Working with Digital Audio

Processing and Storage

Spectral Representation

To explore the working of filtering and digital audio reproduction more fully, this section will touch on some principles of spectral representation and digital signal processing.

0 Hz = Direct Current

A spectral component at 0 Hz is often referred to by an electronics term. There are two types of electrical current. *Alternating current,* ac, is current that oscillates as the electrons move back and forth within a wire. This is the type of current supplied by power companies, available through wall sockets. *Direct current,* dc, is current that does not oscillate but moves constantly in one direction. This is the type of current produced by batteries. Because it has no oscillation, with the electrons moving in one direction only, dc has a frequency of 0 Hz, indicating that there is no oscillation present in the current. Figure 10–1 compares ac and dc. The terms "dc" and "0 Hz" are often used interchangeably.

There are times when a current or a signal has a constant added at all times. For example, the equation

$$y = 0.5 + \sin(x)$$

describes a sine wave with a value of 0.5 added to all values. This means that the sine wave does not oscillate equally above and below the value of zero, but rather above and below the value of 0.5. The presence of this constant value is termed "dc content" or "dc offset."

To use a maritime analogy, ac is similar to the height of waves in water; dc content represents the tide level, as shown in Figure 10–2.

Spectra of Digital Signals

The Fourier transform was introduced in Chapter 2. It states that any periodic signal may be expressed as the sum of a series of sinusoidal waves. All are harmonics of the fundamental frequency of the signal, and each is at a particular amplitude and phase.

Figure 10–1

Alternating vs. Direct
Current

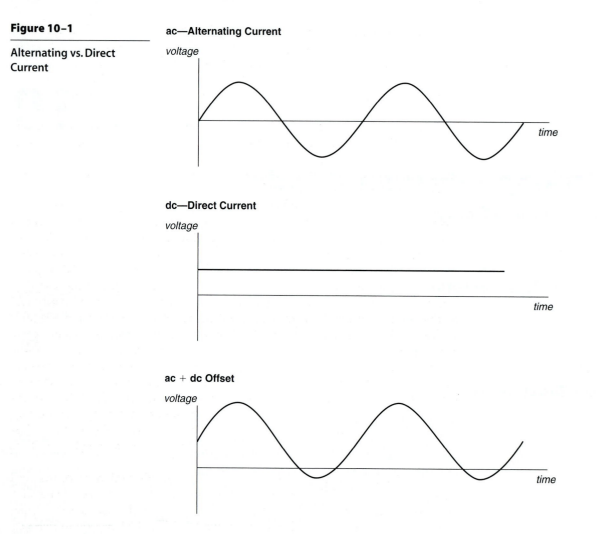

ac—Alternating Current

voltage

time

dc—Direct Current

voltage

time

ac + dc Offset

voltage

time

For discrete digital signals, the mathematics of the Fourier transform have been adapted to a process known as the Discrete Fourier Transform (DFT). This section will treat the DFT process as a "black box." Interested readers may consult the references for extremely accessible explanations of the mathematics involved. This brief description will simply consider the results of the process.

Figure 10–2

Comparison of Current to
Wave and Tide Levels

Waves at High Tide

Tide
level

Waves at Low Tide

Tide
level

The signal of N values is considered to be one period of an infinitely repeating waveform. With this assumption, all past and future positions of the signal may be known, due to its periodicity. The DFT transforms N time domain samples into N spectral values. The fundamental frequency is what the signal as a whole represents: 1 cycle per N samples. The successive spectral values represent multiples of this frequency: 2 cycles per N samples, 3 cycles per N samples, and so on. In other words, the DFT yields spectral values—amplitude and phase—of 0 Hz and $N-1$ harmonics. As stated in Chapter 2, a Fourier transform is completely reversible. A transform may be done to a set of samples to derive spectral information on the values. An inverse transform may be performed that creates exactly the same series of time domain samples.

The DFT produces a spectrum that is symmetrical. The precise reason has to do with the mathematics of the transform, but conceptually, this symmetry may be considered as resulting from the fact that N samples produce N spectral components, but two samples are required to identify a single frequency's peak and trough, as was shown in Figure 9–5. In the same way, a DFT produces two values for each spectral component, one positive and the other negative, with the amplitude divided between the two. This symmetry is well represented by the polar diagram shown in Figure 9–8. Since the information of the positive and negative components is identical, the negative frequencies are commonly discarded and the amplitudes of the positive frequencies are doubled. For some applications, it may be appropriate to illustrate all frequencies resulting from the transform, both positive and negative. Sometimes the complete results are plotted with the 0 Hz component in the middle position of the graph; other times the negative frequencies are shown to the right of the positive frequencies. The different representations are shown in Figure 10–3. The figure also shows how increasing the value of N increases the resolution of the transform.

The DFT is computationally intensive. A more efficient version, the *Fast Fourier Transform (FFT)*, is fast enough for spectra to be derived and manipulated in real time, meaning that the results can be displayed as music is being generated. The results are identical to those of the DFT. The FFT algorithm relies on repeatedly breaking the mathematics of the transform into two parts, so a requirement of the FFT algorithm is that the length of the signal analyzed must be some power of 2.

Convolution

What Is It?

Convolution is a vector operation that involves sliding one vector over another, multiplying overlapping members and taking the sum of all multiplications, then sliding by another increment.

As a real-world analogy, consider a practice common in junior sports leagues. After a game of soccer or tee ball, there is the important exercise of sportsmanship: both teams line up, with team A facing team B. Both lines walk forward, and as players pass each other, each player gives a high five to each member of the opposing team. Now, simply imagine that the players are numbers, that they advance in perfect synchronization, and that each high five is a multiplication. All high fives occur simultaneously. With each step forward, listeners hear the collective sound of all overlapping players high-fiving.

Figure 10–3

Representations of the Discrete Fourier Transform

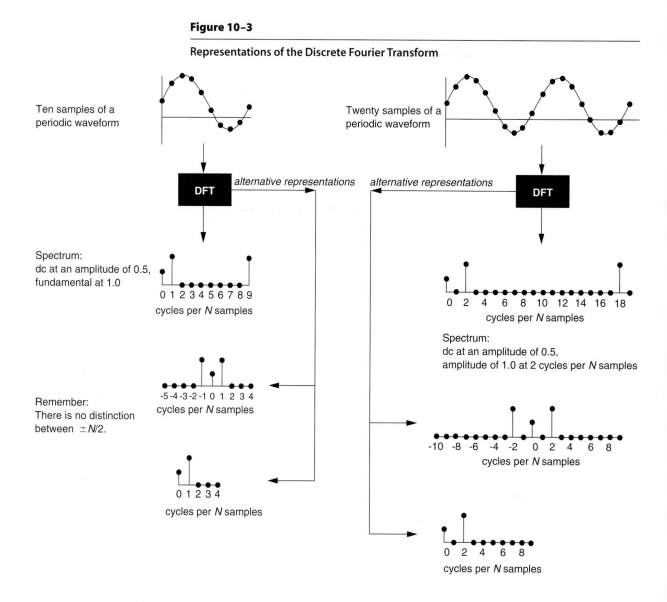

Figure 10–4 illustrates an example with two sequences, $x[n]$ and $y[n]$. The symbol "*" denotes convolution. Notice that it is the same process as was illustrated in Tables 9–1 and 9–2. Two facts may be observed:

1. The process is commutative. It does not matter which sequence is reversed; the results will be the same. (Try it!)

2. The length of the convolved sequence is the sum of the lengths of the two sequences, minus 1.

Figure 10–5 generalizes the process, using index values in place of numbers.

If the definition of any two sequences is extended to include an infinite number of zeroes before and after the values listed, a further observation can be made:

At any time n, the output is the product of $x_m y_{n-m}$, for values of m from zero to n.

Figure 10–4

Convolution of Two Sequences of Numbers

$x[n] = [1, 2, 3, 4, 5]$

$y[n] = [6, 7, 8, 9]$

$x[n] * y[n] = [6, 19, 30, 92, 100, 94, 76, 45]$

Time (n)	Output	
0	$(1 \times 6) = $ **6**	$[6, 7, 8, 9]$ $[5, 4, 3, 2, 1]$
1	$(1 \times 7) + (2 \times 6) = $ **19**	$[6, 7, 8, 9]$ $[5, 4, 3, 2, 1]$
2	$(1 \times 8) + (2 \times 7) + (3 \times 6) = $ **30**	$[6, 7, 8, 9]$ $[5, 4, 3, 2, 1]$
3	$(1 \times 9) + (2 \times 8) + (3 \times 7) + (4 \times 6) = $ **92**	$[6, 7, 8, 9]$ $[5, 4, 3, 2, 1]$
4	$(2 \times 9) + (3 \times 8) + (4 \times 7) + (5 \times 6) = $ **100**	$[6, 7, 8, 9]$ $[5, 4, 3, 2, 1]$
5	$(3 \times 9) + (4 \times 8) + (5 \times 7) = $ **94**	$[6, 7, 8, 9]$ $[5, 4, 3, 2, 1]$
6	$(4 \times 9) + (5 \times 8) = $ **76**	$[6, 7, 8, 9]$ $[5, 4, 3, 2, 1]$
7	$(5 \times 9) = $ **45**	$[6, 7, 8, 9]$ $[5, 4, 3, 2, 1]$

This may be written in mathematical notation as follows:

$$x[n] * y[n] = \sum_{m=0}^{n} x[m]y[n - m] \qquad n = 0, 1, 2, . . . \qquad 10\text{--}1$$

Note that convolving two sequences is quite a different process from multiplying two sequences. Multiplication simply involves multiplying corresponding members of two sequences to form a third sequence:

$$x[n] = [x_0, x_1, x_2, x_3, . . .] \qquad y[n] = [y_0, y_1, y_2, y_3, . . .]$$
$$x[n] \times y[n] = [x_0 y_0, x_1 y_1, x_2 y_2, x_3 y_3, . . .]$$

(Imagine the two junior sports league teams standing in two opposite lines, with each member giving one high five only to the facing player.)

Figure 10–6 gives a graphic view of convolution. Based on this view, convolution may also be described in this way: when sequence A is convolved with sequence B, every member of sequence B produces a scaled duplication of each member of sequence A. When one sequence consists of single impulses spaced widely apart, as in the top part of the figure, the result is discrete copies of the other sequence, scaled accordingly. When the sequences are close together, as in the bottom part of the figure, the discrete copies become superimposed.

Figure 10–5

Generalized View of the Convolution Process

$x[n] = [x_0, x_1, x_2, x_3, x_4]$

$y[n] = [y_0, y_1, y_2, y_3]$

<u>Time (n)</u>	<u>Output</u>	
0	x_0y_0	$[x_4, x_3, x_2, x_1, x_0]$ $[y_0, y_1, y_2, y_3]$
1	$x_1y_0 + x_0y_1$	$[x_4, x_3, x_2, x_1, x_0]$ $[y_0, y_1, y_2, y_3]$
2	$x_2y_0 + x_1y_1 + x_0y_2$	$[x_4, x_3, x_2, x_1, x_0]$ $[y_0, y_1, y_2, y_3]$
3	$x_3y_0 + x_2y_1 + x_1y_2 + x_0y_3$	$[x_4, x_3, x_2, x_1, x_0]$ $[y_0, y_1, y_2, y_3]$
4	$x_4y_0 + x_3y_1 + x_2y_2 + x_1y_3$	$[x_4, x_3, x_2, x_1, x_0]$ $[y_0, y_1, y_2, y_3]$
5	$x_4y_1 + x_3y_2 + x_2y_3$	$[x_4, x_3, x_2, x_1, x_0]$ $[y_0, y_1, y_2, y_3]$
6	$x_4y_2 + x_3y_3$	$[x_4, x_3, x_2, x_1, x_0]$ $[y_0, y_1, y_2, y_3]$
7	x_4y_3	$[x_4, x_3, x_2, x_1, x_0]$ $[y_0, y_1, y_2, y_3]$

Figure 10–6

Graphic Illustration of the Convolution Process

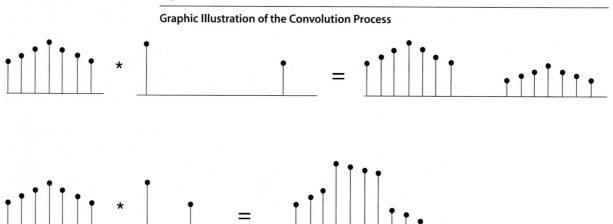

Why Is Convolution Important?

Convolution is a critical process in signal processing due to the following tenet:

> When two time domain signals are multiplied, their spectra are convolved.

The converse is also true:

> When two time domain signals are convolved, their spectra are multiplied.

Two examples will demonstrate these tenets.

**Time Domain
Multiplication:
Ring Modulation**

This is a classic effect of analog synthesis in which two signals are multiplied. When translated into the domain of digital signals, ring modulation exemplifies spectral convolution. Figure 10–7 illustrates how the multiplication of two sine wave signals results in copies of a signal's spectral components, centered around and scaled by the components of another signal. Thus, a time domain multiplication results in a spectral convolution. Ring modulation will be discussed further in Chapter 12.

**Time Domain
Convolution: Filtering**

The discussion on filtering included the definition of the filter difference equation (Equations 9–2 and 9–3). Recall that the values of the coefficients and their time delay determine the frequency response of the filter.

Filters are often analyzed in terms of their *impulse response.* An impulse signal is one that consists of a single pulse and nothing else:

$$[1, 0, 0, 0, \ldots]$$

A DFT of an impulse yields a sequence of

$$[1, 1, 1, 1, 1, \ldots]$$

Thus, the impulse response is useful because its spectrum consists of all harmonics at equal amplitude. If a spectrum consisting of all frequencies is sent into a filter, the filter may be described in terms of how it affects each spectral component of the input signal.

The coefficients of a filter difference equation may be considered as a vector of scaled impulse values. An impulse signal sent into a filter results in output of exactly those coefficients (Figure 10–8). Thus, a filter's coefficients are also termed its *impulse response.* A feedforward filter is also called a *finite impulse response (FIR)* filter, since the output is an infinite series of zeroes after all coefficients have been multiplied by the impulse. Recalling Table 9–2, the case is different with a feedback filter. Since the output is constantly fed back into the filter, it theoretically could continue infinitely. Thus, a feedback filter is also called an *infinite impulse response (IIR)* filter. Care must be taken in the design of IIR filters that their coefficients produce output values of 1 or less so that the feedback continually outputs attenuated values; otherwise, the filter may "blow up" as the signal recirculates endlessly and snowballs with each pass.

The operation of filtering, then, is that an input signal is convolved with a filter's impulse response. The result, as discussed earlier, is spectral shaping. That is,

Figure 10–7

Ring Modulation: Spectral Convolution

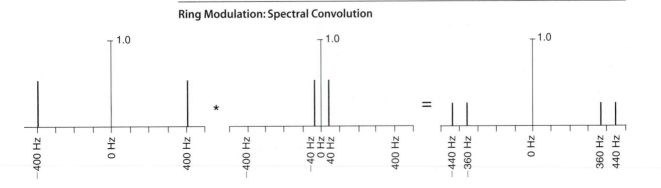

Figure 10–8

Impulse Response

Assume that a filter difference equation is:

$$y[n] = 0.5x[n] + 0.75x[n-1] - 0.2x[n-3]$$

Impulse signal $= [1, 0, 0, 0, \ldots]$

Filter coefficients = [0.5,	0.75,	0,	−0.2]
Time: n	$n-1$	$n-2$	$n-3$

Given an input signal of a single impulse,
the output will be the coefficients:

Time (n)	Output	
0	0.5	[. . ., 0, 0, 0, 1.0] [0.5, 0.75, 0, −0.2]
1	0.75	[. . ., 0, 0, 0.0, 1.00] [0.5, 0.75, 0, −0.2]
2	0	[. . ., 0, 0.0, 0.00, 1] [0.5, 0.75, 0, −0.2]
3	−0.2	[. . ., 0.0, 0.00, 0, 1.0] [0.5, 0.75, 0, −0.2]
4	0	[. . ., 0.00, 0, 0.0, 1.0] [0.5, 0.75, 0, −0.2]
.		
.		
.		

the spectrum of the input signal is multiplied by the spectrum of the filter's frequency response, which is defined by the coefficients. The spectrum of each signal may also be represented as a vector of amplitude values. Corresponding spectral values of the input signal and the filter frequency response are multiplied, as was described in the section on convolution. Thus, a time domain convolution results in a spectral multiplication.

Time Domain Localization vs. Spectral Resolution

A discrete Fourier series is theoretical in that a finite signal is assumed to represent one period of a signal with an infinite length. The Fourier transform is accomplished by convolving the input signal with a series of signals that represent harmonics of the input. Through the resultant spectral multiplications, the contribution of each harmonic to the signal may be determined. Thus, a Fourier transform is analogous to the output of a set of bandpass filters at a fixed bandwidth.

These harmonics may be termed a *basis set,* which is a term describing a set of linked (dependent) basis vectors in a system. Any point in the system may be described as a linear combination of these basis vectors; conversely, these basis vectors are able to describe any point in the system. For example, Cartesian geometry describes points in space based on a system of two basis vectors (the x and y axes) or three basis vectors (with the addition of a z axis). All points in two- or three-dimensional space may be described in terms of two or three basis vectors that represent axes in the Cartesian system.

The Fourier transform of a continuous time signal has a basis set consisting of an infinite number of vectors that are able to describe any possible frequency component of the analog signal. The Fourier transform of a discrete time signal of N points has a basis set consisting of N vectors, which represent 0 Hz and $N - 1$ harmonics of the signal.

The infinite theoretical length of the signals makes the DFT an effective process to describe stable (*stationary*) signals, but it has shortcomings in the description of irregular (*nonstationary*) signals. Any transient behavior in the signal is interpreted as resulting from frequency components whose contributions of constructive and destructive interference over the total length of the signal produce the transient. The nonstationary nature of the transient is thus translated as a coincidence brought about by the amplitudes and phases of a number of stationary components, with the result that its transient nature is lost in the Fourier transform. Thus, it is said that a Fourier transform loses *time localization* of events in a signal, resulting in a tension between time and frequency resolution. A longer signal contains more points, and thus a Fourier transform reveals the presence of more harmonics, with any nonstationary activity "smeared" over the length of the signal. The transform of a shorter signal is better able to describe the timing of an event but, due to its fewer data points, is interpreted as containing fewer frequency components. Thus, there is an inverse relationship between time and frequency resolution. This trade-off is analogous to the *uncertainty principle* in physics, which states that the better a particle's position can be observed, the less accurately its velocity can be estimated, whereas a more accurate measurement of its velocity, by definition, introduces more uncertainty as to its precise position.

One solution to this trade-off is to divide a signal into shorter pieces, called *windows,* and to perform a *Short Time Fourier Transform* (STFT) of each window. A suitable window length must be found to provide a workable compromise, since the shorter window divides the spectrum into fewer components. Each window, representing one period of a waveform, thus has a higher fundamental frequency (due to its shorter wavelength) than the entire signal would have if it were to be transformed. To avoid discontinuities, windows are typically made of overlapping segments of samples: samples that end one window are repeated at the beginning of the next window.

The literature on spectral operations often describes them in terms of the window length. For example, a given analysis might involve a 512-point FFT. What, then, are the implications of a 512-point FFT?

Each window of 512 samples is treated as one cycle of an infinitely repeating wave. This cycle is a multiplication of the sampling period. For CD audio, the sampling period is $1/44,100$ seconds. Multiplying this value by 512 produces a period of 0.01161 seconds. In Chapter 2, Equation 2–1, it was discussed that the frequency of a cyclic wave is the inverse of its period. Thus, the frequency of the cycle is the sampling frequency divided by the window length. In the case of a 512-point window applied to CD audio, this is

$$\frac{44,100 \text{ samples/second}}{512 \text{ samples/cycle}} = 86.132 \text{ cycles/second}$$

This value is interpreted as the fundamental frequency of the signal. The transform produces 512 harmonics of this frequency, frequencies that are integer multiples of the fundamental, from 86.132 Hz to 44,100 Hz. (Recall the polar diagram of Figure 9–8. Because the sampling rate is equivalent to dc in a digital audio system, this is the same as saying that the harmonics will range from 0 Hz to 511 times the fundamental.)

The frequency components resulting directly from the transform are problematic, however, due to the practical reality that most signals contain many frequencies that are not integer multiples of 86.132 Hz. The result of these frequencies is spectral "leakage," which refers to amplitude values assigned to frequency components of the transform that are not actually part of the audio signal. An additional processing step involves the use of a *window function,* which is applied to each transform window to reduce the inevitable presence of leaky components.

Oversampling and Noiseshaping

The concepts of spectra and convolution allow a closer look at what happens to a signal that is recorded and played back (Figure 10–9). An analog signal that is lowpass filtered to remove frequencies above the Nyquist frequency has a symmetrical spectrum after it is sampled and represented in discrete form (10–9a). Sampling effectively consists of a *sampling signal,* a series of pulses occurring at each sampling period. Due to the spectrum of an impulse train (Figure 2–8), the spectrum of the sampling signal consists of harmonics at multiples of the sampling rate (10–9b). The sampling process involves multiplying each value held by the sample and hold circuit by a pulse of the sampling signal. Thus, the time domain multiplication of the audio signal and the sampling signal produces a spectral convolution, with the result that the stored signal consists of multiple images of the audio signal's spectrum, centered at harmonics of the sampling signal (10–9c).

At the digital-to-analog conversion stage, the output lowpass filter has the demanding job of removing these spectral images with a cutoff slope sharp enough to leave the frequencies below the Nyquist frequency unaltered. These are considerable design restraints, as shown in Figures 9–26 and 9–27. Demands on the filtering process are made more practical with the use of oversampling. As was discussed in the section on playback on Chapter 9, oversampling is a process that places intermediate samples between the stored samples in the audio signal, with a corresponding increase in the sampling rate. This process gives a smoother rendition of the audio signal, and more. Although oversampling does not increase the frequency bandwidth of the original audio, it raises the Nyquist frequency accordingly and with it the spectral images of the signal (Figure10–9d). Following conversion to analog, a simple analog FIR lowpass filter with a flat passband and long cutoff region is sufficient to remove the spectral images (Figure 10–9e).

At the same time, potential quantization error noise introduced by the digital-to-analog conversion is, by definition, spread evenly throughout the spectrum of the signal. By increasing the signal's spectral range through oversampling, the error is spread to higher frequencies that are inaudible and possibly removed by the lowpass filter. The redistribution of quantization error is aided by noiseshaping. Noiseshaping combines the present sample with quantization error accumulated with earlier samples and manipulates the present sample plus accumulated error in a manner that amounts to a highpass filter applied to the quantization error distortion. Thus, the error is redistributed to the high end of the spectrum, often above the audio range. Watkinson suggests the term "quantizing error spectrum shaping" as an alternative to "noiseshaping."

Figure 10–9

Spectral View of the Digital Recording Process

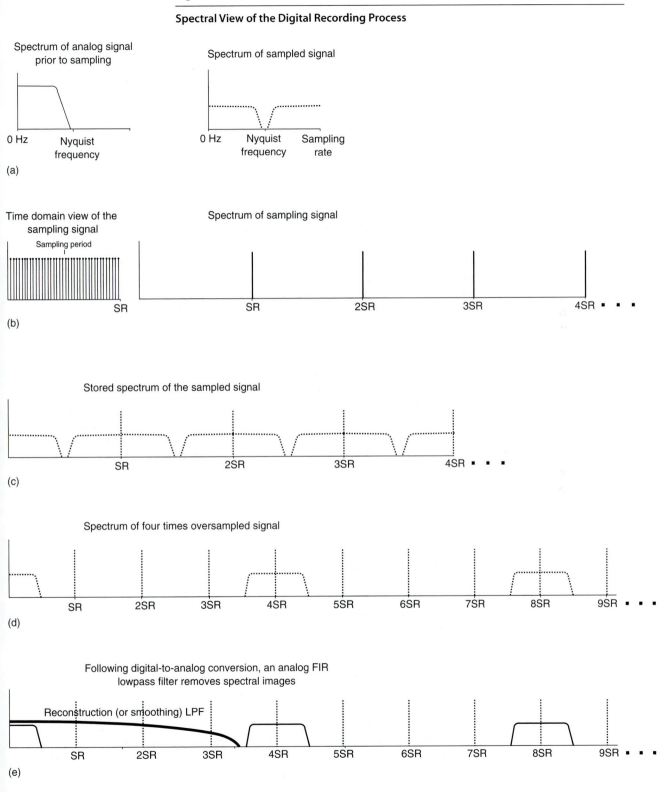

Oversampling, in summary, not only smooths the audio wave and removes spectral images but it also can help to reduce the noise caused by quantization error. The term *oversampling* as an advertised feature of an audio component is a general term that tends to include not only the oversampling plus reconstruction (or smoothing) just discussed but also some form of noiseshaping. The two steps occur in tandem, prior to digital-to-analog conversion, which occurs at the higher sampling rate.

Perceptual Coding

The sampling process, as described above, creates a description of an audio waveform as accurately as possible and transmits it as a PCM signal. As was discussed earlier, at CD sampling rate and bit depth, this produces files on the order of 10 MB/minute. Chapter 3 discussed some examples of differences between what may be accurately measured and what may actually be perceived. The field of perceptual coding takes these measurable-perceptual disparities a step further. Perceptual coding attempts to reduce the size of audio files by considering two questions:

1. To what degree does the auditory system perceive the complexities of an audio signal?

2. How much may be removed from an audio signal with no noticeable effect?

Data reduction techniques involving perceptual coding seek to create algorithms that imitate the processes of the auditory system, eliminating from the bitstream elements that the auditory system would ignore in an acoustic signal.

Psychoacoustics

Early work in digital synthesis involved the analysis of recorded instrumental sounds. The work of Moorer and Grey at Stanford University involved the analysis of the amplitude and frequency envelopes of partials in trumpet tones (Figure 10–10). Theirs was a valuable study of timbre, yielding information about the separate changes that individual partials undergo over time. A significant element of the study involved reducing the large amounts of data needed for accurate representations of the complex amplitude fluctuations. They discovered that line segment approximations of each partial's amplitude envelope could reduce the amount of data significantly, yet there was no great difference reported by listeners between synthesized tones created from the complex and the simplified amplitude envelopes. Thus, a good deal of the sounds' natural complexity is lost on the auditory system, and creating highly accurate renditions of these envelope shapes for purposes of audition uses essentially unnecessary bandwidth.

Psychoacoustics is the study of auditory perception. Researchers such as Diana Deutsch and Albert S. Bregman have produced extensive studies of how the auditory system responds to various stimuli. The responses often differ from the actual nature of the stimulus, one classic example being Deutsch's "scale illusion" (Figure 10–11). The ability to "trick" the auditory system with demonstrations

Figure 10–10

Envelope Segment Reductions

From James A. Moorer, John Grey. "Lexicon of Analyzed Tones, Part 3." *Computer Music Journal* 2(2), Sept. 1978. Reprinted courtesy of James Moorer.

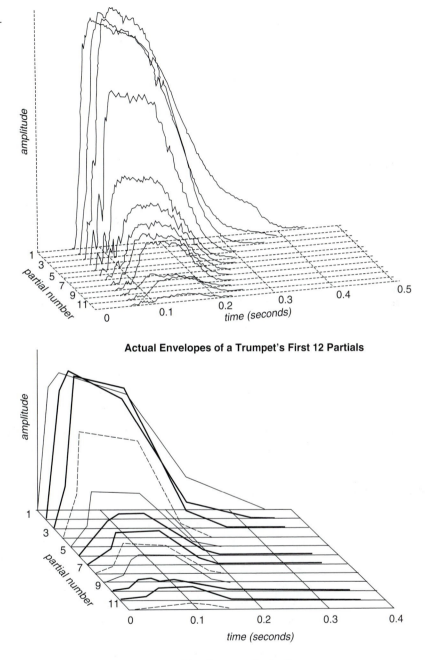

Actual Envelopes of a Trumpet's First 12 Partials

Line Segment Reductions

such as this shows that what is transmitted to the brain via the auditory system is in fact an interpretation of what the ear receives, and not an objective representation. Perceptual coding attempts to employ these interpretations to reduce the data required to produce audio signals. The basis of much of this work involves the use of masking.

Figure 10–11

The Scale Illusion (Discovered by Diana Deutsch)

Listeners report tones grouped by frequency proximity, rather than the actual ear of presentation.

Figure from "Grouping Mechanisms in Music" by Diana Deutsch in *The Psychology of Music,* Second Edition, edited by Diana Deutsch, copyright © 1999 by Academic Press, reproduced by permission of the publisher.

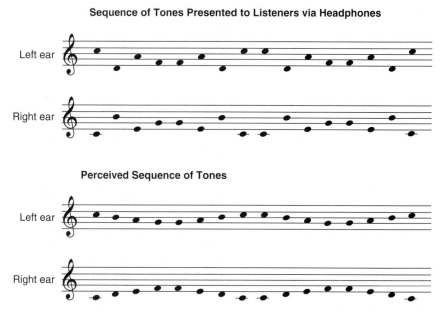

Sequence of Tones Presented to Listeners via Headphones

Left ear

Right ear

Perceived Sequence of Tones

Left ear

Right ear

Masking

Masking refers to a phenomenon of certain sounds causing other sounds to disappear (to be "masked") perceptually. Anyone who has tried to have a conversation while walking along a city street is likely to have been frustrated by the frequent intrusion of loud noise from passing vehicles that masks the sound of a person's voice. More precise analyses of masking show it to be related to the physiology of frequency perception.

The eardrum converts incoming sound waves into mechanical energy. This mechanical energy is then transduced into electrical impulses in the cochlea, located in the inner ear. Within the cochlea, roughly 30,000 hair cells are arranged in rows. These hair cells fire electrical impulses that are interpreted by the brain as auditory signals. Not all cells fire simultaneously, however. Different regions of the hair cells fire when vibrations at different frequencies are received. A given frequency causes a given region of cells to fire. The width of the region that is activated by a given frequency is called a *critical band*. A given frequency creates maximum excitation in a small set of hair cells, plus lesser amounts of excitation in neighboring cells. The term *critical band* also refers to the frequency range to which all of these cells respond. The relationship of critical bands to frequency is not linear, but logarithmic. Equivalent lengths of hair cells are stimulated by wider ranges of high frequencies than those stimulated by lower frequencies, Thus, for example, a frequency of 350 Hz may stimulate the region of cells that responds to frequencies from 300 to 400 Hz. But a frequency of 4000 Hz may excite a region of cells that responds to frequencies within the range of 3700 to 4400 Hz.

Perceptual Masking

Critical bands and the threshold of hearing shown by the Robinson–Dadson curves (Figure 3–4) come into play when masking phenomena are analyzed. The presence of a loud tone at a given frequency raises the hearing threshold for other frequencies within the tone's critical band (Figure 10–12). Data reduction techniques that utilize perceptual masking perform spectral analyses on blocks of samples. Low-level frequencies that would be masked by louder neighboring frequencies may be eliminated.

Quantization Distortion Masking

Other techniques involve reducing the bit depth assigned to some frequencies. An analysis is made of low-level frequencies. Those that are deemed less perceptually salient may be allocated fewer bits when the inverse transform is performed. This loss of resolution will necessarily lead to quantization error in these frequencies. A masking analysis model makes an estimation of how much quantization error may be masked within the critical band of louder frequencies. This allows the bitstream to be reduced by dynamic allocation of bits according to how prominent certain frequencies are within a block of samples.

Temporal Masking

Temporal masking addresses the question of time domain masking that occurs within the proximity of transients. A noisy transient may mask softer tones that occur either prior to it (*premasking*) or immediately following it (*postmasking*).

Data Reduction

Audio data may be reduced in size by combinations of the three types of masking just discussed. Blocks of successive samples are analyzed in comparison with a psychoacoustic model, and reductions are made where material is deemed expendable. Block size is an important consideration, given the trade-off in time localization and frequency resolution discussed in the section "Time Domain Localization vs. Spectral Resolution." Any quantization distortion that results from data reduction extends over the length of a block. Should a block contain silence followed by a transient, the added distortion may act as a pre-echo of the upcoming transient.

In a process known as *subband coding*, short blocks of samples are applied to a bank of bandpass filters. The output of each filter is then put through a spectral analysis. Comparison of the activity in each band allows masked spectral

Figure 10–12

Perceptual Masking

From *Principles of Digital Audio*, 3rd ed., by Ken Pohlmann (1995), McGraw-Hill. Reprinted with the permission of The McGraw-Hill Companies.

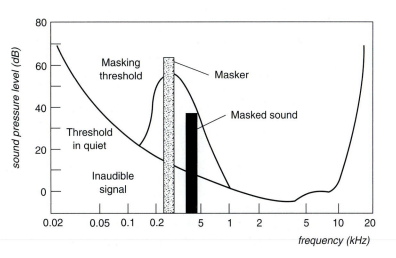

components to be removed and allows the bit depth of each band to be allocated based on its activity and whether the quantization error distortion would be masked by activity in the other bands. Subband coding tends to be stronger in time localization and weaker in spectral resolution.

In *transform coding,* longer blocks of successive samples are subjected to an FFT that yields a more detailed spectral view than that of subband coding. Elimination of inaudible components and coarser quantization of low-level components is determined based on this more detailed spectral representation. Transform coding tends to be stronger in spectral resolution and weaker in time localization.

The effectiveness of data reduction algorithms is difficult to gauge objectively. The results depend on the audio used for testing, the DACs of the playback equipment, and who is being asked to evaluate the quality. Serious audiophiles, who are concerned with maximum listening experience, are likely to find data-reduced files to be lacking, with the compression resulting in a significantly degraded listening experience. Web or multimedia developers, who are concerned with transmitting or storing large amounts of material that may also include images and animation, are likely to find uncompressed audio files needlessly bloated in size, with little perceptual advantage.

Storage Media

This section will discuss how digital information is stored on various media and how it is retrieved for playback.

Compact Disc

Retrieving Data

Binary values are stored on optical disc by the use of microscopic holes, known as *pits,* in the disc surface; the areas between the holes are called *lands.* The length of the pits and lands is variable; it is the length of a given pit or land that translates into a binary value in a manner that will be described shortly. The pits and lands are laid out in a spiral starting from the inner edge of the disc, as shown in Figure 10–13. If the pit track on a standard-sized audio compact disc (a diameter of 12 cm, or 4.72″) were laid out in a straight line, it would extend approximately $3\frac{1}{2}$ miles (5.6 km). (A brief housekeeping note: given the spiral layout of CD data, when cleaning compact discs it is advisable to use a cloth and wipe the disc in a line along the disk's radius, from the center out. Wiping in a circular motion runs the risk of damaging consecutive data should any scratches result. Wiping along the disk's radius is less likely to damage consecutive areas of data, and any scratches are more likely to be correctable with error correction.)

A compact disc holds a maximum of 783 MB of data, allowing a playback time of 74 minutes of audio material. Some variation in the format, such as squeezing the pit/land spiral a bit tighter, allows for playback of 80 minutes or more.

The fact that the data is read from the inner area of the disc outward (the opposite path of a needle on a vinyl record) means that the diameter of optical discs is arbitrary. Smaller-sized discs can work in the same CD players or CD-ROM drives as standard-sized discs. Some people now use coin-sized CD-ROMs as business cards rather than paper, allowing a small multimedia presentation to represent them rather than simply a printed name and address. Similarly, some digital cameras

Figure 10–13

Pits and Lands on the
Surface of a CD

have small CD storage drives where they store photographs. These CDs may be removed from the camera and placed into a computer CD-ROM drive for transferring the pictures to the computer.

Data is retrieved from a CD by an optical system. A fine laser beam is focused along the pit/land track, as shown in Figure 10–14, and is reflected to an optical pickup that translates the intensity of the reflected beam to an electrical signal. The coating that covers the surface of the disc causes the laser beam to refract, reflecting away from the disc at an angle toward the pickup. When the beam is focused on a flat area within a pit or on a land, the wave is reflected intact. This is not the case, however, when the beam is focused at an edge between a pit and a land, when part of the beam reflects from the land and part of the beam reflects from the pit. The depth of the pit is one quarter of the wavelength of the laser. Thus, the laser beam begins reflecting from the pit one-quarter wavelength later than the beam reflecting from the land; it then takes another quarter wavelength before the reflections from the pit join the reflections from the land. Thus, the reflections from the pit are one-half wavelength out of phase with those from the land, and the reflection is largely cancelled, sending a lower-intensity reflection to the pickup.

Pits and lands do not correspond directly to the binary digits of 1 and 0. Rather, the interpretation of a binary digit depends on the intensity of the reflection reaching the pickup. Low-intensity reflections from a pit edge are translated into a digit of 1, and high-intensity reflections from a pit or land are translated into a digit of 0.

The mechanism of laser beam and electrical pickup is what makes the optical disc a much more robust medium than vinyl and tape. Both of these earlier media types rely on friction to create the playback signal, and the friction causes the media to degrade with repeated playings. A needle running over the grooves of a vinyl phonograph record creates friction. The up-and-down shape of the groove track corresponds to the amplitude of one stereo channel of the signal, while the left-and-right motion corresponds to the amplitude of the other stereo channel. Over time, the friction of the needle against the grooves causes them to

Figure 10–14

Optical System for Reading Data from a CD

(a) The beam reflected from a pit or a land is reflected away from it and is read as a 0. (b) When the beam is focused on a pit edge, the reflection from the pit cancels out the reflection from the land. This is read as a 1. (c) Comparison of a sequence of pits and lands, the waveform derived from the laser, and the resulting binary values.

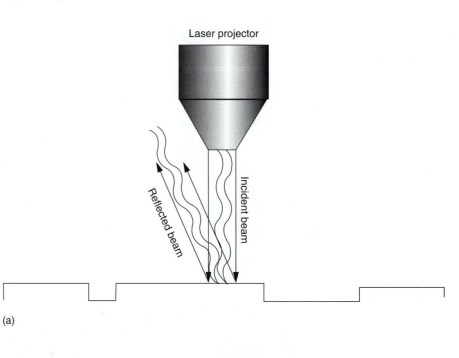

(a)

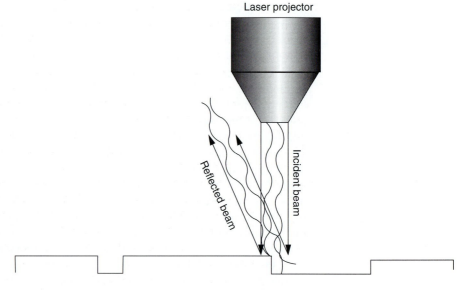

(b)

become dull, degrading the signal that may be played back. Tape has magnetic particles lying along its surface. As the tape is run over the playback head of a tape deck, the magnetic orientation of the particles is transduced into an electrical signal that corresponds to the audio signal. (The nature of tape storage will be discussed further in the section on DAT tapes.) Over repeated playings, the particles dislodge from the tape, so that over time the tape loses fidelity. The optical system of the compact disc involves no such friction, so there is no degradation in the media with repeated playings.

Figure 10–14, cont'd

Binary values

1 0 0 1 0 0 0 0 1 0 0 0 1 0 0 0 0 0 1 0 0 1 0 0 1

Pits and lands on CD surface

NRZI waveform

(c)

The Form of the Data   Prior to being stored to disc, the data values representing audio samples and the associated bookkeeping (described in the section on digital recording in Chapter 9) are encoded to optimize later retrieval from the disc surface. For two-channel stereo audio, each sampling period yields two 16-bit audio samples, one for the left channel and the other for the right. Each frame has 16 of these values, 8 for each channel. At the encoding stage, the values are broken into 8-bit bytes and interleaved (as discussed in the section on error correction in Chapter 9).

Playback is a time-critical process. Values must be read at a constant rate, whether they are taken from the inner or the outer regions of the disc. Thus, the motor on the CD player causes it to spin quickly, at 500 rpm, when data is read from the extreme inner edge. As the laser moves outward, the spinning speed gradually slows to 200 rpm. As the laser focuses over the length of the pit/land track, its progress must be carefully clocked so that values are retrieved accurately. This could present a problem if a long series of the same digit had to be reproduced. The laser tracker would have to be extremely accurate across a long land or pit region to transmit the beginnings and ends of bits accurately. To ease demands on the tracker, the stored values are encoded so that transitions between the two digits happen with some frequency; thus the sequence of bits itself helps to ensure the tracker's timing accuracy. The PCM wave shown in Figure 10–14 is a transmission format called NRZI (nonreturn to zero inverted) code. With this type of coding, there is no requirement that the amplitude return to zero level with each sampling period and that only values of 1 are represented by an amplitude transition and values of 0 are not.

To achieve this timing accuracy from regular amplitude transitions, each 8-bit byte is translated into a 14-bit byte that meets the following two conditions:

1. Successive digits of 1 must be separated by at least two digits of 0.
2. There can never be more than 10 consecutive 0 digits.

Each of the 256 possible 8-bit binary numbers is translated into a 14-bit binary number that meets these two criteria. The translation is done by simple lookup table, so that each 8-bit value has a 14-bit counterpart.

In order to ensure that successive bytes of data do not violate these rules (for example, if a particular byte ended with a 1, followed by a byte beginning with a 1),

3 extra bits are placed between each 14-bit word. These extra bits are calculated on a byte-by-byte basis to ensure that the bit sequence follows the conditions of the encoding and that the average the high and low values of the resulting NRZI waveform maintains a balance between the high and low levels. Thus, every 8 bits of data from the original audio is represented by 17 bits of data encoded on the CD. The increased number of stored bits means that, on playback, bits must be read at a rate much faster than the sampling rate: 17-bit values must be translated back into 8-bit values, checked for error, and still produce audio samples at a rate of 44,100 per second.

CD Recorders

A CD recorder stores data on a disc by melting pit and land patterns into its surface. A write-once (WO) recorder can perform this process only one time. Other drives have the capability to erase a CD's data by smoothing the surface with heat, after which the disc may have new pit/land patterns imprinted.

Digital Audio Tape (DAT)

The nature of tape recording is drastically different in the digital domain than in the analog domain due to the fact that it is not an analog waveform that is put onto the tape, but rather a numerical representation of the signal.

Recording tape is made of plastic backing and a coating of microscopic, cigar-shaped magnetic particles called *domains.* Magnetic particles are characterized by *polarity,* that is, according to one of two directions in which electrons travel within these particles. On blank tape, the polarity of the particles is random, as shown in Figure 10–15. When an analog signal is recorded, a magnetic field from the record head of the tape track saturates the tape, altering the average polarity of the particles to match the amplitude level of the signal. On playback, the particles cause a corresponding current to be generated from the play head.

In digital recording, there is a much higher level of saturation of the particles. Within a given tape region, all particles are oriented in one direction or the other, representing a binary 0 or 1. Thus, a digital recording is much denser than an analog recording. An analog recording, with its literal representation of the signal fluctuations, needs to have the capacity to represent the fluctuations of audible frequencies up to 20 kHz or so. In a digital recording, the polarity of the particles represents the individual bits. Thus, the fluctuations are not those of the audio signal, but rather of 44,100 samples times 16 bits per second, with additional overhead for error correction and subcode information. This makes the requirement for digital tape close to 1 million bits per second per stereo channel, and digital tape must have the capacity to store fluctuations that change at this rate. Thus, digital tape requires 50 times the bandwidth of analog recordings.

This high bandwidth creates problems in tape deck design. The area of tape representing each bit must be as small as possible to make recordings feasible without inordinately long lengths of tape. Digital Audio Stationary Head (DASH) recorders with record and play heads small enough to work with manageable amounts of tape run in the five-figure price range. A less-expensive solution is offered by *rotary head* tape decks, on which the play/record head rotates at high speeds at an angle to the tape. Thus, the speed at which data may be read is determined not only by the tape speed but also the rotation speed of the head. This allows the head to be much

Figure 10–15

Polarity of Magnetic Particles on Recording Tape

Blank tape—random polarity

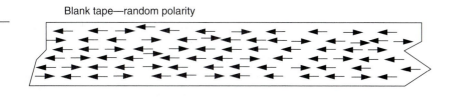

Analog tape—average polarity follows the signal's wave shape

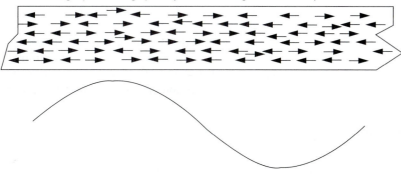

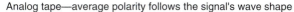

Digital tape—polarity reflects two absolute states completely

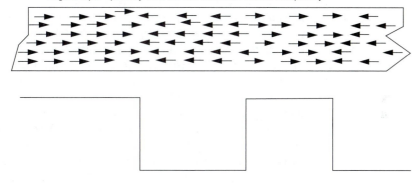

larger, and thus much less costly. The disadvantage of rotary head tapes is that they cannot be cut and spliced, as can analog and DASH tapes.

Video tape recorders have rotary heads to increase the amount of data that may be stored on the tape, hence the angled data pattern shown in Figure 9–9. This is the reason that the first digital recordings were stored on video tape and, by extension, was the basis for the audio sampling rate standard, as discussed in the section "The Sampling Rate of CD Audio and Its Origin." DAT players also use rotary heads. However, a DAT player is an entirely different type of machine from a video recorder. DAT cassettes are smaller than video cassettes. Given the small size, the density of data on the tape is extraordinary, combining CD-quality audio with extensive error correction and subcode. Other innovations of DAT tape include an internal audio tone that acts as a tracking guide so that, should the tone waver, the machine can correct the tape's position against the heads by internally comparing the level of the two tones. Many DAT recorders are small and easily portable. Those with digital output allow the data to be transferred easily into a computer equipped with the appropriate audio hardware, where the material may be edited and copied to another tape or to CD. Computer audio editing systems will be covered presently.

The small size of DAT cassettes makes them somewhat fragile, however. Each binary digit is represented by an area of tape that has a width of about $\frac{1}{20}$ of a human hair. So the tiniest bit of damage to the tape is likely to result in significant data loss. Also, since tape is a flexible medium, DAT output is sometimes prone to timing errors due to mechanical irregularities in the tape transport. These irregularities can lead to the counterintuitive situation of a recording being made on DAT, transferred to CD, and sounding better on the CD duplicate than on the DAT original.

It is advisable not to convert recordings back and forth between the digital and analog domains repeatedly. Excessive conversions between analog to digital also run the risk of distorting the material due to *jitter*. Jitter refers to clock timing irregularities that create errors in the bit transmission rate. The result is that samples are not produced with precise regularity, and distortion may be audible. Jitter is not a problem if a transfer is digital. But any conversion from digital tape to analog has the potential of adding jitter distortion to the audio signal.

MiniDisc

The MiniDisc, created by the Sony Corporation, was the next evolutionary step following the creation of the CD standard. Meant to replace the analog cassette, the MiniDisc is a smaller disc format than the CD, measuring 64 mm (2.5″) in diameter, with a storage capacity of approximately 140 MB. A MiniDisc player can function in two data reading modes, depending on whether it is reading prerecorded or user-recorded material.

Prerecorded MiniDiscs are encoded with a pit/land track similar in design to that of a CD. A laser is focused on the track, and the differences in reflection, depending on whether the reflection is from a flat area or a pit/land transition, are interpreted by an electrical pickup as binary digits. The encoding and error correction methods are also the same as those used for CDs.

Recordable MiniDiscs employ a different system of optics to store and read the data. The recordable data storage method involves *polarization*. Polarization may be summarized as follows: light and other forms of radiant energy travel in transverse waves, meaning that the wave oscillations are perpendicular to the direction of the wave's propagation. Another example of transverse waves is water waves (see Figure 1–3). However, water waves oscillate on one perpendicular angle to the propagation, toward and away from the earth. Light waves, in contrast, oscillate in a potentially infinite number of tilt angles that are perpendicular to the direction of propagation. Imagine attaching one end of a rope to a wall and shaking the other end. The direction of propagation is along the rope. The rope moves toward and away from its equilibrium position at varying degrees of left, right, up, and down tilt. Similarly, light waves are emitted at many tilt angles. A polarizing filter applied to light restricts transmission to oscillations along one axis only. For example, reflected sunlight is typically at a different angle than direct sunlight; Polaroid sunglasses reduce glare by allowing light waves along only one axis to pass through the lenses.

A recordable MiniDisc does not operate by imprinting pits and lands, but rather by changing the orientation of magnetic particles within a magneto-optical surface (Figure 10–16). The magnetic particles are arranged vertically. When in record mode, the laser beam operates at much higher power than in playback mode. The higher-power laser beam heats the particles it focuses on. When the magnetic particles are heated to sufficient temperatures, their *coercivity* is lowered, meaning that little or no magnetic energy is required to change their orientation. A recording coil emitting a magnetic field makes contact with the particles during recording and can change the orientation of the heated particles. The orientation of the recorded particles corresponds to transitions, resulting in binary digits of 1.

During playback, the laser returns to normal power, which is not powerful enough to heat the particles and weaken their orientation. The normally powered laser beam reflects off the particles and is sent into a polarizing prism that acts as a filter, only letting reflections at a certain polarization angle pass through. The particles that have had their orientation reversed during recording reflect the laser at a different polarization angle, and these reflections do not pass through the prism. The output of the prism is read by an electrical pickup and translated to voltage levels based on the binary values.

A disc may be erased by reversing the direction of the magnetic field, thus realigning the orientation of heated particles to their prerecorded direction. Although the MiniDisc recording process does involve contact with the magnetic head, this friction is far less than that involved in vinyl or tape recording and playback. MiniDiscs reportedly may be recorded and erased millions of times before any degradation occurs.

MiniDiscs have a more complex subcode system than CD or DAT formats in order to allow the degree of bookkeeping necessary for selections to be recorded and erased. The magneto-optical surface of MiniDiscs is not flat, but is oriented within a spiral groove that guides the laser during recording and playback. The spiral is not perfectly circular, but has a wobble pattern (a "spiral squiggle"). The wobbles are used to identify address coordinates that are stored in the disc's table of

Figure 10–16

MiniDisc Recording

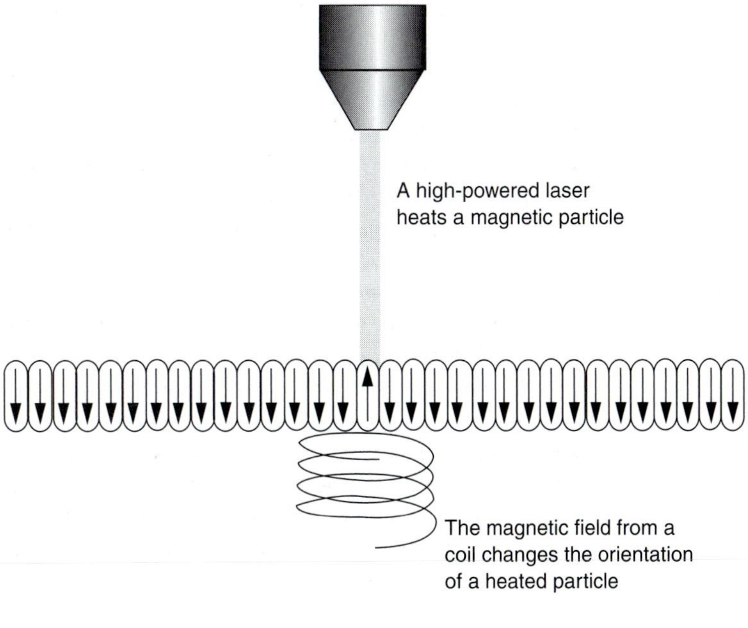

A high-powered laser heats a magnetic particle

The magnetic field from a coil changes the orientation of a heated particle contents. When changes are made, such as deleting or recording new material, the coordinates are updated in the disc's table of contents.

To address the issue of portability, MiniDisc players employ extensive buffering so that 10 to 40 seconds of material are stored prior to playback. Should a physical disturbance disrupt the laser during playback, audio can continue uninterrupted provided the laser can be realigned before the buffer's contents are emptied. The buffer system also allows new material to be stored on noncontiguous areas of the disc. If a selection is erased, any new recording may begin at this erased segment. Should the new recording require more area than this blank space, the data may be stored elsewhere on the disc. The buffer allows the laser to move from one region of the disc to another as necessary during recording and playback without interrupting the continuity of the audio material.

MiniDisc data is reduced by the ATRAC (adaptive transform acoustic coding) algorithm, which reduces data to $\frac{1}{5}$ its original size. Thus, the small MiniDisc may hold as much audio material as the larger CD. With ATRAC, the sampling rate remains at 44.1 kHz, but modifications are made to the bit depth according to tolerable quantization distortion levels as determined by a psychoacoustic model. The signal is split into three frequency bands and a spectral analysis is done on each band. The spectrum is not divided into equal increments, but in a pattern similar to the layout of the critical bands within the inner ear. More resolution is given to lower frequencies than to higher frequencies. Prominent spectral components are given longer word lengths, while masked components are given shorter word lengths. The number of samples in each transform block is variable. A "short block mode" allows attack transients to be encoded without pre-echo, while a "longer block mode" allows greater frequency resolution for segments not characterized by transients (as described in the earlier section "Perceptual Coding").

Many MiniDisc players have both analog and digital inputs and outputs. Some MiniDisc players also allow encoded data to be transmitted directly from player to player. Without such capability, there is the potential for MiniDisc recordings to lose quality over successive duplications. Even if the audio is transmitted digitally, the transmission occurs after decoding. A receiving MiniDisc then reencodes the signal, thus compounding the losses and quantization error inherent in the compression process.

Consumer-level MiniDisc players may also employ serial copy management system (SCMS) protocols to prevent unauthorized duplication of material. Such players may not allow digital recordings to be made from audio CDs. In addition, digital transmission from these players includes identification of a digital source, possibly preventing digital copies from being made with other players. Typically, a SCMS does not limit the number of copies that may be made of a source, but digital copies are so marked, so that copies may not be made from copies. The documentation of a player should detail whether SCMS is used on a particular model or whether it may be enabled or disabled by the user.

DVD

The DVD disc (which originally stood for "digital video disc," then "digital versatile disc," and now does not stand for anything) is meant to address the larger capacity storage needs of video and audio material for film and multimedia releases.

The laser disc succeeded video tape as a medium for storing multimedia, but its video content was in analog form, rendering it incompatible with computer storage and editing. The video compact disc (VCD), popular in Asia, allows films to be stored, but at decreased visual resolution. DVD is intended to store material at high resolution. The format is meant to function similarly to a CD-ROM, but with increased memory. Although identical in dimensions to the compact disc, a more compact pit/land track and a more focused laser provide a storage capacity of 4.7 GB, allowing storage of 120 to 135 minutes of high-quality audio and video. At the same time, DVD players are meant to be backward compatible, allowing audio CDs to be played in them.

The release of films in DVD format is changing the nature of film packaging. With the added storage capability of DVD, there is often room for extra material. This may include deleted scenes or interviews, multiple language tracks, text tracks for subtitles, extra audio tracks to describe the action for visually impaired viewers, or audio with enhanced intelligibility for hearing-impaired viewers. Interactive possibilities include multiple story lines that a user may choose or the ability to view the same scene from different camera angles.

In addition to high-quality video, DVDs are designed to store 5.1 channel, stereo CD-quality audio. This is the stereo format used in cinema and high-definition television (HDTV). The "5" refers to three front channels (left, right, and center) and two surround channels (left surround and right surround). In movie theatres, the surround channels are typically distributed to banks of speakers hung along the side walls. The ".1" refers to a subwoofer channel reserved for frequencies under 120 Hz. Since these low frequencies are theoretically nondirectional due to their long wavelengths, and since the capacity to produce them requires added capability in the main channels, the low frequencies are directed to a separate channel that is not full bandwidth. Thus, the subwoofer channel is referred to as "one tenth of a channel." The subwoofer speaker is typically placed on the floor, anywhere within the viewing room, to enhance the sound of explosions, stampedes, earthquakes, and the like.

The audio component on a DVD-video disc is encoded with the AC-3 compression format developed by the Dolby Corporation. Like the ATRAC algorithm, AC-3 treats the signal dynamically. Blocks of samples are analyzed. Based on how active or steady the material is, the algorithm determines which of three methods of spectral resolution to employ in analyzing the block. Factors include masked components and tolerable levels of quantization distortion.

In addition to AC-3's proprietary psychoacoustic model and method of encoding values, additional measures are taken to treat the discrete stereo channels. The 5.1 channels may often be consolidated, given that they may share the same material at different amplitudes to achieve phantom imaging effects (see Chapter 3). Similarly, Dolby's engineers capitalized on the results of psychoacoustic experiments which found that the auditory system is weak at localizing sounds close in frequency in the high ranges above 2 kHz. Thus, the redundant portions as well as the high-frequency portions of each channel may be combined into a common channel when the audio is encoded. At the decoding stage, this common channel may be sent to the five discrete channels with amplitude information for each. With AC-3, the six audio channels may be reduced to a data amount of less than one-third the volume of stereo CD audio.

DVD-Audio

A separate DVD audio-only format is meant to allow higher-quality audio recordings. These discs contain audio sampled at 96 kHz with a 24-bit word length. This is meant to bring DVD-audio to the level of the highest-fidelity vinyl and tape audio. Listeners in comparison tests have reported that recordings made at the higher sampling rate are more satisfying due to greater clarity of higher instruments such as cymbals and triangles, sharper attacks, greater clarity of fast staccato passages, and enhanced localization that gives a stronger impression of stage depth.

Although it might seem that this higher Nyquist frequency of 48 kHz would be superfluous, given the maximum audible frequency of 20 kHz, research shows otherwise. A study by Tsutomu Oohashi observed subjects connected to EEG monitors listening to recordings at sampling rates of 96 kHz and 44.1 kHz. The study showed that there was increased alpha wave activity during the higher-bandwidth selections. Other studies have investigated enhanced localization of signals recorded at high sampling rates, resulting in a sensation of greater clarity when listening to material sampled at 96 kHz or 192 kHz. Based on these studies, it seems that capping human frequency perception at 20 kHz may be an oversimplification. Although humans may not be able to perceive sine tones above 20 kHz, this appears to be only one aspect of the perception of audio.

Super Audio CD (SACD)

As this book goes to print, a new format is emerging to rival DVD-audio as the top high-fidelity standard. The Philips and Sony corporations, which created the original PCM format for CD audio, have created a format that improves on the 44.1 kHz sampling rate and 16-bit resolution of PCM storage. The new format relies on an encoding system known as Direct Stream Digital® (DSD®), which is being touted as the next step forward in digital audio encoding. PCM recording is not employed at all; another method is used, called *delta-sigma* encoding (or *sigma-delta* encoding). The DSD delta-sigma recording utilizes a sampling rate of 64 times the CD sampling rate (2.8224 MHz) and a word size of one bit. The single bit at each sampling interval functions as a sign bit: a digit of 1 means that the audio wave ascends, and a digit of 0 means that the wave descends (Figure 10–17). Each digit is sent to an *integrator* that keeps a running total of the sample level. At each sampling period, the audio level is compared to the level stored in the integrator. If the audio level is above the integrator level, a value of 1 is output. If the audio level is below the integrator level, a value of 0 is output. With sharp increases or decreases, an ascending wave produces a stream of the value 1, and a descending wave produces a stream of the value 0. A wave that remains at a constant level is approximated with each sampling period. The integrator value is alternately above and below the audio level, producing alternating values of 1 and 0. Thus, the density of the pulses represents the shape of the wave. This type of encoding is also known as *pulse density modulation* (PDM).

As discussed in Chapter 9, PCM recording relies on ensuring that an audio wave is sampled at its peak and its trough, with an analog lowpass filter ensuring that the analog signal's bandwidth is within the Nyquist frequency. When the samples are played, another analog lowpass filter is required to smooth the staircase wave. With delta-sigma recording, the aim is to re-create the analog waveform as accurately as

Figure 10–17

Delta-Sigma Modulation
Sampling

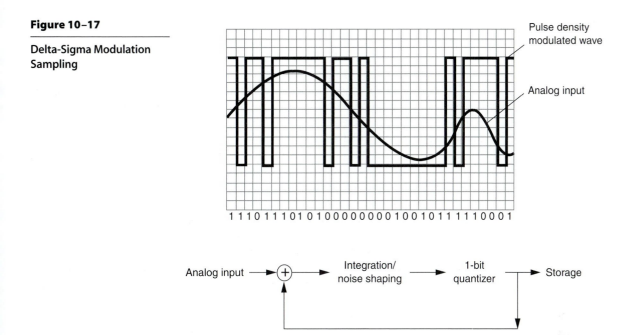

possible, and the Nyquist frequency is no longer at its basis. This reconsideration of the sampling process eliminates the need for the analog filtering stages, which bring about added levels of noise. While single-bit resolution has the potential for greater error than PCM recording, advanced noise-shaping processes are employed to push the error noise above the audible frequency ranges. The necessary processing is all done in the digital domain, eliminating noise introduced by analog processing.

SACDs promise increased dynamic range (resolution of loudness levels) and a frequency response of 100 kHz, doubling the range of the highest quality analog recording. The discs are designed to hold up to 4.74 GB of data. A hybrid disc format allows different versions of the material to be stored so that a 2-channel stereo or a 5.1-channel surround arrangement may be realized, depending on the user's configuration. SACD discs are not compatible with CD players, but SACD players can play both SACD discs and discs with the original CD format.

Hard-Disk Recording—The Convergence of Multimedia

Digital Workstations

As the price of computer memory storage drops and processor speeds rise, computer hard drives have become increasingly common as a storage medium for large video and audio files. Hard-disk recording offers the added advantage of random access: the ability to jump instantly to any point in an audio file without having to fast-forward or rewind. Random access allows extreme flexibility in editing, just as software MIDI sequencers offered advantages over hardware sequencers. Audio may be cut and pasted as easily as text is manipulated in a word processing program. Volume and stereo pan controls may be automated, typically by drawing an envelope over a graphic of the track's waveform. Crossfades may be specified between two audio segments on the same track, allowing separate sound elements to be integrated seamlessly. Filtering and other effects may be implemented as part of an audio editing software package.

Digital editing software typically works with an interface similar to a MIDI sequencer, with independent control of parallel tracks of audio. Thus, audio software works similarly to a multitrack tape deck, allowing separate audio streams to be combined. Figure 10–18 shows a set of screens from a digital audio editing session. Tracks 1 and 2 comprise a two-channel stereo pair. The pan envelope for both tracks is displayed, with the result that the waveform view is grayed out. Both channels are panned hard right and left, so the pan envelope simply consists of a solid line at the top of track 1's display and at the bottom of track 2's display. Track 3 is a mono file with the volume envelope displayed. The file fades up approximately 10 seconds into the file and fades out again after approximately 28 seconds. Tracks 4 and 5 also comprise a stereo pair. These tracks are shown in waveform view, with a segment highlighted that may then be cut, copied, or pasted elsewhere.

Given the size of audio files, files in these programs do not contain audio information per se, but rather reference (make use of) external audio files. A segment of audio that is used more than once is not copied each time it is reused; rather, the program references the same file as many times as it is used. Thus, audio data is kept separate from editing operations, a marked departure from an environment such as tape, where use of the same audio requires copying a section of tape and use of a small portion of audio requires razor-blade editing. In a software environment, editing operations do not affect the original audio files. Thus, all edits are nondestructive. A splice or a crossfade may be undone without affecting the audio data. Different versions of the same operation may be stored in memory before a final selection is made.

Just as audio may be digitized and stored on hard disk, so may video and animation. An editing program is likely to allow audio and visual elements to be combined, so that multimedia projects may be realized on one computer workstation. Thus, the ability to digitize media blurs the distinctions among different media types, allowing them to be combined in new ways. Many processes that have commonly been performed by dedicated hardware are now available in software form.

The capabilities of many audio editing programs are made expandable via *plug-ins,* specialized software modules that may be used in conjunction with a larger program to provide certain processing operations. For example, while most audio editors come with a number of effects, it is often possible to use even more effects available as separately purchased plug-ins. (Effects will be covered in detail in Chapter 12.)

Transferring Data Among Devices

Digital information may be transferred among storage devices directly, without analog conversion, through two PCM protocols, AES/EBU or S/PDIF. PCM, as discussed earlier, is a means of transmitting information through two voltage levels representing binary 1s and 0s.

AES/EBU (Audio Engineering Society and European Broadcasting Union) is a transmission format allowing two-channel data to be transferred. The physical connection is usually via a three-pin balanced connector, the same type used for professional microphones. This is meant to be the "professional" format, capable of

Figure 10-18

Digital Audio Editing Software

Printed courtesy of BIAS Inc.

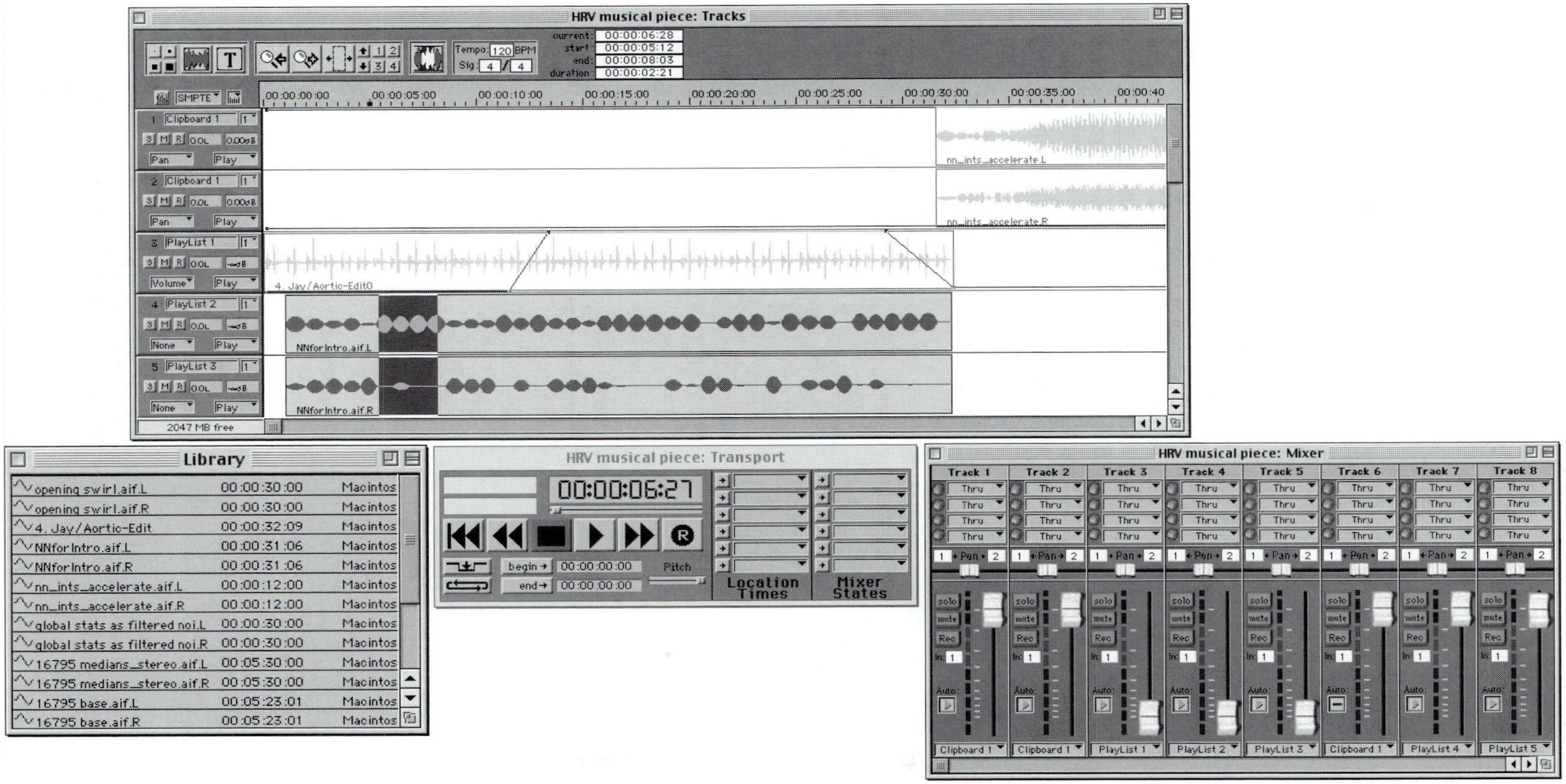

transmission over long distances (up to 100 meters, or longer if extra processing is introduced) and low in jitter.

S/PDIF (Sony/Philips Digital InterFace), like AES/EBU, transmits two channels of digital audio. S/PDIF also can transmit extra information to allow copy protection in some devices, enabling producers of material to build in prohibitions against copying. This is the type of transmission typically used on consumer-grade equipment, with a jitter potential slightly higher than that of AES/EBU. It is typically transmitted over RCA cables (such as those used in home stereo systems to connect devices to the amplifier) and is not meant to be transmitted over long distances. A S/PDIF connector may also be labeled "Digital i/o."

Transferring data among devices is a synchronized procedure. Steps must be taken to ensure that bit start and stop times in the sending device match bit start and stop times in the receiver. The source device must be placed into a mode that defines it as the clock master, and all receiving devices must be placed into a slave mode, with the clock source determined by AES/EBU or S/PDIF input, depending on the source device. Accidentally keeping a receiving device on an internal clock mode (as would be appropriate when recording an analog signal) may result in distortion due to mismatches between sender and receiver of bit start and end times.

Audio Files

To be available to hard-disk editing systems, audio files must exist as a defined file type. There is no one standard audio file type; audio files come in a variety of formats. The different types arose from the differences in storage and processing requirements for different computer platforms. However, the differences among them have become largely historical. Any incompatibilities are easily overcome, as any software sound utility is likely to be able to convert an audio file from one format to another. For example, different formats may store samples within different number ranges, in which case converting to the other format involves performing a multiplication on each sample.

In addition to requiring number conversions, there may also be bookkeeping differences among file types. Audio files are differentiated by a header portion of the file that precedes the actual sample values. Some file types require a series of different header types, known as "chunks." The header(s) give information about the file, such as the sampling rate, quantization level, number of stereo channels, and so on. Converting from one file type to another may mean altering header information as well as converting samples.

The differences among file types are negligible to the average musician and ultimately immaterial, aside from requiring the occasional extra step of converting files to whatever type is necessary. Some of the more common file types are described next.

NeXT/Sun

This is the earliest audio file format type and was intended for Unix computers, primarily for voice files and telephone transmission. These files can typically be identified by the extension ".au" or ".snd." The format supports four sampling rates: 8,000, 8,012, 22,050 and 44,100, although the lower rates are more typical. The bit depth is also variable, with samples stored as 8- or 16-bit words. When 2-byte samples are used, they are stored with the most significant byte listed first ("big endian"). The sample values are stored as floating-point numbers, which means that there is a decimal point with some number of places for the number's fractional value, such as 0.0975. Files are compressed with a variable quantization algorithm that assigns more bits to lower levels than to higher levels. The mu-law compression algorithm was adopted in North America and Japan. An alternative format, a-law compression, the standard adopted by the International Telecommunications Union, is used in Europe.

AIFF

AIFF (Audio Interchange File Format) is a format native to Macintosh and SGI platforms and is meant to store high-quality audio. These files typically have the extension ".aiff" or ".aif." AIFF stores stereo channels in interleaved format, which means that samples are transmitted serially, with alternating samples belonging to different channels. For example, in a two-channel file, the samples will follow a succession of

[(sample n, left), (sample n, right), (sample $n + 1$, left),

(sample $n + 1$, right), . . .]

Each set of successive of samples to be played simultaneously on different channels is termed a *sample frame.* The file header contains information about the number of channels, sample rate, sample size, and the number of samples contained in the file. Samples in AIFF format are stored as integer values. Two-byte samples are stored with the most significant byte listed first ("big endian"). The header also specifies the size of the file, meaning that its length is fixed. This aspect of the header may make AIFF files too inflexible to be used in some editing environments.

AIFF can store loop point markers, allowing them to be used in sampling instruments (samplers will be discussed further in Chapter 13). The ability to store loop points along with audio data is meant to make the AIFF format sampler-ready. AIFF files may also contain MIDI data, which could contain SysEx data. This represents an attempt to foresee new developments in instrument design. For example, the AIFF format may contain information about two loop points in a sample. Typically, the loop points represent the steady-state portion of an audio wave. The samples between the loop points are repeated until a Note Off message is received. Should an instrument be created that features more than two loop points, presumably this information will be accessible via SysEx, and information about these loops could be stored in the MIDI segment of an AIFF file.

A more general form of this file type is AIFC (Audio Interchange File Format Extension for Compression), which allows sample data to be either uncompressed or compressed. AIFF files are uncompressed by definition. A variety of compression types are recognized by the AIFC standard and are identified in the appropriate chunk of bookkeeping information about the file.

SDII

SDII (Sound Designer II) files are also native to Macintosh computers. They typically are named with the extension ".sdii." SDII originated from the digital editing program Sound Designer, one of the first audio editors created for the personal computer. Stereo channels are stored as separate files that are meant to be played simultaneously. Information about the file is also kept separate from the audio samples, not in a chunk that must precede them. SDII files are thus less fixed in form than AIFF files and are more suited to editing environments such as multitrack editing programs. Many audio editing programs convert AIFF files to SDII files when they are imported. On completing editing work, users may choose to export the audio to a consolidated AIFF file.

WAVE

The RIFF WAVE (Resource Interchange File Format Waveform) was created by Microsoft and is native to Intel platforms (Windows machines). Files are often named with the extension ".wav" and have a structure similar to an AIFF file, with added bookkeeping to aid in buffering samples in advance of playback and minor differences in data storage, such as storing 2-byte sample values with the least significant byte listed first ("little endian"). As in the AIFF format, samples are stored as integers, and like AIFC files, the RIFF WAVE specification also allows for a variety of compression types, including mu-law and a-law.

MP3

This is a compression format for audio and video material and is a popular format for Internet audio. The ".mp3" extension refers to layer 3 of the MPEG-1 standard created by the Motion Picture Experts Group (a group formed from the International Standards Organization and the International Electrotechnical Commission). The three layers are variations on the compression method. They differ in terms of complexity and efficiency. Layer 3 gives the best results for audio material, with compression to $\frac{1}{10}$ the original data volume. The psychoacoustic model employed in MP3 compression is based on the same principle as other forms of compression: determining masked components and tolerable levels of quantization error and allocating word sizes accordingly. A variable window length allows dynamic compromises to be made between time and frequency resolution. Redundant stereo information is encoded only once and on playback is sent to both channels with amplitude instructions. An extension of the standard allows encoding of 5.1 audio channels. It is likely, however, that multichannel Internet audio will utilize the MP4 format, which is emerging as this book goes to press. In addition to support for multichannel audio (up to 48 tracks), MP4 promises more efficient compression and decoding plus higher resolution audio that exceeds the quality of MP3 audio.

Streamed Files

Streaming was discussed in Chapter 4. The topic is inserted here as a placeholder for those downloading audio files from the Internet. Often, sites do not allow files to be downloaded, but only streamed. Selecting the file on the Web page may cause a file icon to appear on a user's computer that might be confused with an audio file. In fact, it is not an audio file at all, but simply a reference to a file on the Internet that may be downloaded into a streaming player.

CHAPTER 11

Acquiring Audio

Chapters 11 and 12 cover the steps of acquiring and processing audio in a music production or recording environment. The big picture is as follows:

- A room is selected to function as a performance space.
- Audio signals are acquired by means of a microphone.
- When more than one microphone signal make up the final product, the separate signals may be combined in a mixer.
- In the process of mixing, some signals may be enhanced by filtering, reverberation, or other special effects.

Room Acoustics

Direct and Reflected Sound

Chapters 1 through 3 discussed physical principles of acoustics as they relate to music. Here, the subject of acoustics will be explored further in an architectural sense—how performance/recording spaces treat acoustic energy. The performance space is inseparable from the musical material performed within it, as both combine to create the listener's impression. If music is analogous to a painting, the acoustic characteristics of the performance space are analogous to the canvas, lighting, and frame.

In Chapter 9, it was stated that everything is a filter. This includes rooms. All rooms have a characteristic sound that is based on how they treat the relationship between *direct* sound and *reflected* sound. Direct sound refers to acoustic energy originating from the instrument itself. Reflected sound refers to acoustic energy interacting with the boundaries of the performance space and objects within it. Direct sound attenuates with distance according to the inverse square law, as shown in Chapter 3 (Equation 3–2). As the distance doubles, the sound's intensity drops by one quarter, or 6 dB:

$$I \propto \frac{1}{D^2} \Rightarrow I \propto \frac{1}{2^2} = \frac{1}{4} = -6 \text{ dB in intensity}$$

Since pressure is proportional to the square root of intensity (as shown in Chapter 2, Equations 2–8 to 2–12), the pressure is halved as the distance doubles, dropping 6 dB in pressure level:

$$A^2 \propto I \Rightarrow A \propto \sqrt{I}$$

$$I = \frac{1}{4}$$

$$A = \frac{1}{\sqrt{4}} = \frac{1}{2} = -6 \text{ dB in pressure}$$

Given the quick drop in the intensity of direct sound with distance, virtually all sound reaching listeners is a combination of direct and reflected sound. At greater distances, there is a much higher proportion of reflected sound. A room's treatment of reflected sound depends on its size, shape, wall and ceiling treatment, and the presence or absence of objects within the room. Acoustic reflections within a performance space filter all sound that propagates within it. The nature of "room filtering" differs somewhat between large and small performance spaces, so the two will be discussed separately.

Large Performance Spaces

The discussion of large performance spaces will begin with an overview of three stages of sound propagation. Many of the issues described in the overview will be refined further in a subsequent discussion of types of sound reflection. Finally, the issue of sound absorption by construction materials will be taken up.

Stages of Sound Propagation

Sound propagation in large spaces is often described in three stages: *direct sound, early reflections,* and *diffuse reverberations.*

Direct Sound   Direct sound travels directly from the source to the listener. As mentioned, the direct sound attenuates rapidly as the distance from the source increases. However, the direct sound is usually the first wavefront to reach the listener. No matter how faint the direct sound may be compared to subsequent reflections, the auditory system determines location by the direction of the first wavefront, a phenomenon known as the *precedence effect* (also called the *Haas effect*). Thus, the direct sound provides the primary impression of the sound's location.

Early Reflections   Early reflections are first-order reflections that reach the listener after reflecting once from the floor, ceiling, or walls. Early reflections arriving within 35 ms of the first wavefront have been found to reinforce the direct sound, adding to its clarity and intelligibility. In a study of 54 concert halls (Beranek, 1962), it was found that those commonly described as sounding "intimate" had as a significant characteristic first-order reflections of less than 20 ms. First-order reflections are most likely to come from the walls, although seats located near the center of a hall may receive first reflections from the ceiling. In especially large halls, suspended reflectors are often installed with the intention of providing early reflections to center seats.

Longer first-reflection times result from longer distances from source to listener. Therefore, besides providing a sense of reinforcement and added clarity, first-order reflections are also a cue by which the auditory system makes a judgement of a room's size.

Reverberation   Reverberation refers to second- (and higher) order reflections. As first-order reflections continue to reflect off of a room's surfaces, a wash of reflected sound results that eventually dies down as the sound's energy is absorbed by the walls, ceiling, and objects in the room. The *reverberation time* is the time required for the sound pressure level to drop 60 dB ($\frac{1}{2^{10}}$, or approximately $\frac{1}{1000}$ of its initial pressure level). The reverberation time is generally proportional to the ratio of a room's volume to the combined area of its surfaces and any objects:

$$\text{reverberation time} = 0.16 \frac{\text{volume (m}^3)}{\text{area (m}^2)} \qquad 11\text{--}1$$

Thus, a larger room is likely to have a longer reverberation time than a smaller room. Reverberation time, however, is frequency dependent. Higher frequencies are usually absorbed more quickly by air than lower frequencies, so longer reverberation times tend to contain a greater proportion of lower frequencies. Different materials in the room also tend to absorb different frequencies (the subject of an upcoming section). Equation 11–1 is sometimes useful as a rough estimate, usually describing the reverberation time of a sound at 500–1000 Hz. A more precise description of a room is a graph plotting reverberation time as a function of frequency.

Since rooms filter sound, it is not surprising that acousticians describe the sound of a room by its *impulse response,* just as electrical engineers describe filters in terms of their impulse response. Before digital analysis was possible by impulse signals (as described in Chapter 9), impulses were created with a short sound burst (hand clap, flick of a lighter, click from a toy). The room could then be characterized by the intensity and timing of its reflections.

Types of Reflection: Specular and Diffuse

Wave reflection was discussed in Chapter 1. Figure 1–5 illustrated the principle that angle of incidence equals the angle of reflection. This holds true for reflections off a surface that is smooth and regular. Reflections of this type are called *specular reflections.*

However, reflective surfaces are often irregular, with the result that the simple relationship exhibited by specular reflections does not apply. When waves come into contact with an irregular surface, reflections are scattered in all directions, and the nature of the reflections is dependent on the angle of the incident wave. *Lambert's cosine law,* illustrated in Figure 11–1, states that the intensity of the reflections is proportional to the cosine of the angle of incidence with a line perpendicular to the surface (the perpendicular line is termed a *normal*). This principle is important in the study of 3D modeling and shading. If a flashlight is aimed at a painted wall, for example, it is reflected with greater intensity if it is pointed directly at the wall (perpendicular to it) than if its light strikes the wall at an angle. Diffuse reflections are no less important in the study of room acoustics.

Diffuse reflections have two important differences from specular reflections. First, the intensity of specular reflections is dependent on the observer's position as well as the angle of incidence. Diffuse reflections are independent of the observer's position. Second, diffuse reflections radiate from a larger area of the reflective surface, rather than from a single point (Figure 11–2).

Figure 11–1

Lambert's Cosine Law

Intensity of reflection ∝ intensity of incidence × cosine (angle of incidence to surface normal).

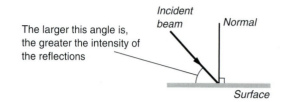

The larger this angle is, the greater the intensity of the reflections

Incident beam   *Normal*

Surface

Examples: Size of the angle represented by the height *h*

Since diffuse acoustic reflections are scattered, a listener at any given position receives many reflections of a single sound event. These duplications have a number of consequences. There is an overall smoothing of amplitude transients. There is also a frequency response—recall that filtering involves the combination of an input signal with a delay, which implies that these multiple reflections necessarily filter the acoustic energy. These consequences result in a faster buildup toward the reverberation stage of sound propagation and a more uniform reverberant field than that of simple specular reflections. Diffuse reflections also increase the likelihood of low *interaural cross-correlation* (IACC), meaning that the acoustic energy reaching each ear is likely to differ. This is a desirable characteristic, as it improves localization of sound sources and contributes to an impression commonly described as "spacious."

Thus, the nature of diffuse reflections is a significant factor in characterizing the most highly rated concert halls. Prior to 1900, theatres were commonly designed with Greek/Roman-styled aesthetic enhancements. Fluted pillars, mouldings, sculptures, and the like often served to create diffuse reflections and thus positively affect the space's acoustics. Since the turn of the twentieth century, the "Inter-

Figure 11–2

Diffuse Reflections

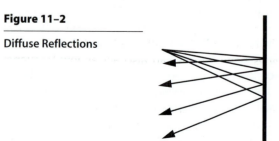

national Style" of architecture, coupled with economic considerations that encourage fast construction and increased seating capacities, have led to sparser spaces characterized by large, flat surfaces. These spaces do not promote diffuse reflections to the degree that earlier designs did. Consequently, the creation of idealized diffuse reflections is a topic of serious consideration in contemporary acoustics.

Absorption

As stated, reverberation characterizes the sound of a room, and reverberation is frequency dependent. Therefore, the character of a room may be described in terms of which frequencies are allowed to reverberate and which frequencies are more easily absorbed.

The degree to which any given frequency is reflected depends on the materials and objects within the performance space. One factor is size. Small obstacles reflect high frequencies, while larger obstacles are needed to reflect low frequencies. Another factor is material. Different materials tend to absorb different frequencies. A certain material's tendency to absorb a given frequency is described by the material's *absorption coefficient:*

$$\text{absorption coefficient} = \frac{\text{absorbed sound}}{\text{incident sound}} \qquad 11\text{–}2$$

A low absorption coefficient indicates that the majority of sound energy striking a surface is reflected away from it. In contrast, an open window does not reflect any incident sound, so it is considered to be 100% absorptive. In Equation 11–2, an open window yields an absorption coefficient of 1.0. Figure 11–3 plots absorption coefficients as a function of frequency for a variety of materials.

Highly Reflective Surfaces   Heavy, stiff materials—such as unpainted concrete and shower tiles—have low absorption coefficients and tend to reflect all frequencies equally.

High-Frequency Absorbers (500–1000 Hz)   Soft porous materials—such as curtains, clothing, or carpet—are high-frequency absorbers. The thicker and more porous the materials are, the lower the frequencies they are likely to absorb. Since clothing tends to absorb high frequencies, stone churches and cathedrals tend to be much more reverberant in high frequencies when they are empty. Modern concert halls address this problem with seats designed to match the absorptive characteristics of clothing so that they are as absorptive when empty as they are when they are full.

Low-Frequency Absorbers (300–500 Hz)   Materials that can vibrate—such as windows, plaster walls on widely spaced beams, or wooden floors on widely spaced beams—can be brought into vibration by low frequencies. Thus, they act as resonators for frequencies near their resonant frequency. The energy required to bring these surfaces into a state of vibration results in an attenuation of these frequencies within the room. Air cavities behind walls can also act as low-frequency resonators.

Midfrequency Absorbers (300–1000 Hz)   A combination of high- and low-frequency absorptive material can be employed to absorb midrange frequencies. An example is a wall made of a porous material with regularly spaced wood panels placed over it.

Figure 11–3

Absorption

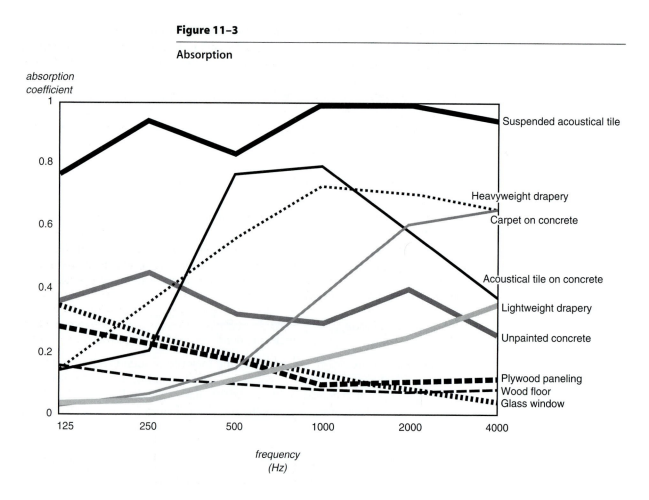

absorption coefficient

frequency (Hz)

Absorption and Sound Propagation   Typically, it is desirable to use a combination of low-, mid-, and high-frequency absorbers. A room with only high-frequency absorbers is likely to sound dull, and a room with only low-frequency absorbers is likely to sound thin.

Performers should be placed with due consideration to the acoustic properties of their immediate surroundings. A reflective surface near a performer can be advantageous, as the early reflections can enhance the sound. Placing an ensemble on a carpet or under a wooden ceiling is likely to be counterproductive, as much of the sound will be absorbed. On the other hand, a reflective wall or ceiling can be an enhancement, provided that efforts are made to ensure that the reflections are sufficiently diffused in order that the resulting enhancements are uniformly spread and suited to the space's overall acoustic environment.

Small Performance Spaces

Room Modes   The behavior of waves in a tube was discussed in Chapter 1. Small performance spaces have the potential to act as closed tubes in that pressure can maximize at the walls as air molecules are abruptly stopped in their motion and crowd together. Thus, the walls of the room may act as pressure nodes, and standing waves may be produced if steady-state tones are played that have wavelengths at twice the dimensions of the room or at harmonics of this frequency. The result is that certain frequencies are amplified due to the room's dimensions. This phenomenon is termed *modal enhancement,* and the frequencies that may produce standing waves are termed *room modes.* There are three types of room modes: *axial modes, tangential modes,* and *oblique modes,* as shown in Figure 11–4.

Room modes can dramatically affect the frequency response of a small room, particularly at low frequencies. If the room is a perfect cube, the same resonances

Figure 11–4

Room Modes

(a) *Axial: AB, AD, AE.* Axial room modes are possible with wavelengths at $m_1 = AB \times 2$; $m_2 = AD \times 2$; $m_3 = AE \times 2$, plus all harmonics of these three frequencies. (b) *Tangential: AF, AC, AH.* Fundamental frequencies of tangential room modes may be calculated using the Pythagorean theorem: $m_1 = \sqrt{AD^2 + DC^2}$; $m_2 = \sqrt{AB^2 + BF^2}$; $m_3 = \sqrt{AD^2 + DH^2}$. Harmonics of these frequencies also resonate. (c) *Oblique: AG.* The fundamental frequencies of the primary oblique room modes may be calculated using the Pythagorean theorem applied to three dimensions: $m_1 = \sqrt{AB^2 + AD^2 + AE^2}$. Harmonics of this frequency also resonate.

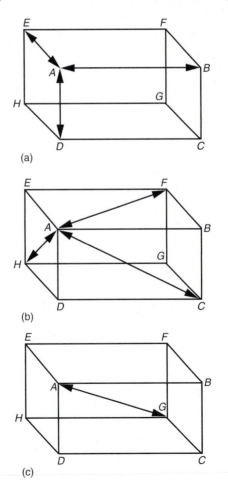

(a)

(b)

(c)

may be amplified on all three axial modes, creating a cumulative amplification. The same problem can be encountered when a room is based on simple relationships. If one dimension is exactly two times another dimension, for example, the fundamental of the shorter dimension corresponds to the second harmonic of the longer dimension, again creating a cumulative amplification. Ideally, small rooms are designed without simple relations, thus avoiding this problem.

The placement of an instrument in a small room can determine its low-end frequency response. Placed in a corner, a cello has the potential to create pronounced low-end resonances; moving the player into the room can reduce the effect. The same is true for microphone placement. Placing a microphone within a pressure node can exaggerate a standing wave, while moving the microphone a short distance, out of the node, can eliminate the problem.

Due to room modes, sound levels are not consistent throughout a room for resonant frequencies. By moving short distances, one can walk through nodes and antinodes and notice the changes in sound level. For high frequencies, it may be enough simply to tilt one's head. The effect is often more pronounced when the audio is being picked up by a microphone for recording or broadcast.

Room modes are not a factor in the acoustics of large rooms because the air temperature tends to vary over the room's volume. For example, the ceiling tends to be warmer than the floor. The result is that sound waves do not propagate at consistent speeds throughout the space of the auditorium (recall from Chapter 1 that the speed of sound depends on temperature). Thus, pressure waves cannot oscillate consistently enough to cause room resonances in large spaces.

Flutter Echo

While sustained tones can cause standing waves in small rooms, impulsive sounds can cause *flutter echoes,* which are the result of a pressure wave bouncing back and forth between two surfaces. These have the character of a "reverberation tail." Flutter echoes are often noticeable when you first move into a house or apartment and the rooms have no furniture or carpeting. Rooms with parallel walls are particularly prone to flutter echo effects.

Comb Filtering

Along with flutter echo, the combination of acoustic energy with a specular reflection leads to a type of sound coloration known as *comb filtering.* This refers to an uneven frequency response due to regular frequency cancellations that can result when a signal is combined with a delayed version of itself. Two examples of undesirable comb filtering are shown in Figure 11–5. Comb filtering will be discussed in detail in the section on effects in Chapter 12.

Acoustic Treatment of Small Spaces

Although it may be ideal to construct performance rooms without parallel walls, this is often impractical, particularly when a preexisting space is made to function as a studio or practice room. However, a number of steps may be taken to reduce standing wave and flutter echo effects. Treating the room with absorptive material can reduce resonances. On the other hand, it can also create a "dead" sound if reflections are eliminated altogether. Rather than attempting to absorb certain frequencies, another approach is to ensure that reflections are diffused. Acoustic companies produce a variety of diffusion products that are meant to enhance or reduce certain frequency ranges. A less-expensive approach to creating diffuse reflections might simply be to place a bookshelf against a wall or to place some chairs in the middle of the room.

Figure 11–5

Accidental Comb Filtering

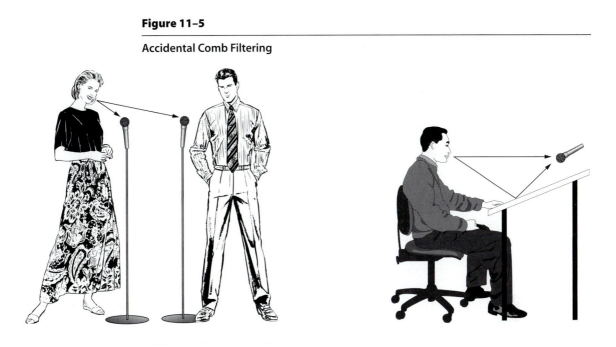

Microphones

The initial step of storing or transmitting audio material necessitates use of a microphone. A microphone may be considered an analog of the ear. A diaphragm inside acts as a *receptor,* responding in the same fashion as the eardrum: it vibrates in response to changes in air pressure, and the vibrations are converted (*transduced*) to electricity. Microphones may be discussed according to:

- Receptor type
- Transducer type
- Directionality

Receptor Types

The diaphragm of a microphone is usually an extremely thin sheet of mylar that is coated with gold, aluminum, or nickel. The receptor configuration of a microphone describes the mechanics of the diaphragm and how it responds to diaphragm displacement (changes in the position of the diaphragm) as air comes into contact with the diaphragm through openings in the microphone capsule. Receptors fall into two categories: *pressure* and *pressure gradient* (sometimes simply referred to as *gradient*).

Pressure

Pressure microphones contain a diaphragm that responds to sound pressure changes on only one side of the diaphragm (Figure 11–6). There is nothing in the diaphragm's response that indicates the direction of the sound source.

Figure 11–6

Pressure Receptor

A pressure receptor is sensitive to pressure waves arriving from the front only.

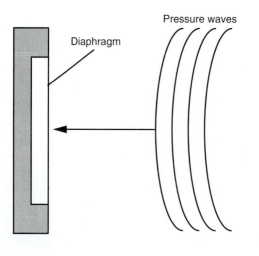

Pressure Gradient (Velocity)

The diaphragm of a pressure gradient microphone responds to pressure changes arriving from the front and rear (Figure 11–7). Sound pressure waves arriving from the front diffract around the microphone and, after some delay, strike the diaphragm again from the rear. Similarly, pressure waves arriving from the rear also reach the front of the diaphragm after the same delay time. The signal produced is determined by the difference (gradient) of pressures arriving from either side of the diaphragm. For long wavelengths, air particle velocity is proportional to the pressure gradient in the vicinity of the diaphragm, so an older term for this receptor type is *velocity*.

Figure 11–7

Pressure Gradient Receptor

A pressure gradient is sensitive to pressure waves arriving from the front and the rear.

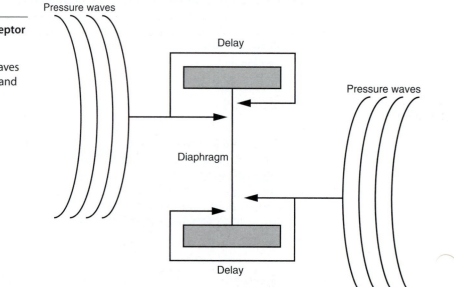

Transducer Types

The transducer type of a microphone determines how the motion of the diaphragm is converted into electrical oscillations. Like receptors, microphone transducers also fall into two categories: *dynamic* and *condenser.*

Dynamic (Electrodynamic, Electromagnetic, Ribbon, Moving Coil)

A dynamic microphone transducer works according to the principle of *magnetic induction,* which states that when a wire (conductor) is made to move within a magnetic field, an electrical current is produced within the conductor. The voltage level of the current depends on the strength of the magnetic field, the velocity of the conductor's motion, and the length of the conductor. In a dynamic microphone, the strength of the magnetic field and the length of the conductor are constant, so the voltage levels in the resultant current are due entirely to velocity changes. Coils attached to the diaphragm extend into an area within a magnetic field. As the diaphragm moves back and forth in response to air pressure changes, the corresponding motion of the coils produces an electrical current with voltage levels that are proportional to pressure changes, as shown in Figure 11–8. A classic dynamic pressure gradient microphone is a design commonly known as the *ribbon microphone.* In a ribbon microphone, the diaphragm consists of a thin metal ribbon, typically made of corrugated aluminum, suspended vertically within a magnetic field (Figure 11–9).

Dynamic microphones have the advantage of being simple in design. They are inexpensive and sturdy, well suited for live performances of popular music or for home recording studios.

Condenser (Capacitor)

The second transducer type works by means of an electrical capacitor. Simply put, an electrical capacitor consists of two metal plates in close proximity to each other that are opposite in charge. As a result, there is an attraction between the negatively charged plate (possessing an excess of electrons) and the positively charged plate (possessing a shortage of electrons). When the two plates are brought closer together, the level of attraction increases. As a result, the negatively charged plate

Figure 11–8

Dynamic Transducer

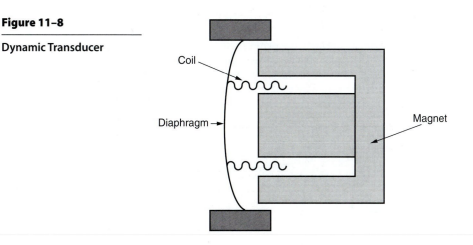

Figure 11–9

**Ribbon Microphone
(Side View)**

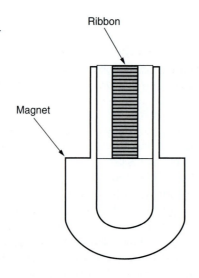

Ribbon

Magnet

gains an increased capacity for electrons, and a current of electrons flows into the negative plate. When the plates are moved farther apart, the attraction decreases. Consequently, there is less capacity for the negatively charged plate to store electrons, and the extra electrons flow away from the plate. In a condenser microphone, one plate of the capacitor is the microphone diaphragm; the other plate of the capacitor is called the *backplate*. As the proximity between the plates changes due to changes in air pressure, a current is produced (Figure 11–10).

Condenser microphones are characterized by sharper transients than dynamic microphones, making them well suited for percussive instruments such as drums and pianos. Their design is more complicated than that of dynamic microphones, making condenser microphones more expensive. The charge of the plates may need to be maintained by an external power source, known as *phantom power*. Phantom power is often supplied by a mixer and will be discussed in the section on mixing in Chapter 12.

Figure 11–10

Capacitor Transducer

(a) At closer proximity between the plates, there is greater attraction, and greater capacitance (ability to store electrons) in the negative plate, thus producing a current into the negative plate. (b) When the plates are moved apart, there is less attraction, and less capacitance (ability to store electrons) in the negative plate, thus producing a current away from the negative plate.

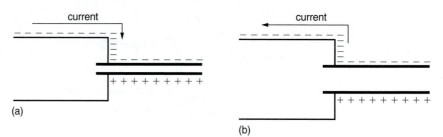

current

current

(a)

(b)

Directionality

The *directionality* of a microphone describes the magnitude of a microphone's response to pressure changes arriving at different angles. It is often expressed as a polar equation with magnitude as a function of a given angle, where 0° represents the position directly in front of the microphone.

Omnidirectional

This classification indicates that the microphone responds with equal magnitude to pressure changes from all angles. The description may be written as a polar equation:

$$\rho = 1 \qquad\qquad\qquad 11\text{--}3$$

which indicates that the microphone is 100% responsive, regardless of the sound source's angle in relation to the microphone. A polar directional plot is shown in Figure 11–11.

By definition, pressure microphones are omnidirectional, since only one side of the diaphragm responds to air pressure changes (as shown in Figure 11–6). But it is more accurate to describe pressure microphones as omnidirectional *within certain limits*. Lower frequencies diffract around the body of the microphone and are able to reach the diaphragm without attenuation. Higher frequencies, with their smaller wavelengths, tend to reflect away from the microphone, causing a rolloff of higher frequencies (typically starting at 8 kHz) not originating from a frontward direction. Thus, smaller pressure microphones allow better omnidirectionality of high frequencies.

Bidirectional

This pattern describes a figure-eight magnitude response, in which the response is maximum for pressure changes from both front and back and zero for changes from the side. The polar equation for a bidirectional pattern is

$$\rho = \cos\theta \qquad\qquad\qquad 11\text{--}4$$

Figure 11–11

Omnidirectional Polar Plot

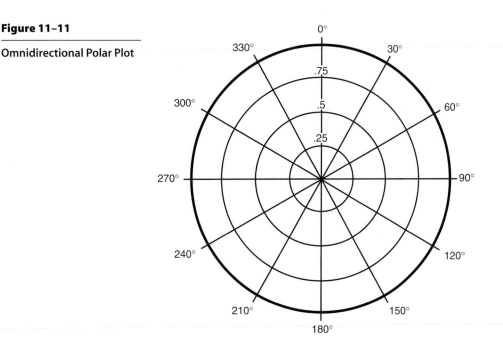

where θ represents the polar angle of the sound's position relative to the front of the microphone. A bidirectional polar plot is shown in Figure 11–12. Pressure gradient microphones are, by definition, bidirectional because both sides of the diaphragm respond to air pressure changes (as shown in Figure 11–7). Although the magnitude of the response is equal from the front and rear lobes of the diaphragm, the polarity of the response is opposite with each lobe. (Polarity was discussed in Chapter 1.) The front lobe is assigned positive polarity and negative polarity to the rear lobe.

Most early ribbon microphones were bidirectional. The hanging ribbon responded to sound pressure changes arriving from the front or rear directions, whereas sounds from the left or right produced equal pressure on both sides of the ribbon and caused little or no displacement. Bidirectional ribbon microphones date back to the early days of broadcasting. They were ideal for interview situations when the questioner and subject sat facing each other, to the front and rear of the ribbon. (The microphone in the logo for the Larry King show is a ribbon microphone.) Ribbon microphones have been largely replaced by more recent microphone designs that feature changeable directional patterns.

First-Order Directional Microphones

The most common directional microphones in professional use may be classified as *first-order cardioid*. "Cardioid" refers to a heart-shaped directional pattern; "first order" refers to the polar response equation of these microphones, which contains a cosine term to the first power. The directional patterns are obtained by combining pressure and pressure gradient elements in varying proportions. The variety of directional patterns in this class are derived from combinations of their respective omni- and bidirectional patterns. The positive and negative polarities of the bidirectional component cancel and reinforce the positive omnidirectional component, producing variations on the cardioid shape of the directional plot.

Figure 11–12

Bidirectional Polar Plot

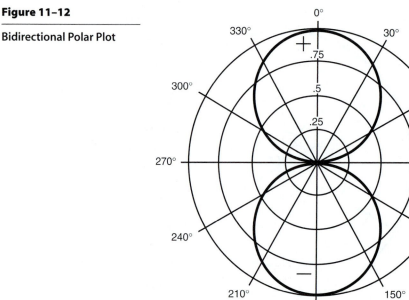

First-order directional microphones have a generalized polar equation of

$$\rho = A + B \cos \theta \qquad\qquad 11\text{--}5$$

where $A + B = 1$. The A term describes the omnidirectional component, and the B term describes the bidirectional component. The most common first-order combinations are shown in Figure 11–13.

Figure 11–13

Derivation of First-Order Cardioid Patterns

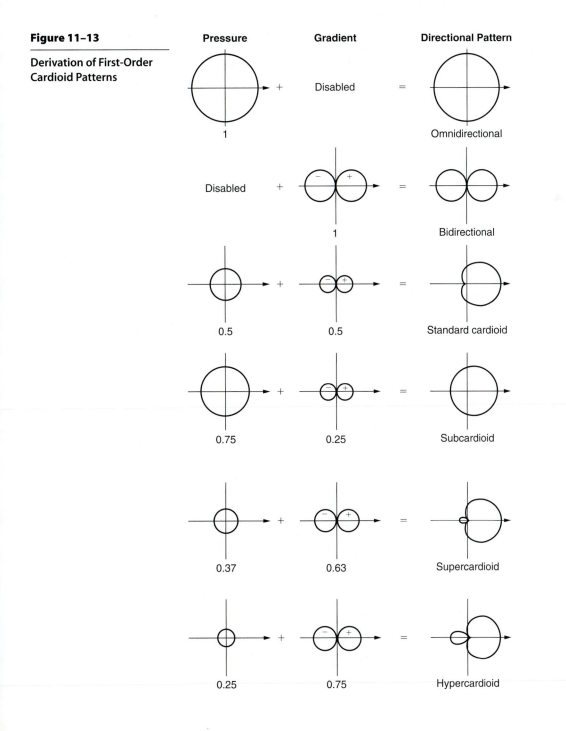

Pressure		Gradient		Directional Pattern
1	+	Disabled	=	Omnidirectional
Disabled	+	1	=	Bidirectional
0.5	+	0.5	=	Standard cardioid
0.75	+	0.25	=	Subcardioid
0.37	+	0.63	=	Supercardioid
0.25	+	0.75	=	Hypercardioid

Standard Cardioid This is the most common directional pattern. It is the result of an equivalent combination of omni- and bidirectional components, as described by Equation 11–6:

$$\rho = 0.5 + 0.5 \cos \theta \qquad\qquad 11\text{–}6$$

The emphasis in magnitude on sounds originating from the front is due to the combination of the omnidirectional component with the positive lobe of the bidirectional component. A directional plot is shown in Figure 11–14.

Subcardioid Also referred to as the *forward-oriented omni*, this type has become popular in classical music recording. It is most often represented by the polar equation

$$\rho = 0.75 + 0.25 \cos \theta \qquad\qquad 11\text{–}7$$

A directional plot is shown in Figure 11–15.

Supercardioid This pattern has a somewhat tighter front response than the standard and subcardioid patterns and is represented by the equation

$$\rho = 0.37 + 0.63 \cos \theta \qquad\qquad 11\text{–}8$$

and is illustrated in Figure 11–16.

Hypercardioid This type has the tightest forward-magnitude response. It is represented by the equation

$$\rho = 0.25 + 0.75 \cos \theta \qquad\qquad 11\text{–}9$$

and is illustrated in Figure 11–17.

Figure 11–14

**Standard Cardioid
Directional Polar Plot**

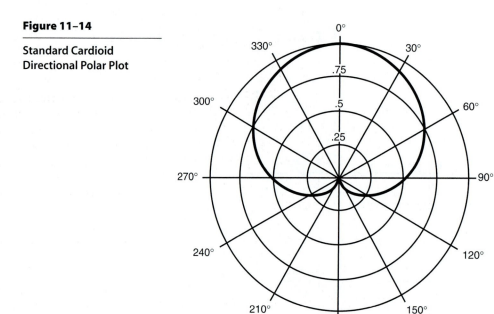

Figure 11–15

Subcardioid Directional
Polar Plot

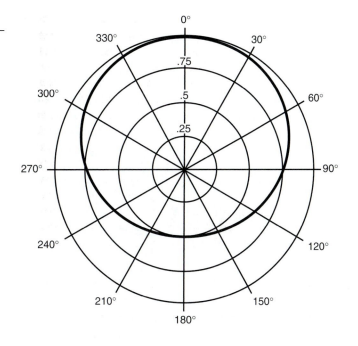

Directionality and Frequency Response Because the directionality of microphones
varies with the frequency of the audio material, as discussed in the section on omnidirectional microphones, specifications for cardioid microphones typically include
a polar plot with superimposed patterns that illustrate the response of the microphone to different frequencies (Figure 11–18).

Figure 11–16

Supercardioid Directional
Polar Plot

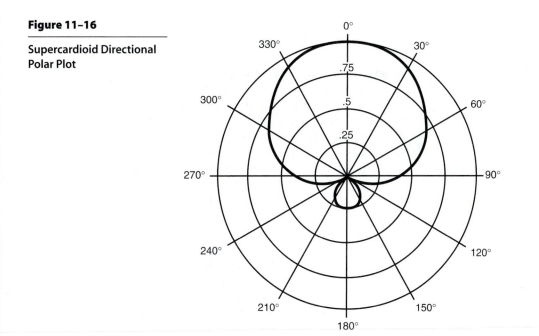

Figure 11–17

Hypercardioid Directional
Polar Plot

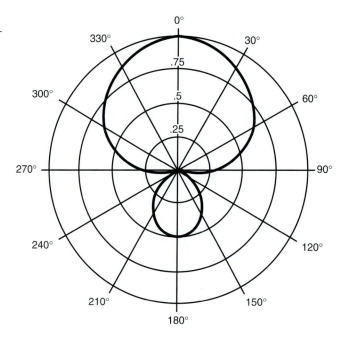

Figure 11–18

Cardioid Polar Plot with Frequency Response

Frequency response plots of the Microtech MV 692/M 70 model microphone.

Printed with permission of G Prime Limited.

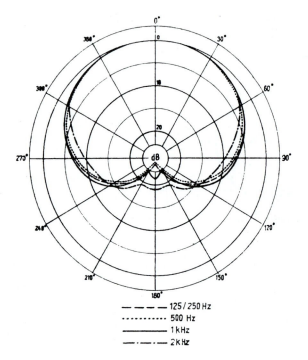

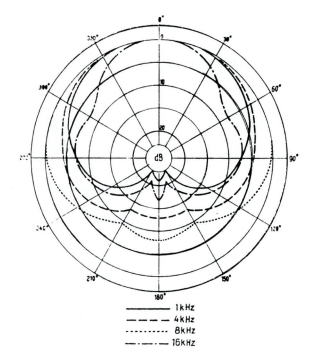

Direct vs. Diffuse Sound Responses   Inherent in the various microphone directional patterns is the way each pattern type treats direct and diffuse sound. The balance of direct and diffuse sound is a major factor in the selection of microphones by professional recording engineers.

Random energy efficiency (REE), sometimes termed *random efficiency* (RE), is a comparison of a microphone's response to sounds arriving from the front to sounds with equivalent power arriving from other directions, which are presumably diffuse reflections. For example, a 0.25 REE of a hypercardioid microphone indicates that its signal consists of one-quarter off-axis reverberations, and three-quarters on-axis direct sound. The REE of the various directional patterns is summarized in Figure 11–19.

Figure 11–19

**Random Energy Efficiency
of First-Order Directional
Microphones**

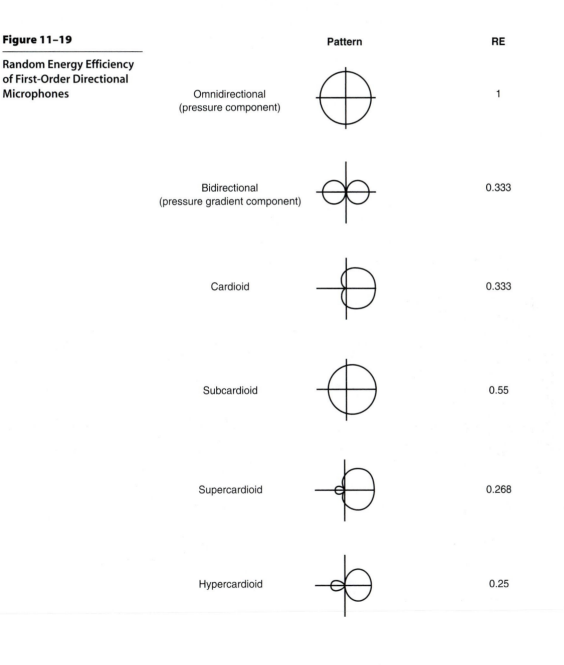

	Pattern	RE
Omnidirectional (pressure component)		1
Bidirectional (pressure gradient component)		0.333
Cardioid		0.333
Subcardioid		0.55
Supercardioid		0.268
Hypercardioid		0.25

A related measurement is the *distance factor* (or *reach*) of a microphone. This is a comparison of the relative distance a microphone may be placed from a sound source, compared to an omnidirectional microphone, to produce the same direct-to-reverberant response. For example, a hypercardioid, with its reach value of 2, may be placed twice as far from a sound source as an omnidirectional microphone to obtain a signal with the same direct-to-reverberant ratio. The distance factor of the various directional patterns is summarized in Figure 11–20.

Design of Cardioid Microphones   Figure 11–21 illustrates the construction of a dynamic cardioid microphone, a common microphone used for vocal performances. It is similar to the pressure gradient design shown in Figure 11–7, with openings in the side of the capsule that cause the back side of the diaphragm to respond to pressure changes arriving from the rear as well as changes arriving from the front after a delay time. This delay time, determined by the distance of the openings from the front opening, determines the cardioid pattern response of the microphone.

Figure 11–20

Distance Factor of First-Order Directional Microphones

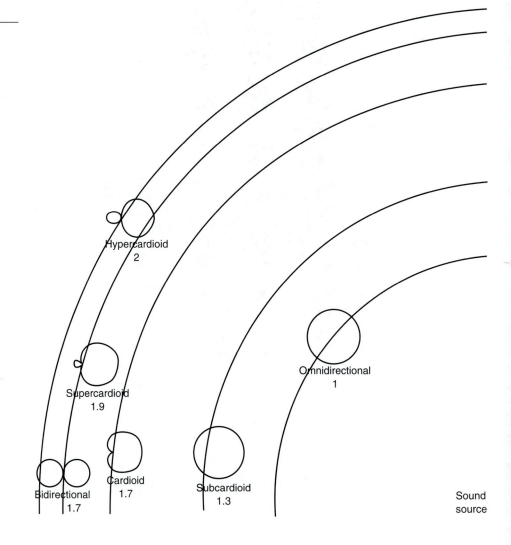

Figure 11–21

Construction of a Dynamic Cardioid Microphone

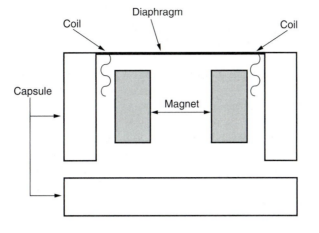

Condenser cardioid microphones also operate via openings in the side of the capsule but with an internal delay applied to the signal from the back (negative polarity lobe) of the diaphragm. For pressure changes arriving from the front, the internal delay is added to the acoustic delay. For pressure changes arriving from the sides, there is no acoustic delay, so a moderate gradient results from the internal delay. For pressure changes arriving from the rear, the acoustic delay resulting from the longer path to the front of the diaphragm is matched by the internal delay, so there is little or no gradient. The specific directional response pattern of the microphone is dependent on the time of this internal delay.

Variable pattern microphones allow users to change the directional response pattern. *Single-diaphragm* variable pattern microphones allow the acoustic delay time to be changed by either lengthening the capsule or by placing an adapter over the microphone. Far more common, however, is the *Braunmühl–Weber dual-diaphragm* variable pattern design. This is a condenser design in which two diaphragms are placed on opposite sides of a single backplate. By various combinations of the cardioid patterns from each diaphragm, virtually all first-order patterns can be produced (Figure 11–22).

Microphone Configurations

Recording music rarely involves just one microphone. It is far more common for engineers to use a number of microphones in tandem. Optimal microphone configurations vary according to context. The size of the room, type of ensemble, and style of music are all factors that determine the precise type and positions of microphones. Recording is a refined art, just as is an instrumentalist's ability to interpret a written score. The configurations discussed here are meant to provide starting points for common recording contexts. They can all be refined further through experience and experimentation.

The simplest multimicrophone configuration is that of a separate, directional microphone for each instrument in an ensemble. The signals are then combined at a mixing board, where adjustments of relative volumes, stereo positioning, and appropriate filtering and effects are applied. Thus, an artificial stage picture is created in postproduction. This method is commonly used in recordings of popular music.

Figure 11–22

Directional Plots Resulting from the Combination of Two Cardioids

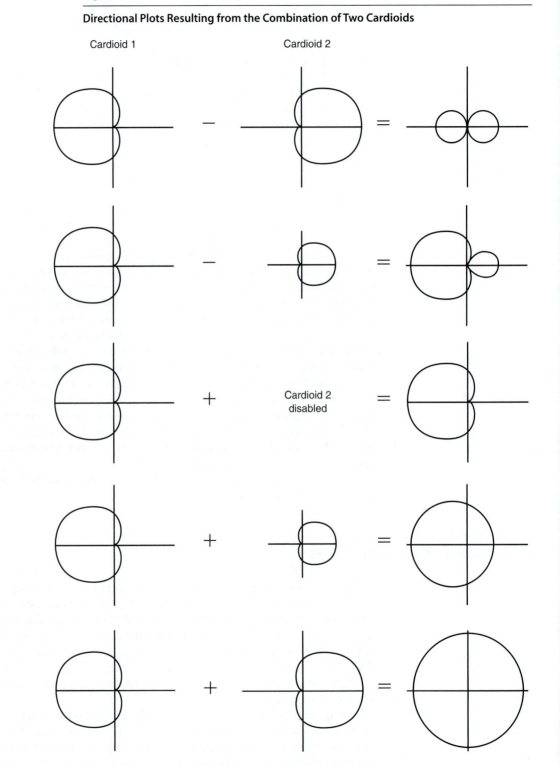

This section will examine configurations that are meant to capture the authentic sound of a performing ensemble, creating a lifelike sense of volume balance, stage position, and sound characteristics of the performance space. These types of multimicrophone configurations determine the stereophonic imaging and the balance between direct and diffuse sound present in the recording.

As discussed earlier, virtually all sound reaching audience members is a combination of direct and diffuse sound. Normally, it is desirable to place microphones near the *reverberation radius,* the point at which the intensities of direct and reverberant sound are equal. An estimate of the reverberation radius can be obtained as follows:

$$\text{reverberation radius} = 0.056 \sqrt{\frac{\text{volume (m}^3)}{\text{reverb time}}} \qquad \text{11–10}$$

The precise distance, however, varies with microphone type, with microphones of higher directionality possessing a greater reverberation radius than those of lower directionality.

Direct sound without diffuse sound is only present in the immediate vicinity of the instrument. It can be a surprising experience to move through the area in close proximity to a musician who is playing, since instruments do not produce the same timbral quality in all directions and heights. Listening carefully to the tone quality at the front, rear, and sides, as well as comparing the sound near the floor with that at normal standing height, can reveal a wide variation in tone quality. A close microphone, then, can bring about very different results depending on its height and position relative to the player. The references at the end of this book provide recommendations on microphone placement for specific instrument types.

As is the case with any recording, diffuse sound may be added at the production stage (reverberation will be discussed in the section on effects in Chapter 12). When the aim of a recording is to reproduce the sound of a performance space, direct sound normally predominates, with a sufficient proportion of reverberant sound to add an element of "liveness."

The two broad approaches to stereophonic recording are based on *time of arrival* and *intensity.*

Time-of-Arrival Stereophony

This method involves spaced microphones, typically in an arc in front of a large ensemble. The difference in arrival times of each instrument's wavefronts reaching the separate microphones produces phantom imaging between the stereo channels. Time-of-arrival recordings provide a good sense of space and are suitable for ensembles in large rooms. The stereo imaging tends to be less precise than with intensity recording, and in some cases instruments may appear to change position when they play different pitches. The shift in position is due to varying degrees of phase cancellation for the wavefronts of different frequencies at the separate microphones.

Although it is seldom a problem with contemporary audio playback equipment, in the early days of stereophonic recording it was often necessary to produce monophonic versions for playback over radio or phonographs that were not stereo. Combining the signals from both channels of an intensity recording had the potential for phase cancellation problems.

Time-of-arrival recording is typically done with omnidirectional microphones placed at a distance of 20 cm to 150 cm (8″ to 60″) apart. For highly reverberant rooms or rooms with pronounced audience noise, cardioid microphones may be preferred.

Intensity Stereophony

Also known as *coincident microphone* recording, this method involves two closely spaced directional microphones placed at the same location and oriented in different directions from each other. The stereo imaging is due to differences in pressure reaching the two microphones. Thus, localization is due to differences in amplitude rather than time. Coincident microphones tend to produce more precise spatial imaging than spaced microphones, the trade-off being a decreased sense of room spaciousness. Coincident microphone techniques may be divided into two main categories, XY and MS.

XY Microphone Configuration

With an XY configuration, two directional microphones with identical directional sensitivities are placed at the same spot, one directly on top of the other, at an angle. A common configuration consists of two bidirectional microphones placed at 90°, as shown in Figure 11–23. This is also called a *Blumlein configuration,* after its creator, Alan Blumlein. It has the advantage of providing precise stereo imaging from sound sources in front of the microphones plus reverberation that reaches the microphones from the rear. Cardioid microphones also may be used in XY configurations. Depending on the microphones used, the separation angle may range from 90°

Figure 11–23

XY Configuration

(a) Two coincident bidirectional microphones, oriented at 90° to each other; (b) combined directional characteristics.

90°

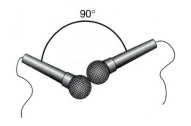

(a)

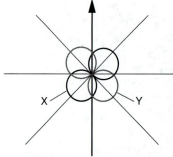

(b)

to 130°. The signals from the two XY microphones provide left and right stereo signals. The angle of the microphones, plus the panning separation of the two signals adjusted on the mixer, provide the overall width of the apparent stage picture.

MS Microphone Configuration

An MS configuration (the M standing for mono, main, or middle; the S standing for side or stereo) consists of two coincident microphones, typically with differing directional characteristics. The M component is usually a cardioid microphone pointed toward the sound source. The S component is usually a bidirectional microphone that is oriented perpendicular to the M microphone (Figure 11–24). Unlike the signals from XY configurations, the signals from MS configurations do not create two corresponding stereo channels. Rather, the channels are created from combinations of the two microphones, which may be achieved in two ways. One way requires an additional hardware component known as a *matrixer* that combines incoming signals. In the case of MS stereophony, the matrixer creates sum and difference combinations from the two microphones, which in turn form the left and right stereo signals that are sent to the mixer. Level controls on the matrixer for each microphone allow the stereo image to be controlled. Varying the level of the S component allows the

Figure 11–24

MS Configuration

(a) A cardioid plus a bidirectional; (b) combined directional characteristics.

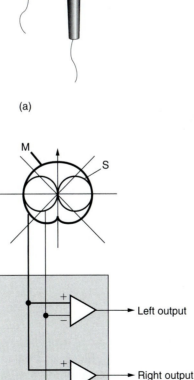

(a)

(b)

apparent width of the soundfield to be altered. If a monophonic recording is required, the S component may be eliminated entirely.

If a matrixer is unavailable, a similar effect may be achieved if the microphones are plugged into a *patchbay* that is able to split an input into two outputs. Some mixers also allow the input of one channel to be sent elsewhere; in this case, the bidirectional microphone may be directed to one input channel, which in turn sends the signal to another input channel. The polarity should be opposite in the two channels. Many mixers allow a signal to be polarity inverted; if a mixer does not have this capability, a special cable known as a *polarity-flip cable* can do the job.

Ultimately, the goal is for the M signal to be directed to one channel and panned center and the S signal to be directed to two other channels that are panned left and right and at opposite phase. The two channels with the bidirectional signal may have their volume adjusted in relation to the M channel for stereo imaging. If a monophonic version is required, the bidirectional components may cancel each other out if both channels are panned center, leaving only the M signal.

MS configurations allow more flexibility than XY configurations. With XY configurations, the angle of the microphones is critical in determining the stereo imaging. With MS, the imaging may be controlled through level differences rather than through physical microphone placement. MS also has the advantage of the main microphone facing the center of the soundfield, thus giving a firm foundation (sometimes described as "greater brilliance") to the recording.

Near-Coincident Configurations

Near-coincident (or quasi-coincident) configurations attempt to incorporate elements of spaced and coincident microphone placements. Pairs of directional microphones are placed close together with a separation distance up to 30 cm. These configurations feature the precise imaging of coincident configurations while maintaining some of the sense of spaciousness present with time-of-arrival configurations.

ORTF

This technique, created by the French broadcasting group Office de Radio Télévision Française, involves two cardioid microphones separated by 17 cm (6.7″), the approximate width of the human head. The microphones are each angled 55° away from center. While the directionality is meant to simulate the sensation that would reach a listener's ears, the open space between the microphones allows each microphone to pick up the full range of frequencies without the spectral shadowing that the head produces (see Chapter 3 for a discussion of spatial cues).

Spherical Stereo Microphones

Another technique involves placing two omnidirectional microphones in a sphere that is roughly the size of a human head, with the microphones placed on opposite sides to correspond to the position of the ears. Spherical microphones create interaural delay and spectral shadowing similar to that perceived by the auditory system. Spherical microphones have the advantage of being easy to set up and provide good stereo imaging and ambient sound.

Support Microphones

Under some circumstances, it may be desirable to add additional microphones close to selected instruments in order to accent the presence of a soloist, an interesting secondary musical line, or a soft instrument that may be lost in the overall signal picked up by the main microphones. The additional audio signal allows the instrument's contribution to be controlled at the mixing board by controlling its volume and pan position. Another factor that highlights a support microphone signal is the shorter distance between the instrument and the support microphone in comparison to the distance between the ensemble and the main microphones. The support signal is received earlier than the main signal, causing the instrument to stand out from the rest of the ensemble. Although this added prominence may be helpful in some circumstances, too much reliance on support microphones can throw off the balance of the overall sound. The support signals do not share the direct-to-diffuse balance of the main microphones and run the risk of destroying the sensation of spaciousness and "flattening" the sound. These undesirable effects can be lessened somewhat by sending the support signal through a delay of a few milliseconds, so that its sound is more in synch with that of the rest of the ensemble.

5.1 Channel Configurations

The 5.1 channel format, described in Chapter 10, is still in its infancy, and microphone configurations for it are still in experimental stages. Early work in the new format, however, gives good indication that surround recordings offer enhanced "presence" or "immediacy" to music recordings, giving listeners a stronger sensation of being present in the concert environment. In general, the methodology is to consider front (right, center, left) and surround (left-surround, right-surround) sound sources separately. The front microphones are used as main microphones, with the added center channel providing increased localizability. The surround microphones are used for reverberant sound. This section will describe three microphone configurations, shown in Figure 11–25, that may become the basis of future standards.

INA 5

The most straightforward configuration is the *Ideale Nierenanordnung* ("ideal cardioid"), created by Ulf Herrmann and Volker Henkels of Dusseldorf. Five cardioid microphones are oriented in five directions to supply the five channels.

The Fukada Tree

Developed by Akira Fukada of Nippon Hoso Kyokai (NHK), the Japanese Broadcasting Corporation, this configuration builds on the INA 5 configuration by employing seven microphones. Five cardioid microphones pick up the five channels. In addition, two omnidirectional microphones are placed outside of the five directional microphones, and their signals are equally shared between the left/left surround and right/right surround channels. The added right-of-right and left-of-left omnidirectional signals are meant to supply an expanded spatial impression.

OCT Surround

This configuration is an expansion of the OCT (optimized cardioid triangle), a recently proposed two-channel stereo configuration that is still subject to some refinement. A front-facing cardioid microphone is combined with two hypercardioids that face 90° to the left and right. Given the variety of established techniques for recording two-channel stereo, it is perhaps most likely that this configuration will be

Figure 11–25

5.1 Channel Microphone Configurations

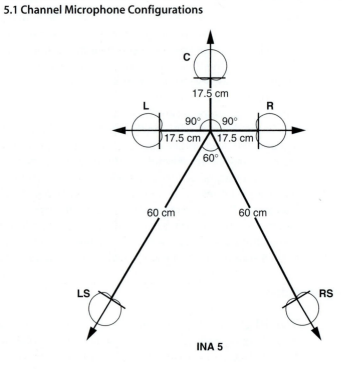

INA 5

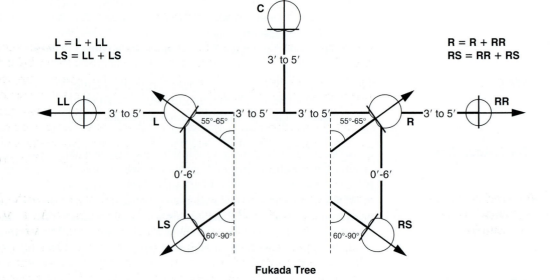

Fukada Tree

Figure 11–25, cont'd

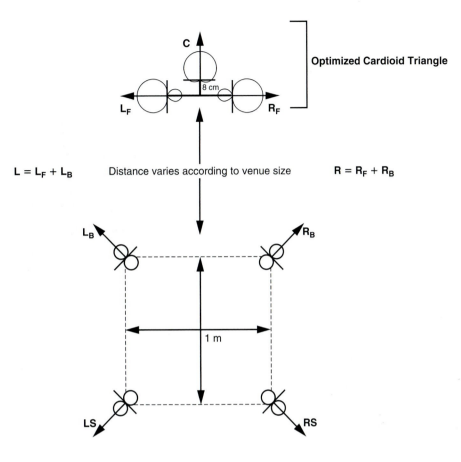

Optimized Cardioid Triangle

$L = L_F + L_B$ Distance varies according to venue size $R = R_F + R_B$

OCT Surround

used in its expanded form for 5.1 channel recording. The basic triangle is supplemented by a square of four microphones placed some distance behind the front triangle. The exact distance is subject to the size of the performance space. The rear square is meant to pick up diffuse sounds that complement the directional sounds picked up by the triangle. The square may consist of bidirectional, omnidirectional, or cardioid microphones. The rear microphones of the square are sent to the surround channels, while the left and right channels are combinations of the front microphones of the square and the left and right microphones of the forward triangle.

Expansions of the Spherical Stereo Microphone

Some stereo spherical microphones (described in the previous section) offer the option of an expanded configuration that includes two bidirectional microphones in addition to the two omnidirectional microphones within the sphere. The bidirectional microphones are attached beneath the sphere and face forward. Five channels may then be derived from these four microphones. A center channel may be created by summing the signals from the two omnidirectional microphones. The four corners may be created by treating the omni–bidirectional pair on each side as an MS configuration, with the front corners resulting from the sum of the pair and the rear corners resulting from the differences. This treatment is meant to give the impression of front and back sound sources.

CHAPTER 12

Treating and Mixing Audio

Effects: Introduction

All music that is recorded or amplified relies on effects to enhance its sound. Music delivered to a concert hall through a PA system needs to be filtered to compensate for the room's frequency response. Many recordings made in studios are done in small, dry-sounding rooms. In postproduction, the recording is given character through the use of reverberation, equalization, and other types of effects. In short, effects are essential just to make electronic audio signals resemble natural sound. A further step is the use of special effects to remold the sound. Pop music guitarists typically perform with an array of foot-activated effect units in front of them. Recording studios have stacks of rack-mounted effects processors. This section will cover some of fundamental types of effects and sound enhancement.

Effects = Filtering

Most effects are the result of filter combinations. There are two basic ways to combine filters (Figure 12–1):

1. *Parallel:* An input signal is split and each copy of the signal is sent through one or more filters; then the signals are recombined. The frequency responses of the filters are *added* at the output. (Note that a crude bandpass filter could be constructed by using a highpass filter and a lowpass filter in parallel.)
2. *Series (or Cascade):* An input signal is sent through a succession of filters. The frequency responses of the filters are *multiplied* at the output.

Filtering = Delay

As noted in Chapter 9, digital filtering involves combining a signal with a delayed version of itself. The result of this delay depends largely on how much time is involved. Time delays may be broken into three categories:

1. Delay > 50 ms: audible echoes
2. Delay < 10 ms: coloration, filtering
3. 10 ms < delay < 50 ms: enhancement, increase in volume

Figure 12–1

Filter Combinations

(a) *Parallel:* The filters' frequency responses are added. (b) *Series:* The filters' frequency responses are multiplied.

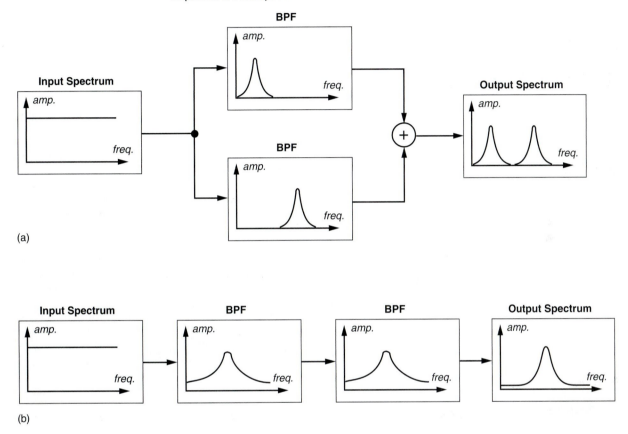

(a)

(b)

Effects Processors and Word Length

Many digital audio processors boast high-bit processing (e.g., "32-bit internal processing"). Since CD audio is 16 bits (or 24 bits for DVD audio), this may lead to some confusion. The key word to bear in mind is *internal*.

Recall that filtering is achieved by arithmetic operations on audio samples. These operations frequently add bits, as in the following equations involving binary numbers:

$$100 \times 100 = 10000$$
$$100 + 111 = 1011$$

If the result of a calculation requires more than the available number of bits, the only way to proceed is to *truncate* (chop off) the least significant bits before moving on to the next calculation. Thus, each calculation potentially introduces more error. High-bit internal processing allows more bits for each calculation involved in processing the final output sample. The truncation is saved until the very last step, when the final output is reduced to 16-bit audio. But there is no accumulated error—only one potential error at the last processing step.

Figure 12–2

Simple Delay

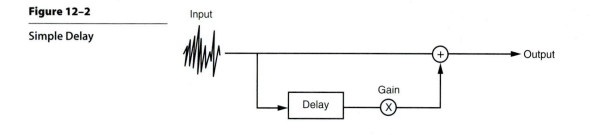

Long Delays: Audible Echoes

The first group of effects involves the first of the three categories just listed: longer delays resulting in echo effects.

Simple Delay

In this most basic delay-based effect type, the signal is combined with a delayed version of itself, resulting in an echo (Figure 12–2). Users can typically set the delay time and the volume (gain) of the delayed signal.

Multitap Delay

This is a series of simple delays. The name is an analogy to plumbing. Picture water flowing through a pipe. If water is drawn from different points along the pipe by inserting taps along its length, it might be described as a multitap plumbing system. Translating the analogy to audio, the output is combined with a succession of delays. Users may set the time (tap location along the pipe) and gain (tap width) of each tap (Figure 12–3).

Feedback Delay

As with a feedback filter, a feedback delay combines the delayed output with the input signal. This gives a decaying series of echoes, such as might be heard when shouting into a canyon. Users may typically set the delay time and the echo decay time (Figure 12–4).

Figure 12–3

Multitap Delay

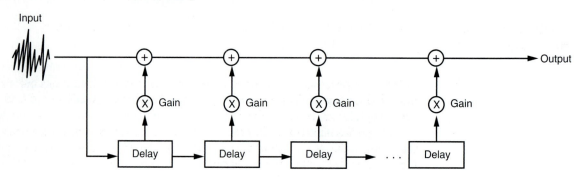

Figure 12–4

Feedback Delay

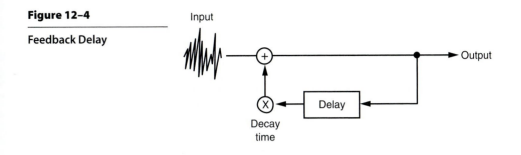

Input

Output

Decay
time

Building Blocks of Delay-Based Effects: Comb and Allpass Filters

Comb Filters

Undesirable comb filtering was mentioned in Chapter 11, in the discussion of sound propagation in small rooms. While accidental comb filtering can lead to undesirable results, intentional comb filtering is the basis of a variety of effects treatments. A comb filter is a generalization of the filters discussed in Chapter 9. In a basic comb filter, the current sample is combined with a delayed sample, as in the following filter difference equation:

$$y[n] = x[n] + a \times x[n - D] \qquad\qquad 12\text{--}1$$

where D is some number of samples. This is similar to the simple lowpass filter discussed in Chapter 9 (Equation 9–4), except that the delay is longer than one sample.

The delay time imposed by the filter is D/SR seconds (the number of delayed samples over the sampling rate). The result of this delay has a pronounced effect on harmonics of the frequency having a period of twice the delay time. As shown in Figure 12–5, the even harmonics of this frequency are reinforced, and the odd harmonics of this frequency are canceled. Frequencies between harmonics are attenuated. The result is a frequency response consisting of a series of regularly spaced spectral peaks and nulls, resembling a comb.

Comb filters may be feedforward or feedback, and may be either *positive sum* (when the delayed sample is added to the current sample) or *negative sum* (when the delayed sample is subtracted from the current sample).

Feedforward Comb Filter (Inverted Comb Filter)

The positive-sum comb filter (Figure 12–6) has the difference equation

$$y[n] = x[n] + x[n - D] \qquad\qquad 12\text{--}2$$

This filter type produces peaks at nSR/D Hz and nulls at $(2n - 1)SR/2D$ Hz. In other words, spectral peaks are produced at harmonics of SR/D Hz, with nulls occurring halfway between the peaks.

A positive-sum comb filter may be considered to resonate in a manner that emulates a tube that is open at both ends. Consider the frequency having a wavelength that is twice the tube's length. As shown in Figure 1–12, a tube's resonances are

Figure 12–5

Reinforcement and Cancellation from Comb Filtering

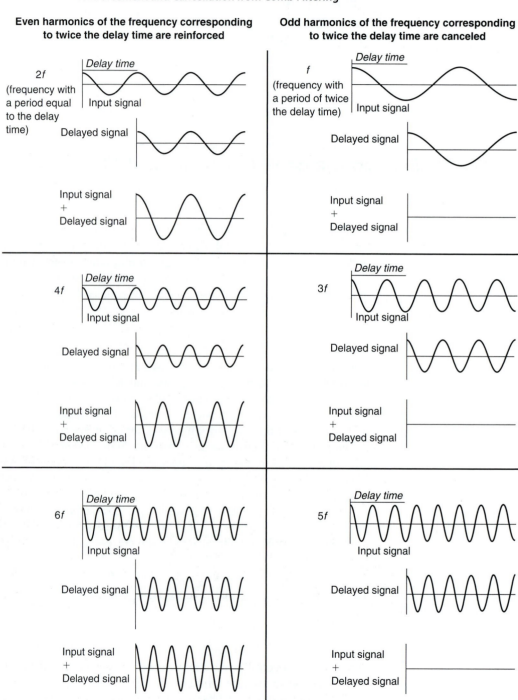

Even harmonics of the frequency corresponding to twice the delay time are reinforced

2f (frequency with a period equal to the delay time)

Delay time
Input signal

Delayed signal

Input signal + Delayed signal

4f
Delay time
Input signal

Delayed signal

Input signal + Delayed signal

6f
Delay time
Input signal

Delayed signal

Input signal + Delayed signal

Odd harmonics of the frequency corresponding to twice the delay time are canceled

f (frequency with a period of twice the delay time)

Delay time
Input signal

Delayed signal

Input signal + Delayed signal

3f
Delay time
Input signal

Delayed signal

Input signal + Delayed signal

5f
Delay time
Input signal

Delayed signal

Input signal + Delayed signal

Figure 12–6

Feedforward Comb Filter Frequency Response

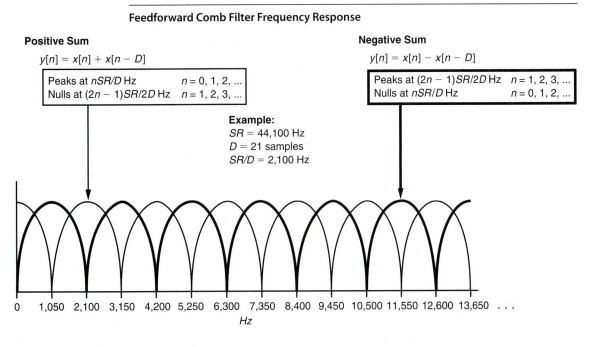

Positive Sum

$y[n] = x[n] + x[n - D]$

| Peaks at nSR/D Hz | $n = 0, 1, 2, ...$ |
| Nulls at $(2n - 1)SR/2D$ Hz | $n = 1, 2, 3, ...$ |

Negative Sum

$y[n] = x[n] - x[n - D]$

| Peaks at $(2n - 1)SR/2D$ Hz | $n = 1, 2, 3, ...$ |
| Nulls at nSR/D Hz | $n = 0, 1, 2, ...$ |

Example:
$SR = 44,100$ Hz
$D = 21$ samples
$SR/D = 2,100$ Hz

0   1,050 2,100 3,150 4,200 5,250 6,300 7,350 8,400 9,450 10,500 11,550 12,600 13,650 . . .

Hz

harmonics of this frequency. Recalling the equation relating frequency and wavelength (2–1), the following comparison may be made to show the relationship between Figures 1–12 and 12–5:

$$\frac{nSR}{D} = f = \frac{nc}{\lambda}$$

where the left ratio describes resonant harmonics of a feedforward comb filter based on the delay time, and the right ratio describes resonant harmonics of a tube based on the tube's length. Thus, the delay time of a comb filter is analogous to the length of a tube.

The longer the delay, the greater the number of peaks and nulls. Recalling the spectral symmetry described in Chapter 10, it can be seen that the simple lowpass filter with a delay of one sample, described in Equation 9–4, produces the same result: the peaks are at 0 Hz and the sampling rate, and the first null is at the Nyquist frequency. The comb filter, with its longer delay, simply "squeezes" this frequency response, producing more peaks and nulls within the same frequency range.

The negative-sum comb filter (Figure 12–6) has a change of sign in the difference equation:

$$y[n] = x[n] - x[n - D] \tag{12–3}$$

With a negative-sum filter, the position of the peaks and nulls is reversed from the frequency response of the feedforward comb filter. The nulls appear at harmonics of SR/D, and the peaks are halfway between the nulls. The simple highpass filter with a one-sample delay described in Chapter 9 (Equation 9–5) also represents this form. The nulls are at 0 Hz and the sampling rate, and the peak is at the Nyquist frequency.

A negative-sum comb filter is analogous to a tube that is closed at one end (Figure 1–13). Consider the frequency with a period of twice the delay time, as in Figure 12–5. The *odd* harmonics of this frequency are reinforced, while its *even* harmonics are canceled. Since these odd harmonics are canceled in a positive-sum comb filter, this implies that the fundamental resonance of the negative-sum comb filter is an octave lower than the fundamental of the positive-sum comb filter, and only odd harmonics are produced. The delay time is analogous to twice the length of a half-open tube.

Feedback Comb Filter

Feedback comb filters (Figure 12–7) combine the present sample with a delayed output sample. The difference equation's positive- and negative-sum versions are

$$y[n] = a \times x[n] + b \times y[n - D] \qquad 0 < a, b < 1 \qquad \text{12–4}$$
(positive sum)

and

$$y[n] = a \times x[n] - b \times y[n - D] \qquad 0 < a, b < 1 \qquad \text{12–5}$$
(negative sum)

Feedback comb filters produce peaks and nulls at the same positions as those produced by feedforward comb filters. The difference is that the shape of the spectrum is inverted, eliminating most frequencies between peaks. The result is a pronounced ringing at SR/D Hz (or an octave lower in the case of the negative-sum filter). The amplitude of the ringing depends on the coefficient b. A feedback comb

Figure 12–7

Feedback Comb Filter Frequency Response

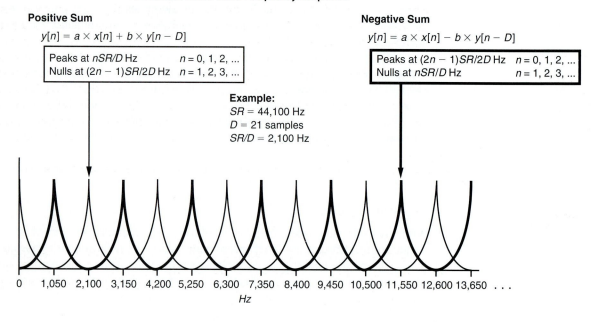

Positive Sum

$$y[n] = a \times x[n] + b \times y[n - D]$$

| Peaks at nSR/D Hz | $n = 0, 1, 2, \ldots$ |
| Nulls at $(2n - 1)SR/2D$ Hz | $n = 1, 2, 3, \ldots$ |

Negative Sum

$$y[n] = a \times x[n] - b \times y[n - D]$$

| Peaks at $(2n - 1)SR/2D$ Hz | $n = 0, 1, 2, \ldots$ |
| Nulls at nSR/D Hz | $n = 1, 2, 3, \ldots$ |

Example:
$SR = 44{,}100$ Hz
$D = 21$ samples
$SR/D = 2{,}100$ Hz

0   1,050   2,100   3,150   4,200   5,250   6,300   7,350   8,400   9,450   10,500   11,550   12,600   13,650   . . .

Hz

filter may be made to ring at a given frequency by setting the delay time to the inverse of the ringing frequency, as shown here:

Given:

f —ringing frequency (cycles per second, or Hz)

D —number of samples delayed (samples per cycle of delay)

SR —sampling rate (samples per second)

t —delay time (seconds)

1. $f = \dfrac{SR}{D} \dfrac{\text{cycles}}{\text{sec}}$

which may be rewritten as:

2. $D = \dfrac{SR}{f} \dfrac{\text{sample}}{\text{cycle}}$

Since

3. $t = \dfrac{D}{SR} \text{ sec}$

(2) and (3) may be combined:

$$t = \frac{D}{SR} = \frac{SR/f}{SR} = \frac{SR}{f} \times \frac{1}{SR} = \frac{1}{f} \text{ sec}$$

Allpass Filters

The difference equation for the allpass filter combines elements of feedforward and feedback comb filters:

$$y[n] = -a \times x[n] + x[n - D] + a \times y[n - D] \qquad \text{12–6}$$

The filter's output during its steady state passes the amplitude of all frequencies equally but alters their phases. This description might lead to the misunderstanding that an allpass filter has no audible effect. However, the nonuniform phase response of an allpass filter means that its transient response alters the phases of the sound's attack spectrum. Since the attack is the definitive portion of an audio signal, an allpass filter audibly colors its input signal. Like the comb filter, an allpass filter produces a ringing at the frequency 1/delay time Hz, where the delay time is D/SR seconds. In contrast to the longer delays discussed earlier, allpass filters produce a delay that is *frequency dependent*.

Delay-Based Effects

Flanging

A flanging unit consists of a feedback comb filter having a short, oscillating delay time—typically in the range of 1 to 10 ms. The delay time oscillations result in a dynamic comb filter with oscillating teeth, continuously expanding and compressing. Flanging is characterized by a pronounced "whooshing" sound.

Chorusing

A chorus unit is similar to a flanger in that it also combines input with an oscillating delay, but there are two differences. In a chorusing unit, the comb filter is typically feedforward rather than feedback, and the delay time is longer, typically on the order of 20–30 ms. Due to the longer delay time, the result is not the coloration of comb filtering, but rather something like a simulation of human singers, who can never sound at exactly the same time and thus have a "group" sound. Chorus units often use a multitap delay, with control over the time and gain of each delay.

Phase Shifting

A phase shifter is another delay effect with modulating delay times, producing "holes" in the spectrum. But unlike flanging, which is based on comb filtering, phase shifters use a series (cascade) of allpass filters. The frequency-dependent oscillating delay results in a gentler sound than flanging that might be described as an "underwater" sound, in contrast with flanging's "whoosh."

Reverberation

A reverberator (or "reverb unit") simulates the natural propagation of sound in an enclosed space. As reverberation is an inherent component of natural sounds, it is considered an essential effect in recorded and amplified audio. In the days of analog recordings, there were three classic methods of simulating reverberation, and there was not a great deal of control over the reverb parameters. Each had its own distinctive, artificial color. However, they became part of the standardized aural vocabulary for recorded music so that today, many digital reverberators now have settings that simulate these vintage simulations.

Reverb Chamber

Audio was played into a highly reflective room and picked up with at least one microphone; the signal from this room was mixed with the original signal (Figure 12–8).

Spring Reverb

Electrical fluctuations were transduced into mechanical fluctuations. These fluctuations were reflected back and forth along a spring. The mechanical fluctuations from the spring were then transduced into electrical fluctuations and mixed with the original signal (Figure 12–9).

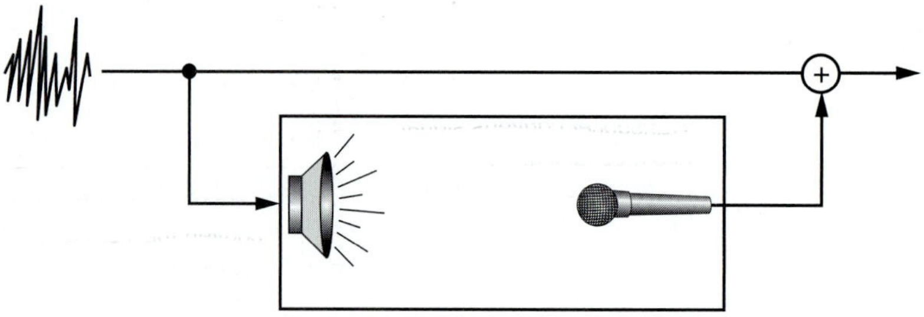

Figure 12–8

Reverb Chamber

Audio is played into a highly reflective room; a signal from this room is mixed with the original signal.

Figure 12–9

Spring Reverb

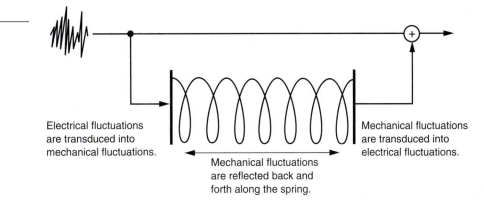

Electrical fluctuations are transduced into mechanical fluctuations.

Mechanical fluctuations are reflected back and forth along the spring.

Mechanical fluctuations are transduced into electrical fluctuations.

Plate Reverb

A transducer converted the audio signal into mechanical vibrations that were spread over a metal plate. Transducers on the plate converted the vibrations into a signal that was mixed with the original (Figure 12–10).

Digital Reverberation

The first computerized reverberation models were introduced in the early 1960s by Manfred Schroeder of Bell Labs. Two basic algorithms formed the basis of digital reverberation, shown in Figure 12–11. In one, a series of five allpass filters creates a ringing similar to that produced by diffuse reflections within a room. The other consists of four parallel comb filters followed by a series of two allpass filters.

Parallel comb filters and allpass filters in series are still considered fundamental building blocks of reverberation algorithms. However, since audio companies invest considerable resources in reverberation and other effects products, the precise algorithms they use tend to be highly confidential industry secrets. Currently, many companies are investigating expansions beyond the classic models, since these simple delays tend to produce primarily specular reflection effects. More satisfying results are being sought that emulate diffuse reflection patterns of actual spaces.

Figure 12–10

Plate Reverb

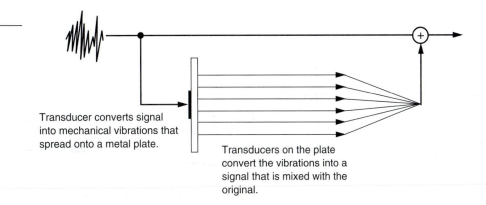

Transducer converts signal into mechanical vibrations that spread onto a metal plate.

Transducers on the plate convert the vibrations into a signal that is mixed with the original.

Figure 12–11

Schroeder Reverberation Algorithms

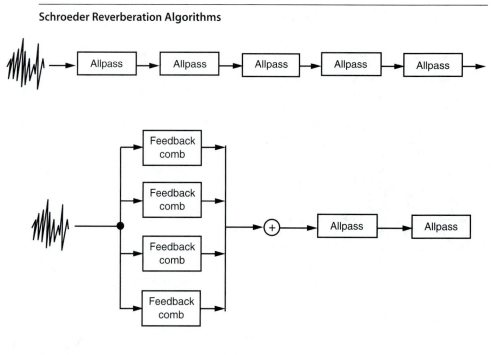

Non-Delay-Based Effects

Ring/Amplitude Modulation

Ring modulation is the multiplication of two signals. The result is spectral *sidebands* at the sum and difference frequencies of the two signals. For digital ring modulation, the sum and difference frequencies represent the spectral convolution that results from the time domain multiplication of two signals, as was discussed in Chapter 10. This agrees with a trigonometric identity that describes the same phenomenon in the analog domain:

$$\cos A \cos B = 0.5[\cos(A + B) + \cos(A - B)] \qquad 12\text{–}7$$

A ring modulator takes an input audio signal. Some can take a second input signal as the multiplier; others produce the multiplier internally as a fixed waveform. With a complex audio input wave, the output is similarly complex and often inharmonic. Every harmonic of the input is duplicated above and below the multiplier, producing a "science fiction" type of mechanical sound. When two signals are input, the result is even more complex, as every harmonic of each signal forms sum and difference frequencies with the harmonics of the other.

Amplitude modulation involves periodically changing the amplitude of a signal. As an example, a sine wave may be used as a control signal that modulates the amplitude of another sine wave. When the modulating oscillator operates at low (subaudio) rates, the result is an oscillation in loudness (tremolo). For example, if the modulator is set to a frequency of 6 Hz, the result is a tremolo that changes in amplitude six times per second. When the frequency of the modulating oscillator is brought to higher values (audio frequencies over 20 Hz), there is a qualitative change in the effect. In addition to the frequency of the audio-producing oscillator, extra frequencies are added to the sound at sum and difference frequencies with the modulator's frequency. The audible result is very similar to that of ring modulation, in that spectral sidebands appear; the difference is that with amplitude modulation the original audio frequency is also maintained.

Looking at amplitude modulation more technically, it can be seen that it is essentially the same process as ring modulation, with the distinction that an offset is added to the modulator. In terms of spectral convolution, as shown in Figure 10–7, this means adding a dc component (0 Hz) to one factor. In terms of the preceding analog equation, it may be described by

$$(1 + \cos A)\cos B = \cos B + \cos A \cos B$$
$$= \cos B + 0.5[\cos(A + B) + \cos(A - B)] \qquad 12\text{–}8$$

This is the same process that is employed in AM radio broadcasting. To broadcast AM signals, a high-frequency carrier wave has its amplitude modulated by a wave representing the broadcast material. Figure 12–12 shows an example of a high-frequency carrier wave whose amplitude is being modulated by a lower-frequency modulating wave. The carrier, being a high-frequency wave, is able to travel long distances when it is emitted as an electromagnetic wave from a station's antenna. Its frequency corresponds to the station number on the AM dial. A receiving antenna may then be tuned so that it resonates at the carrier frequency, and the electromagnetic wave is converted back into electricity in the receiving antenna. The receiver then demodulates the received wave, a process that removes the carrier frequency, leaving only the broadcast material frequencies that then get passed on to the amplifier. Amplitude modulation as a form of music synthesis was an early type of effect that was explored in the radio broadcast facilities that housed many of the first electronic music studios. The difference is that the carrier frequency used for music is generally in the audible frequency range, a good deal lower than radio broadcast carrier frequencies. There is also no demodulation process, so that the modulated carrier wave is used as a musical component.

Compression/Limiting and Expansion/Noise Gating

These two effect types alter a signal's *dynamic range* (the difference between the highest and lowest amplitude levels).

Compressor/Limiter

A compressor/limiter reduces input levels when they exceed a certain threshold. Thus, the dynamic range of the signal is reduced, or *compressed*. The effect may be described by a *transfer function* (Figure 12–13). Below the threshold, the output level matches the input. Above the threshold, the output level is mapped to a value below the input level. The output is described by a ratio that indicates input change over resulting output change—the number of decibels the input must increase to result in an output change of 1 decibel. When the transfer function rises above a value of 10:1, the more extreme effect is called *limiting*.

The output of a compressor/limiter is typically the result of a calculation done on the rms value of a *window* (block of a designated size) of samples. (Chapter 2

Figure 12–12

Amplitude Modulation

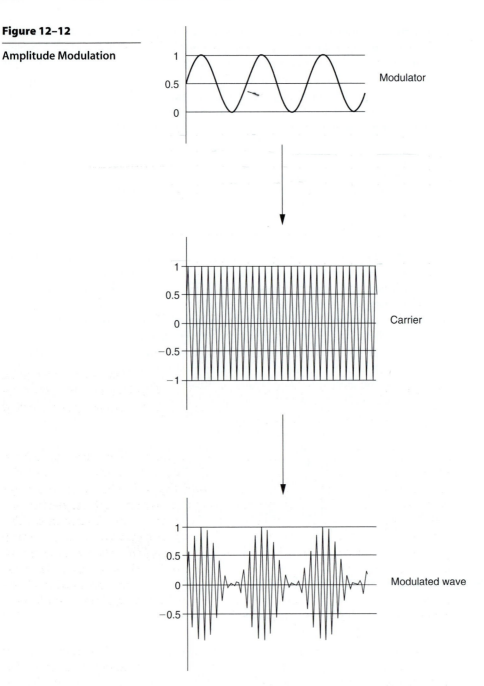

Modulator

Carrier

Modulated wave

discussed rms.) In addition to setting the threshold level and the slope of the transfer function above the threshold, users may typically adjust the attack and release times; that is, the length of time after the input level rises above the threshold until the compression is activated, and how long after the input falls below the threshold the compression stops. A long attack time can blur an instrument's transient, and a long release time can extend an instrument's release if the instrument's natural amplitude level falls below the compression threshold faster than the release time takes to activate.

Figure 12–13

Compressor/Limiter
Transfer Function

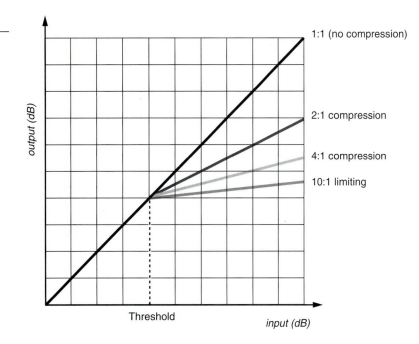

Compression/limiting is useful for evening out an inconsistent signal (such as a player moving about and not maintaining a consistent distance from a microphone). Special effects can be achieved with high attack and release times, creating unnatural-sounding transients or decays.

Expander/Noise Gate

An expander/noise gate performs the opposite function of a compressor/limiter. An input signal is windowed, with processing based on the rms of the amplitudes in each window. As the transfer function shows (Figure 12–14), an expander reduces levels that are below the threshold. The quiet sections of the signal become even quieter, so the dynamic range becomes greater (in a word, it's *expanded*). The *expansion ratio* describes the number of dB that the output will drop for every drop of 1 dB in the input. Levels that fall below the transfer function are eliminated entirely. An extreme level of expansion, greater than 10:1, is called a *noise gate*. As with a compressor/limiter, users may typically choose the threshold level, the expansion ratio, and the attack and release times. The most common uses of expansion are to remove low-level noise from a signal.

Companding

The processes of compression and expansion may be used in combination for noise reduction or transmission over a channel with limited dynamic range. On transmission, a compressor allows the level of the signal to be brought up, thus increasing the signal-to-noise ratio. When the signal is received, an expander restores the original dynamic range, minus the noise.

Mixing

The heart of a multicomponent audio system is the *mixer*, where discrete audio signals are combined and processed. A mixer acts as a traffic director for signals entering and leaving it. Signals are often split and sent to different processing

Figure 12–14

Expander/Noise Gate
Transfer Function

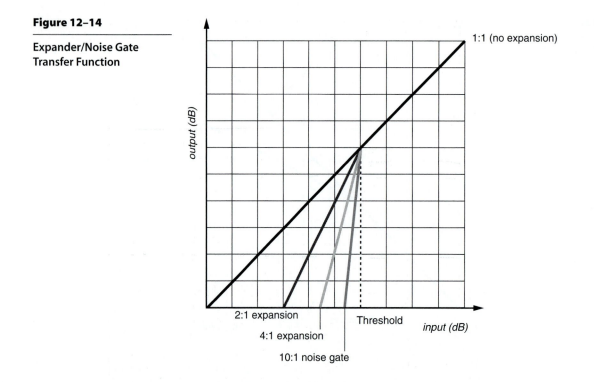

operations, to be recombined later. Sometimes signals are sent out of the mixer and then sent back in again. Figure 12–15 illustrates the physical layout of a "generic" mixer. Figure 12–16 shows a block diagram of the mixer. It is fashioned after the layout of block diagrams in commercial mixer documentation manuals: the signal flow goes from left to right, with the various output routes arranged vertically. This section will give an overview of mixer functions.

A mixer may be analog or digital. An analog mixer routes streams of voltage, or current. A digital mixer has ADCs at the input and DACs at the output, and it routes streams of binary numbers. But both types are the same conceptually. Many digital mixers exist as a software component of a sequencer or of digital editing programs.

Channels

Each input signal is sent to a *channel.* Each channel often corresponds to a different instrument. Some instruments, such as drum sets, may have multiple microphones assigned to them, each of which goes to a separate mixer channel. A large ensemble, such as a choir, may be picked up by several microphones that are suspended over different sections of musicians. Each section may then be sent to a different mixer channel, where the balance among the sections may be controlled.

Most of the controls on a mixer are *channel controls.* Channel controls are arranged in vertical *strips.* Recognizing the repetitiveness of the strips simplifies the array of knobs, sliders, and buttons on the surface of a mixer (just as recognizing the repetitiveness of white and black keys simplifies the layout of a piano keyboard).

Mixers can take two types of input: *line level* and *mic level.* Line level refers to the output level of electronic instruments, such as synthesizers. These instruments

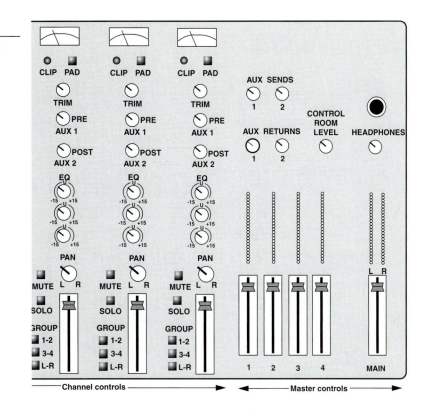

output a signal of higher electrical level, typically transmitted with 1/4″ phone plugs or RCA plugs. Mic level refers to signals from microphones. Microphones output signals of lower electrical level, typically transmitted via three-pin XLR plugs or 1/4″ phone plugs. Some mixers have inputs assigned specifically for line or mic level sources. Others can take either input type and automatically make the appropriate adjustments for signal level. Still others have two jacks at each input, one for each level, such that using one jack overrides the other. The block diagram shows signal paths for one line-level input and one mic-level input.

Mic level inputs typically have a *pot* (*potentiometer*) to adjust the input level, labeled "trim" or "gain." Mic inputs also typically have a *pad* switch to reduce extra "hot" (loud) signals. A *clip light* is a warning signal, usually in red, that turns on when the signal rises to a level that is likely to result in distortion.

Phantom Power

Some microphones require a voltage input to operate. This voltage, *phantom power,* may be typically supplied by the microphone preamplifier in the mixer via the microphone input cable (the audio travels down the cable to the mixer, the phantom power travels up the cable to the microphone). Phantom power may be global for the entire mixer or assigned to only one channel. As a troubleshooting tip, if there is no apparent signal from a microphone, the phantom power may need to be switched on. As a further caution, some devices, such as vintage ribbon microphones, can be damaged or destroyed by phantom power.

Figure 12–16

Mixer Block Diagram

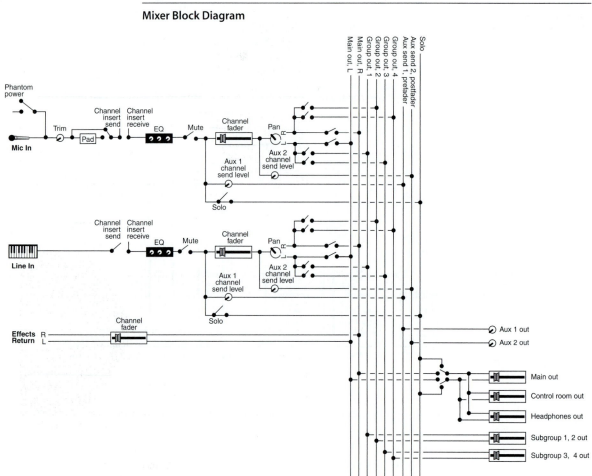

Channel Insert

Many mixers have a channel-level Send/Return route to send an input signal out for immediate processing, such as compression or expansion. Typically, this is done with a single jack that contains the input and output signals. A special Y-shaped cable is often used for channel inserts. The base of the Y is inserted into the Insert jack and is capable both of sending and receiving the audio signal. The two ends of the Y go into input and output jacks of an external processing device.

Equalization

Equalization (EQ) is a set of specialized lowpass, highpass, and bandpass filters. A mixer typically features lowpass and highpass *shelf* filters and one or more midrange band-pass *reciprocal peak dip* filters (Figure 12–17). When an EQ knob is at the 12:00 position, no filtering is being applied. When a signal exits a processor at the same level at which it entered, the processor is said to be operating at *unity gain*. (*Gain*

Figure 12–17

**Highpass and Lowpass
Shelf and Reciprocal Peak
Dip Bandpass Filters**

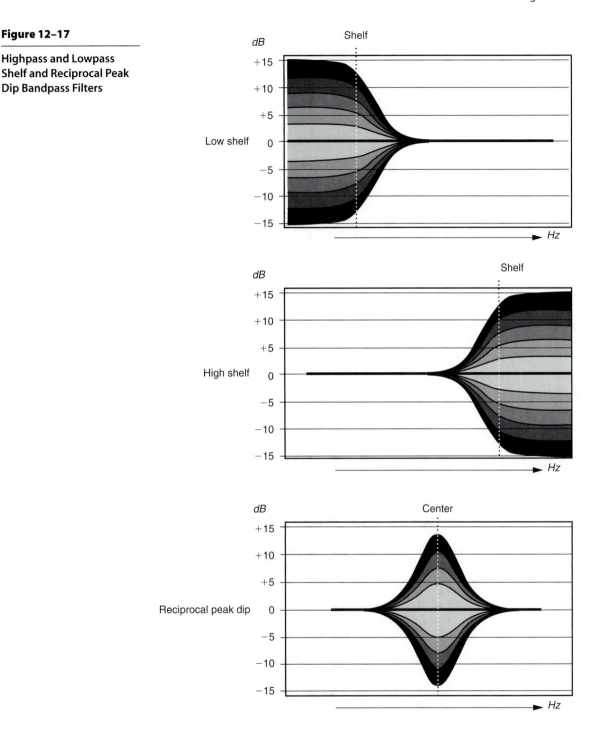

refers to the ratio of a signal's output power to its power on input.) The 12:00 position on an EQ knob is often marked "U" to indicate unity position. Turning the knob to the left or right accentuates or amplifies certain frequency ranges. The "generic mixer" of Figure 12–15 offers a gain of plus or minus 15 dB with each EQ range.

A shelf filter provides a flat amplification or attenuation above or below a given shelf frequency. Most mixers have fixed shelf frequencies for HI EQ and LO

EQ knobs. A low shelf filter affects all frequencies below the shelf frequency. This EQ range can highlight bass drums or bass parts. A high shelf filter affects all frequencies above the shelf frequency. This range can add extra presence to instruments such as cymbals or wood blocks or attenuate background noise.

MID EQ ranges attenuate or amplify frequencies on either side of a center frequency. A reciprocal peak dip filter is a special type is a hybrid filter whose bandwidth varies with gain level. Thus, this filter type is a hybrid of both fixed Q and variable Q filters (as described in Chapter 9). *Semiparametric* filters allow the center frequency to be adjusted. High-end mixers may feature *fully parametric* EQ, which allows both center frequency and Q to be adjusted.

Equalization can provide useful effects, but it is meant to be used in small doses. If all of the EQ knobs are being used in extreme positions, it is comparable to food that needs excessive amounts of salt or pepper to be palatable. It is most likely that there is a problem elsewhere in the signal chain, such as the positioning of a microphone or player.

Channel Fader

This is the volume control for a channel. By adjusting the fader position for each channel, the proper balance among instruments may be set.

Mixer Buses

Signals exit the mixer through *buses*. There are many types of buses. The most straightforward are the main stereo output buses at the final stage of a signal's path. But it is common to send a signal out of the mixer temporarily for additional processing, from which it is sent back into the mixer to be recombined with the rest of the signals.

Auxiliary Buses

The first bus along the signal path is a type called an *auxiliary send*. Auxiliary send ("aux") buses are used to tap the channel. Aux buses are typically used for effects processing and monitor mixes. Depending on the mixer, aux sends may also be labeled "Monitor" or "Effects."

Monitor mixes are useful in live situations where performers need monitor speakers onstage to hear the other players. Some performers may need different mixes (a drummer, for example, may need to hear the bass but not need a strong lead guitar or vocal in the monitor mix). Aux buses allow custom monitor mixes to be created. Mixers have a certain number of aux buses, each of which may correspond to a different monitor mix. The example mixer in Figures 12–15 and 12–16 features two aux buses. Each auxiliary signal tap has a volume control knob on each channel strip. Thus, a channel's signal may be added to a given aux bus via the appropriate volume knob on the channel strip. This allows a channel's signal to be sent to as many aux buses as needed and to the degree needed.

Aux sends are also used to send a signal out of the mixer temporarily for effects processing in an external device. After being sent into the effects device, processed, and sent out of the device, the signal may be returned to the mixer in one of two ways. Some mixers have a special Effects Return jack. The example mixer in the figures features two Effects returns, so that both channels of a stereo processor may be received. Alternatively, a processed signal may be sent into another channel input, allowing control of both the "dry" (unprocessed) and "wet" (processed) signal on separate mixer channels.

An aux send may be either *prefader* or *postfader,* meaning that the signal is tapped either before or after the channel fader sets its output volume. On the example mixer of Figures 12–15 and 12–16, auxiliary send 1 is prefader and auxiliary send 2 is postfader. A monitor send is likely to be prefader, since the monitor mix is set by the volume levels represented by the aux knobs and does not need the extra volume information from a channel fader. An effects send may be either pre- or postfader or it may switchable. A prefader send is the most flexible, as it allows the dry signal to be brought to low volume levels via the channel fader, while the tap sent to the effects devices is at full gain.

Mute/Solo

The Mute switch allows a channel to be silenced without moving its fader position. This allows the role of a channel in a mix to be quickly tested. The Solo switch does the opposite, immediately silencing all channels that do not have the Solo switch depressed.

Pan

All channels are ultimately sent out on a stereo output bus, meaning that the channel's contents are divided between two outputs. The pan pot determines the proportion of the signal that goes to the left (odd) and right (even) output channels. As will be discussed further in the next section, a channel's output may be sent to a number of stereo outputs. When a channel's output is being sent to a subgroup pair, the pan control determines the proportion of the signal level that goes to the odd and even channels of a subgroup. When the channel's output is being sent to the main output, the pan control determines the left-right stereo position.

In Chapter 3, the relative volume levels of a two-channel constant power pan were discussed, with a sinusoidal change in volume required on each channel to create the perceptual effect of a sound source that is moving while maintaining a constant distance from the listener. Mixer pan pots are designed so that a constant power level is divided between the two stereo channels. Thus, the volume range for each channel is a quarter period of a sine and cosine wave for the right and left channels, respectively. The amplitude levels assigned to each channel, based on the position of the pan pot, correspond to sine and cosine measurements of the pan pot's position, as shown in Figure 12–18.

Output Buses

The set of buttons to the left of the channel faders in Figure 12–5 is used to direct each channel to any number of available output buses. The Main Out (or L-R Out) is what is typically connected to a mixdown machine for the final mix, such as a tape deck or CD recorder. Channels may also be sent to *subgroups,* which are also arranged as stereo pairs. Subgroups may be used to send mixer signals to the

Figure 12–18

Output Levels of Left and Right Stereo Channels Based on Pan Pot Position

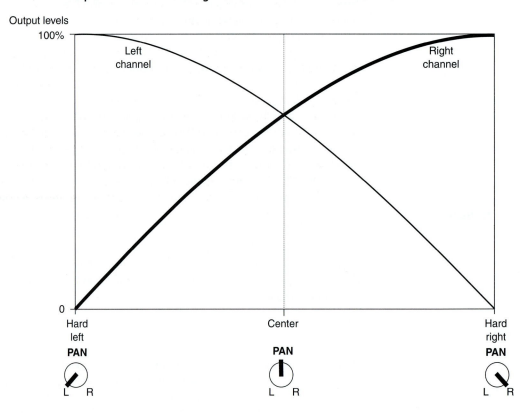

inputs of a multitrack tape deck. Any number of channels may be combined onto one subgroup and sent to one input channel of a tape deck. Thus, if a recording combines a drummer and a choir, each on multiple mixer channels, the drum channels may be combined on one subgroup and sent to one tape track, and the choir channels may be similarly combined and sent to another tape track. The Control Room outputs are meant for monitor speakers in the mixing room. Headphone outputs are meant for headphone monitoring.

Mixers are often classified by the number of channel inputs, the number of subgroups (or group buses), and the number of main outputs (for example, $24 \times 8 \times 2$).

A Final Note on Levels

Mixers and recording devices typically have meters that indicate the signal level (an output gain range of -30 to $+28$ dB is typical). The goal in recording is to keep signal levels high enough that they cover any noise introduced by the audio equipment, yet low enough that the signal does not distort. A level of zero is known as the *nominal level* and is an important reference during recording sessions. However, this nominal level means different things for analog and digital audio equipment.

For analog equipment, the level of zero is what the manufacturer has decided is the optimal level to be handled by that component. It is meant to serve as an *average* level for the audio material. Sometimes signal levels will be somewhat higher, other times they will be somewhat lower, but zero should be the most common reading shown by the meter.

For digital equipment, the level of zero is an absolute cutoff, the *peak level.* Any signal above zero will distort. Therefore, the goal with a digital recording system is to maintain signal levels that come as close as possible to zero without *ever* reaching it.

Care must be taken when using an analog mixer to send audio to a digital recorder, since the meters on the two machines indicate different things. The fastidious solution would be to calibrate the two so that the meter on the analog mixer reflects lower levels than the digital recorder and the two-level displays match in terms of distortion. Few users, however, take their housekeeping habits to this level. The more common solution is simply to adjust levels according to the digital recorder's meters rather than those of the analog mixer.

CHAPTER 13

Digital Instruments

Samplers

Samplers were discussed briefly in Chapter 6. These are instruments that contain recordings that are triggered by MIDI note messages. The earliest pre-MIDI sampling instruments were tape based. The Mellotron, an instrument in vogue in the 1960s and early 1970s, contained strips of audio tape. Depressing different keys activated different strips of tape. Two famous recorded examples were the flutes in the introductions of the Beatles' "Strawberry Fields Forever" and Led Zeppelin's "Stairway to Heaven." Although it could be effective, the Mellotron was an unwieldy instrument, both in size and in maintenance requirements.

In the 1980s, digital samplers became the better option for work with recorded sounds. In samplers, recordings are digital and can be stored on disc or computer hard drive. In terms of computer data, a sampled audio file is no different from a wavetable that describes a timbre (described in Chapter 9). The difference is the source of the samples that make up the wavetable—from a digital recording rather than from sample values calculated by a processor—and in the way the wavetables may be allocated within the instrument.

In the context of these instruments, the wavetables are termed "samples" to refer to the collection of instantaneous amplitude samples that comprises them. A sample can be assigned to a group of MIDI note numbers. One note serves as the "fundamental," which plays the sample back unaltered. Any assigned notes above or below this base note speed up or slow down the sample accordingly. Most samples are only effective over the span of a few notes before they sound "chipmunky" above the base pitch or like an extended rumble below it. A sampled rendition of an instrument, then, necessarily consists of a number of samples, each assigned to a range of about a major third. In some cases, it is advantageous to assign more than one sample to a note number and trigger the different samples according to velocity value. A piano, for example, changes tone depending on the key velocity. Assigning a number of samples to the same note and setting each to be activated by different velocity ranges allows a more expressive overall sound.

Typically, a sample contains *loop points* within its steady-state region. Once the initial transient has played, the steady-state portion can repeat indefinitely until a Note Off message is received. Special effects may be created with multilayered sample banks in which different instruments or sounds are assigned to the same note number so that an ensemble sound is produced. Different sounds may be combined into the same sample in a sequence, with crossfades between them, so that one sample produces a series of different sounds in succession. Most commercial instruments allow such editing to be performed via its front panel or by software that is included with the purchase of the instrument.

Samplers may exist as commercial instruments or as software packages. They have become invaluable not only to musicians but also to sound-effects artists in theatre and cinema. Cinema foley artists, for example, who create sound effects for films, typically work with sequencers and a bank of samples representing footsteps, doors opening and closing, passing cars, and so forth. With a sequencer slaved to a film's synch track, the appropriate sound effects can be triggered at the desired frame of film, allowing sound tracks to be created in a flexible and reliable computing environment.

Sampler Variations

Synthesizers

In the 1980s, there was a distinction between sampling instruments and synthesizers. Today, virtually all commercial synthesizers are hybrids, combining synthesis algorithms with sampled recordings of actual instruments. A synthesis patch may combine the attack from a digital recording and a steady-state portion that is synthesized (a number of common synthesis techniques will be covered in the next section). This hybrid sound may then be combined with synthesis editing functions such as filters, effects, or other wavetables that may be used to accompany the digital recording.

Sound Fonts

Many computer sound cards allow their wavetable banks to be replaced with *Sound Fonts*. These are typically wavetables of sampled instrumental recordings, with the various samples assigned to appropriate key ranges. Sound Fonts may often be downloaded from the Internet as files with the extension ".sf2." The Sound Font files are a series of audio files (typically in ".wav" format) and a text file that maps them to MIDI key ranges. It is often possible to extract the WAV files from the Sound Font files if a musician wishes to work with an individual audio file.

Groove Boxes and Looping Software

Both of these instrument types grew out of drum machines and are common in the creation of dance tracks. Measures are typically depicted as a grid that is subdivided vertically into 8th or 16th notes, with horizontal tracks for different instruments. A rhythmic pattern is created by clicking in the grid to trigger the instruments at certain times. Patterns are typically short, on the order of four measures. Pieces may be created by programming patterns to play in sequences, similar to song mode in a sequencer. Looping software comes with a number of audio samples that may be put into patterns, plus the capability of importing audio files. Some of these files are short samples of instruments; others are recordings of a drummer playing one to four measures. These recordings may be repeated (or *looped,* hence the name) to create a consistent and complex dance beat in short order. A set of audio files, for example, may be single measures of drum beats at a given tempo. These audio files may then be arranged sequentially on a time line. The tempo remains consistent throughout, and variety can be achieved by switching among the loops from measure to measure as desired. Looping software also includes oscillators that produce classic synthesis timbres (oscillators will be discussed further in the next section) and that may be pitched so that they play melodies within the pattern. Instruments or patterns may also be put through filters and effects.

Groove boxes are hardware looping machines, which may be easier to transport into dance clubs than personal computer systems. Some groove boxes allow the tempo to be varied interactively via "tap tempo" mode, by which the musician or DJ taps a pad on the instrument. Some models also feature infrared light sources that affect parameters such as tempo, cutoff frequency, or filter resonance. Hand or body movements within the infrared beam can affect these parameters.

Tracking Software

Tracking software is a means of creating music to be distributed over the Internet as a MOD file. MOD files consist of audio files and instructions for playing them. The instructions are analogous to MIDI instructions, specifying parameters such as pitch or volume. But rather than being specified note numbers, pitches in MOD files are produced by performing mathematical operations on the file to vary its playback speed or amplitude. MOD files were originally meant to be a way to create sound tracks for computer games, but they quickly became popular among computer hobbyists as a means of creating musical compositions that were small enough to be transferred to others via the Internet and Bulletin Board services.

Most tracking software can now convert MIDI input to MOD controls and can import and export to a variety of audio file formats. Many allow songs to be created from a MIDI instrument, by working on a notation view or with a grid onto which samples may be placed on a time line.

Software Synthesis

Sound synthesis, the creation of complex sounds from raw materials, has in many ways come full circle. The first computer audio synthesis programs were acoustic compilers created at Bell Labs in the 1950s by Max Mathews. It was with these programs that the principles of synthesis were first explored and fundamental techniques and algorithms were defined. Digital synthesis remained something available only to facilities able to afford high-end computers until the 1980s, when commercial digital synthesizers were introduced. Synthesis algorithms were encoded into the operating systems of these devices, refined to a high degree by the R&D departments of the companies that produced them. A more-expensive alternative to synthesizers were digital samplers. As memory became cheaper and more plentiful, sampling instruments eclipsed dedicated synthesizers and synthesis-related features became less important in the development of commercial instruments.

Musicians who favor working with synthesizers have turned more and more to the computer as their instrument. Since the mid-1990s, software synthesis programs have become popular on personal computers, giving musicians the generalized synthesis capabilities of early supercomputers. Contemporary computers are much faster than those on which the first software synthesis programs ran, fast enough to realize audio in real time. This means, for example, that instead of using a commercial synthesizer, a musician may assemble synthesis patches of his or her own creation and trigger the audio via MIDI input from an instrument attached to the computer. Audio input may also be processed. A signal taken from an instrument via a microphone may be transmitted to the computer, processed by filters and/or effects, and output virtually instantaneously, so that such processing may be used in concert situations.

Building Blocks of Sound Synthesis

As described in Chapter 9, the techniques of music synthesis were codified by Max Mathews at Bell Labs in the 1950s and 1960s. His concepts of wavetables and modular construction remain the basis of contemporary synthesis engines.

Wavetables

In Chapter 9, wavetables were described as collections of sample values. A wavetable represents these values in a way that facilitates *interpolation*. The process of reading data from a wavetable requires flexibility in both the sampling increment and the method of interpolation.

If each sample in a wavetable is read, the resulting frequency, f, is

$$f = \frac{\text{sampling frequency}}{\text{wavetable size}}$$

13–1

For example, a 512-point table read at the CD audio rate produces a frequency of

$$f = \frac{44,100}{512} = 86.132 \text{ Hz}$$

13–2

To generate a frequency an octave higher, every second sample is skipped, that is, a sampling increment of 2 is used, so the table is traversed twice as fast. As the sampling increment changes, the resulting frequency is

$$f = \frac{\text{sampling increment} \times \text{sampling rate}}{\text{wavetable size}}$$

13–3

To obtain the sampling increment, Equation 13–3 may be rewritten as

$$SI = \text{wavetable size} \times \frac{\text{desired frequency}}{\text{sampling rate}}$$

13–4

For example, a 512-point table with a sampling increment of 4 produces a frequency of 344.53 Hz:

$$SI = 512 \times \frac{344.53}{44,100} = 4$$

13–5

The wavetable is incremented in circular fashion, analogous to the hands of a clock face. Consider a progression of increments of five hours, starting at 12:00.

The resulting hours are 12:00, 5:00, 10:00, 3:00, 8:00, 1:00, and so on. The same type of progression of values occurs when a wavetable is traversed (replacing the 12 hours on a clock face with the number of entries in a wavetable).

The sampling increment determines the frequency produced. In addition, many wavetables are traversed with an additional value of phase. This second value works in conjunction with the sampling increment to produce an offset to each sampling increment position. For example, with a sampling increment of 4 and a phase offset of 3, the values will be taken from the table at points $(0 + 3)$, $(4 + 3)$, $(8 + 3)$, $(12 + 3)$, and so on. Recall from Chapter 1 that *phase* refers to a wave's position. By the same token, the term may also refer to a position (index) within a wavetable.

In the preceding examples, integer sampling increments were chosen that produced noninteger frequencies. By the same token, not all desired frequencies may be produced with integer sampling increments. For example, to produce a frequency of 440 Hz from a 512-point table at the CD audio rate, the sampling increment needs to be

$$SI = 512 \times \frac{440}{44,100} = 5.1083 \hspace{3cm} 13\text{--}6$$

With this sampling increment, the first value is read from the table's phase position zero, the next value is read from phase position 5.1083, the next is read from phase position 10.2168, and so on. Interpolation allows the decimal part of the sampling increment to be accounted for and values to be produced that fall between the table entries. For a phase position of 10.2168, the output sample may be a combination of 21.68% of the value in table index 10 and 78.32% of the value in table index 11. This method of interpolation, called *linear interpolation,* effectively considers a straight line between successive sample values and produces the value of the line at the position of each sampling increment. Signal-processing algorithms may employ a variety of other interpolation methods based on their accuracy and computing efficiency.

Unit Generators and Signal Flow Charts

Analog synthesis used the term *module* to describe building blocks that could be patched together to create complex instruments. Software synthesis systems use the term *unit generator* for these building blocks. A unit generator is an algorithm that creates or modifies an audio signal. Unit generators have one or more input parameters and at least one output. The output of one unit generator may provide the input to another unit generator. Instruments may be illustrated in flowchart notation, which shows connections of unit generators and mathematical operations done on their outputs. Three simple examples are shown in Figure 13–1.

Unlike the orientation of electrical diagrams (such as the mixer block diagram of Figure 12–16), signal flow in synthesizer flowcharts is oriented vertically, with signal flow going from the top down. The unit generators shown in Figure 13–1 are a fundamental unit generator type known as an *oscillator.* An oscillator produces a periodic wave. Most software synthesizers allow musicians to employ oscillators that create the classic wave shapes of Figure 2–8 or to create their own wavetables.

Figure 13–1a is a simple sine wave oscillator. This oscillator has three inputs (sometimes called *arguments*): a frequency of 440 Hz, a phase offset of zero, and an argument for amplitude. The amplitude is controlled by another unit generator,

Figure 13–1

Simple Unit Generator Flow

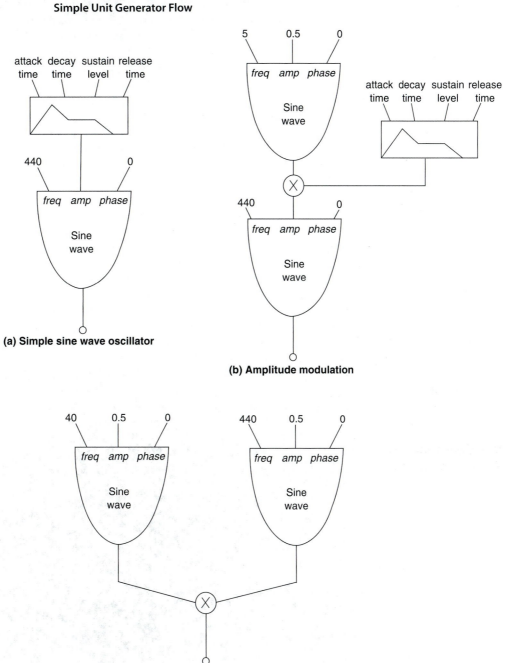

(a) Simple sine wave oscillator

(b) Amplitude modulation

(c) Ring modulation

an *envelope generator.* Envelope generators are used to control output level over time. Like oscillators, they output a series of values over time. The distinction is that the output of an envelope generator does not cycle, as does the output of an oscillator. The envelope generator in the figure is a classic type, with arguments for attack time, decay time, sustain level, and release time (how long it takes a note to fade to silence after it is released). These envelope types are called *ADSR envelopes.*

Figure 13–1b illustrates amplitude modulation, which was described in Chapter 12. A second sine wave oscillator is added to the output of an envelope generator, and their sum controls the amplitude input of the audio oscillator. In principle, there is no difference between the two audio oscillators, although to speed computations many programs offer the capability for modulating oscillators to produce samples at a slower rate than the audio rate of 44.1 kHz. This slower rate is often called the *control rate* to distinguish it from the audio rate. The control oscillator has a frequency of 5 Hz, well below the threshold of human hearing. Thus, in this patch it functions as a *low-frequency oscillator* (LFO); that is, its signal is not meant to be heard, but rather to modulate another oscillator. If the frequency of the modulator were brought to an audio frequency (above 20 Hz), the spectral sidebands described in Chapter 12 would become audible.

Figure 13–1c illustrates ring modulation, also described in Chapter 12. The output of two audio oscillators is multiplied to create sum and difference frequencies of the two oscillators' frequencies.

Another common unit generator is a *noise generator.* These output random sequences of values to create noise signals, such as that shown in Figure 2–1. A simulation of a flute, for example, might combine outputs of a noise generator with a triangle wave. The noise generator might have a shorter envelope time and a lower overall volume than the triangle wave so that it is only heard during the initial onset of a note, just as the sound of breath is audible during the onset of a note from a flute. Percussion instruments typically contain a high degree of noise, so a noise generator sent through various filters may be essential for the creation of percussive sounds.

Additive Synthesis

One computer synthesis technique studied in the 1950s and 1960s employed a methodology now called *additive synthesis* (or *Fourier synthesis*). A series of sine oscillators are used to create each partial of a complex tone. With each oscillator at a different frequency and with a different amplitude envelope, in theory any complex sound can be synthesized, given enough oscillators (Figure 13–2). The trumpet tones in Figure 10–10 were resynthesized using additive synthesis. Similar work was carried out by Jean Risset in the analysis and resynthesis of bell tones. Additive synthesis offers musicians the maximum level of flexibility, but is also data intensive. Dozens of oscillators are needed to synthesize an instrument of any complexity. Because acoustic instruments have spectra that change with their amplitude and pitch range, a library of oscillators and envelopes for different volume ranges would be needed to come up with a satisfying synthesis of an instrument.

Subtractive Synthesis

While additive synthesis was possible in computer music in the 1960s, an opposite approach emerged with the invention of voltage-controlled analog modular synthesizers, which synthesized waveforms through the manipulation of electronic

Figure 13–2

Additive Synthesis

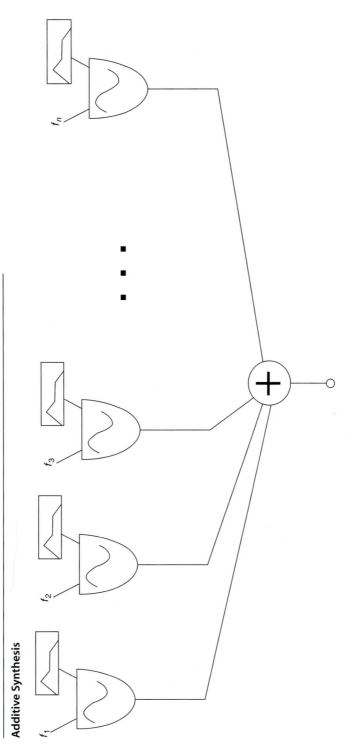

voltage levels. Typical modules included the voltage-controlled oscillator (VCO), voltage-controlled filter (VCF), and voltage-controlled amplifier (VCA). Musicians could purchase these small modules separately and put them together to create larger synthesis systems that created and manipulated waveforms with subtractive synthesis algorithms.

Additive synthesis might be compared to needlepoint, where many strands are assembled to create a greater whole. Subtractive synthesis could similarly be compared to sculpting, where an undefined mass of material has elements removed until an image of something is created. In subtractive synthesis, noise signals and complex waveforms, such as those shown in Figure 2–8, are put through filters to shape a spectrum in broad strokes.

Figure 13–3 is a flowchart illustration of the subtractive patch that was used to create Figure 9–16. A sawtooth wave with a frequency of 220 Hz is the input to a lowpass filter. The filter's cutoff frequency is modulated by an LFO sine oscillator with a frequency of 0.5 Hz. The LFO has an amplitude of 1800, meaning that its values oscillate in the range of ± 1800. Clearly, this is not a range of values intended for an audio oscillator. The LFO's offset value means that 2200 is added to all values generated by the oscillator. With the amplitude and offset combined, the oscillator outputs values that oscillate between 400 and 4000, a useful range for an oscillating filter cutoff frequency. The resonance value produces the spectral peak that is characteristic of feedback filters.

Figure 13–3

**Subtractive Synthesis
Flowchart**

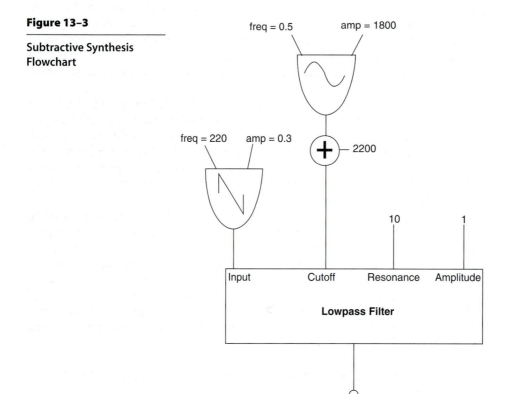

Phase Modulation

A generation of commercial digital synthesizers introduced in the early 1980s relied on *frequency modulation synthesis.* The term refers to a high-frequency vibrato applied to an oscillator so that its output frequency changes in a periodic fashion. Just as the effect of amplitude modulation was derived from broadcast techniques (described in Chapter 12), FM synthesis was derived from techniques of FM radio broadcasting, in which the modulator varies the carrier's frequency rather than its amplitude. Figure 13–4 illustrates the process with a low-frequency sine wave modulating the frequency of a sinusoidal carrier wave. FM broadcasts are less prone to interference from lightning or electromagnetic radiation from the sun since the broadcast wave is kept at a constant amplitude and it is possible to eliminate amplitude fluctuations from such interference at the receiver without affecting any of the broadcast material. Although the properties of frequency-modulated waves had been known for decades, it was not possible to employ FM as a synthesis technique until digital synthesizers, which were not subject to the tuning fluctuations suffered by analog oscillators, became feasible.

While FM revolutionized the music industry and quickly became a household word among synthesists, in fact the term was a misnomer. The actual synthesizer implementation is more accurately termed *phase modulation.* Many more recent synthesis programs use the term "phase modulation" to describe what was formerly termed "frequency modulation." The audible results are equivalent. The distinction is shown and discussed in Figure 13–5.

Phase modulation is the most common example of a class of synthesis algorithms called *nonlinear waveshaping.* If waveshaping is considered a black box that makes changes to an input wave, the term *nonlinear* refers to the fact that more comes out than was put in. While a linear system can alter frequencies and phases of input waves, a nonlinear system generates entirely new spectral components. Other examples were given in Chapter 9, when the effects of distortion were discussed. Nonlinear waveshaping is also termed *modulation synthesis* or *distortion synthesis* in some literature.

Recall that with amplitude modulation (Chapter 12) the result is the carrier frequency with sideband spectral components at the sum and difference of the carrier frequency (f_c) and the modulator frequency (f_m). In phase modulation, the result is many such sideband pairs at integer multiples of the sum and difference frequencies, as shown in Figure 13–6. The number of sideband pairs is theoretically infinite. Practically, the number of significant sideband pairs is the *index of modulation* (amplitude of the modulator) plus 2.

The amplitude of each sideband pair may be determined by the modulation index plus a graph of *Bessel functions of the first kind.* Bessel functions are plotted in terms of an *order.* Figure 13–7 shows plots of Bessel functions ordered 0 through 9. The orders of Bessel functions correspond to the sideband pair. The zero-order function corresponds to the unmodulated carrier, the first order corresponds to the first sideband pair at $f_c \pm f_m$, the second order corresponds to the second sideband pair at $f_c \pm 2f_m$, and so on. The horizontal axis of each graph corresponds to the index of modulation. The amplitude of each sideband pair may be determined by a three-step process:

1. To get the amplitude of sideband pair *n,* select the graph of the Bessel function order *n.*

Figure 13–4

Frequency Modulation

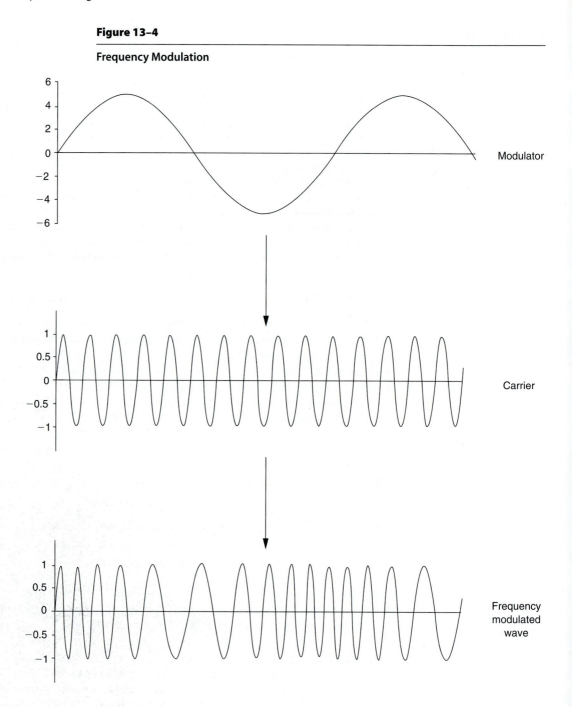

2. Read across the horizontal index to the modulation index value.

3. The value of the curve at that point is the amplitude of the sideband pair.

Because only the first-order Bessel function is not zero at a modulation index of zero, an index of zero produces only the carrier frequency. As the modulation index increases, the power of the carrier frequency is distributed to the sidebands that emerge; thus, the bandwidth increases while the total power produced by the complex wave remains consistent. Since all the Bessel functions oscillate at different

Figure 13–5

Phase Modulation and Frequency Modulation Synthesis

When a wavetable is incremented, the phase refers to the position of the incrementer. Frequency is derived from the rate at which the table is incremented. Therefore, the audible frequency is the result of the incrementer's speed. When the speed of the incrementer is modulated, the audible frequency is also modulated. Frequency is analogous to acceleration, which is the derivative (rate of change) of velocity. (Since the incrementer moves through the table in one direction only, speed is synonymous with velocity in this example.) Therefore, frequency is the derivative of phase. This means that the same audible results may be obtained from both configurations, as long as the derivative of a sine wave (a cosine wave) is used as the modulator in the frequency modulation algorithm. Phase modulation is what has been implemented in most commercial synthesizers. It is a more economical configuration. Phase modulation also makes it more practical to implement cascades of phase modulators. In phase modulation, any dc offset in the chain of modulators only results in a constant phase shift, which is inaudible. In a frequency modulation cascade, any dc offset in the modulators would result in a constant change in frequency, which would be audible.

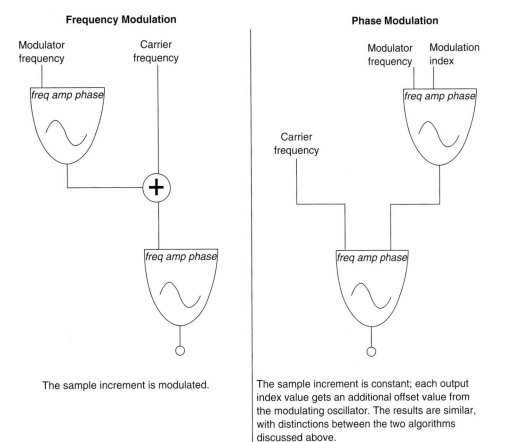

Frequency Modulation

Modulator frequency   Carrier frequency

freq amp phase

freq amp phase

The sample increment is modulated.

Phase Modulation

Modulator frequency   Modulation index

freq amp phase

Carrier frequency

freq amp phase

The sample increment is constant; each output index value gets an additional offset value from the modulating oscillator. The results are similar, with distinctions between the two algorithms discussed above.

rates, changing the modulation index produces many changes in the spectral content as different sideband pairs are amplified or attenuated. A small change in the modulation index can produce complex spectral variations.

For high modulation indexes, it is possible for lower sidebands to extend below 0 Hz. In this case, the situation corresponds to the aliased frequencies represented in the polar graph in Figure 9–8. "Negative" components are "wrapped around"

Figure 13–6

**Spectrum Outline of a
Phase-Modulated Wave**

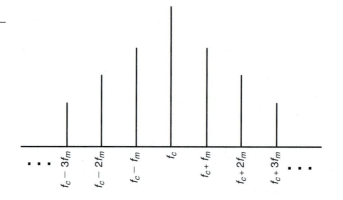

0 Hz to a frequency below the Nyquist frequency and phase inverted. This can have the effect of altering the even spacing of sidebands and producing inharmonic effects. Should the "wrapped" sidebands coincide with any positive sidebands, the phase inversion can cause cancellation or attenuation of the positive sideband.

The resulting spectra can be predicted by considering the ratio of the modulator to the carrier. When the frequencies of both are equal, all harmonics are produced, producing sawtooth-like waveforms. When the modulator frequency is twice the carrier frequency, every second harmonic is produced, thus removing all even harmonics and producing a square-like waveform. In general, if the modulator frequency is N times the carrier frequency, every Nth harmonic is removed from the complex wave, producing pulse-like waveforms. If the ratio is inharmonic, then the sideband pairs do not occur at harmonics of the carrier frequency, and an inharmonic spectrum is produced. Thus, the complex, inharmonic spectrum of a bell or percussion instrument can be produced with just a few oscillators. With an amplitude envelope applied to the modulator, dynamic spectral changes can be produced.

With phase modulation, extremely complex spectra can be produced with just two oscillators, and more variation can be introduced with the use of more than a simple oscillator pair. Sets of oscillator pairs may be combined. Or a single modulator may modulate a group of carriers, all of which are set to different frequencies. Programming one carrier to have a fixed frequency, regardless of any changes from a MIDI note message or any other input, can create formants in the spectrum (formants are discussed in Chapter 2). Other multioscillator configurations contain cascaded modulators that produce even more complex spectral patterns.

Phase modulation represented a quantum leap in digital synthesizers, which revolutionized the music industry in the early 1980s when it was introduced in commercial products. It was an economical form of synthesis that could be implemented in instruments affordable to musicians who had not been signed to lucrative recording contracts. Although sampling has largely outpaced synthesis in terms of market demand, phase modulation is still an efficient algorithm that is applied in many wavetable banks of computer sound cards.

Vector Synthesis

This synthesis type, featured on many commercial instruments and software programs, is actually not a synthesis method per se, but rather a means of combining different types of synthesis algorithms and mixing them dynamically. The mixing

Figure 13–7

**First-Order Bessel
Functions 0 through 9**

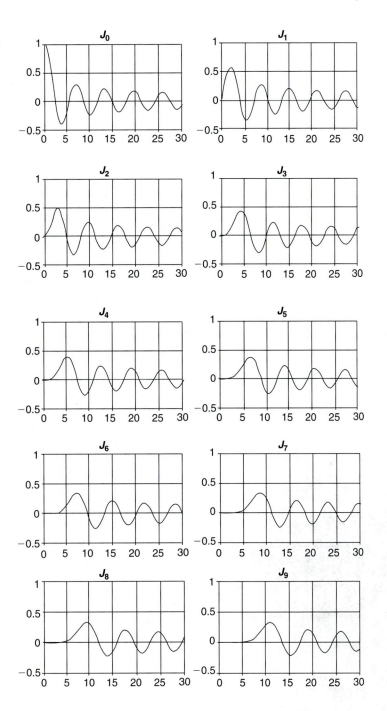

is often done with a joystick, mouse, or some other external controller. The position of the controller defines positions within an *X-Y* Cartesian coordinate system. Four different synthesis algorithms may correspond to the four corners of the joystick span or computer screen, and moving the joystick or mouse results in different blends of the four sounds. If the controller is placed at a corner, only one type of sound is heard. If it is dead center, all four are heard at equal volume. With the controller anywhere else, the loudest sound is that associated with the nearest corner, with the softest sound that associated with the corner farthest from the controller position. A variation on external control is to create a programmable envelope for the different synthesis algorithms or oscillators so that they crossfade automatically.

Latency

As mentioned earlier in this chapter, software synthesis now allows for the possibility of real-time processing of performers in concert situations. The acoustic performance of a musician may be digitized, processed, and output in fractions of a second. The size of this fraction is critical, however, given that the auditory system can sense interonset difference times on the order of milliseconds. At the CD audio rate, the sampling period is 1/44,100 sec, 0.0226757 ms. This, theoretically, is the shortest amount of time necessary for a digital audio system to recognize and output audio. However, it is usually more efficient computationally to fill a block (or buffer) of samples and process them all at once, rather than one at a time. Samples may be, for example, processed in blocks of 64, which means that anything done in response to incoming audio requires at least 64/44,100 sec (1.45125 ms) for the new samples to be generated.

Computer operating systems or sound cards may have built-in audio block sizes, typically at 1024, 2048, or 4096 samples. The more samples are held in buffers, the more efficient the computations and the less conducive the processor is to real-time performance. If live audio is combined with processed audio, large buffers may produce undesirable echoes or comb filtering.

The latency time of a system may be tested by creating an impulse signal on one channel, and recording the impulse on the other channel. Then both channels may be viewed and compared in an audio editing program, and the time difference between the impulse on each channel represents the system's latency.

Afterword

It was stated in the Introduction that music technologies have taken on a variety of meanings and applications in recent years. This text has attempted to show that music technology does not refer simply to concert recording, using sound synthesis in composition, preparing scores with notation programs, or any short definition. Rather, it is all these things and more. Just as digital technology is blurring the lines between traditional media forms, music technologies are redefining the nature of music itself.

One distinction that has often been drawn between music and visual arts is that music is, by definition, nonrepresentational. While visual arts may be pictures or sculptures *of* something (human figures, still lifes, landscapes, and so on), music is an abstraction of emotional content (this is just one of many descriptions that attempt to describe what music *is*). This contention is no longer true, now that acoustic sounds may be sampled and added to a music recording to refer to real-world events. Thus, music technologies allow new levels not only of sonic flexibility but also of communicative power. Just as television and radio redefined popular entertainment with their ability to bring it to people's living rooms, music technologies open up a broad range of aesthetic and sociological questions on the nature of music and its role in culture.

While some may raise concerns that music as an art form is being subsumed by technologies, it must be stressed that computers are no more than tools. Like any tool, the computer can only carry out the actions of the person using it. Any tool may be used conscientiously, poorly, with the best of intentions, or with the worst of intentions. While some may complain that music produced by computers is "inhuman" or "mechanistic," there is no evidence to suggest that more bad music has been produced by computers than by pen and paper. There will always be those who create poor music, and blaming the tools of production is little more than a red herring.

Musicians who avail themselves of the tools that have been created over the last twenty years have unprecedented opportunities for creating new types of music and sound art. Just as music may now enrich work in other fields through computer applications, the field of music may also be enriched by contributions from other areas of research.

Suggested Class Projects

Introductory Exercises

Scavenger Hunt

Many times, students who are new to computers have trouble with file management. They may save files and may not be able to find them again or be unclear how to copy files to or from floppy disks. Or they may be confused by generic files that cannot be launched by double-clicking them, but need to be opened from within another application. Another basic skill is the ability to export files in different formats, for example, to save a word processing file as a simple text document, or to save a sequencer file as a standard MIDI file.

As a preliminary exercise, it might be useful to have a "Search and File Management" assignment, along the following lines:

- Create a simple word processing document. Hide it on all student computers. Have students use the computer's search program to find the file. The file can contain further instructions for them to carry out, such as:
- Type their name in the file and save it to their disk, renaming it and saving it in a simple text format.
- Within the word processing document, include instructions to find another file elsewhere on the computer, perhaps a generic MIDI file. Have them open the file in a sequencer or MIDI player and save it in a new format also on their disk.
- Create a folder on their disk that holds their text file and MIDI file.

Creating Sine Wave Graphs

Figure A–1 illustrates how a sine wave graph may be created in a spreadsheet. Once students are comfortable creating graphs of waves and combinations of waves, a number of useful exercises may be explored:

- Another plot may be created of a sine wave that has a slight difference in frequency. The two plots may be added to show the volume oscillations that result from two pure tones that are close in frequency.
- The harmonics of square, sawtooth, and triangle waves may be created and plotted.

Figure A1-1

Using a Spreadsheet to Plot Sine Wave Graphs

	A	B	C
1	0	=sin(A1*pi()/180)	
2	=A1+1		
3			
4			
5			
6			
7			
8			
9			
10			
11			
12			
13			
14			
15			
16			
17			
18			
19			
20			
21			
22			
23			
24			
25			
26			
27			
28			
29			
30			
31			
32			
33			
34			
35			

1. Select a cell to be the top left corner of your grid. Enter the following:

`0`

2. Go to the cell directly below the top left cell. Enter the following:

`=`

Now, click on the cell directly above (the grid's top left cell). The column and row will appear after the equal sign. Complete this cell's entry by typing:

`+1`

This will cause the second cell to reference the upper cell and add 1 to the upper cell's value.

3. Click in the second cell, and drag your mouse downward, highlighting cells moving down the column. Go to at least 360 cells below the top left cell.

4. With the column of cells selected, select **Fill Down...** from the appropriate menu. This causes each cell to reference the cell above it and add 1 to the value shown in the cell immediately above it.

5. Go to the cell immediately to the right of the top left cell. Enter the following:

`=sin(`

Now, click on the top left cell. Its column and row number will appear. Complete the entry in this cell as follows:

`*pi()/180)`

This will convert the value in the left column from a degree to a radian angle measurement, and take the sine of the value.

6. Repeat steps 3 and 4 in this second column. Highlight the top entry in the column, and drag the mouse downward for the same number of cells that were selected in step 3. Select **Fill down...** from the appropriate menu.

7. Go to the spreadsheet's graphing function and create an X-Y graph with the leftmost column as the horizontal axis and the rightmost column as the values to be plotted. A sine wave graph will be created.

8. Using the formula shown above, graphs at different frequencies and amplitudes may be created. For example, to create a graph at twice the frequency as the first graph, adjust the formula of step 5 as follows:

`= sin(2*A1*pi()/180)`

To create a graph at half the amplitude of the first graph, adjust the formula of step 5 as follows:

`= 0.5*sin(A1*pi()/180)`

9. Plots that are combinations of different waves may easily be created.

For example, if a series of sine values are plotted in column B, as shown above, and column C contains a separate plot of a sine wave at a different amplitude and frequency, the two may be combined in column D by going to cell D1 and entering:

`=B1+C1`

and filling the rest of column D with this same formula, as in step 4. A graph may now be generated from column D that shows the sum of the two other sine waves.

Spectrogram

Have students search on the Internet for programs that are able to create spectrograms of audio. Many are freeware or shareware. Then have them search for sites that have recordings (samples) of musical instruments and download at least one instrumental sample and create a spectrogram of it. Ask, How much of the spectrogram is surprising? How much of it looks the way they would expect it to?

MIDI-Related Exercises

Students should be comfortable doing Internet searches for MIDI files, downloading them, and opening the downloaded standard MIDI file in a sequencing program. Students should also be comfortable recording MIDI data directly from a keyboard, via step entry, and graphically on a piano roll screen.

Basic MIDI Editing

Starting with a favorite song as a downloaded MIDI file may be an effective introduction to the workings of a sequencer. Allow students to manipulate the MIDI data in a variety of ways: adding program change messages to change instruments, transposing parts, copying a track and modifying it by transposition, remapping of notes, and so on.

Song Mode

Have students create a musical composition out of short component sequences in Song Mode.

Sequencing + Notation

Have students enter one line of a two-voice invention in a sequencer in the manner with which they are most comfortable. When the line is complete, have them export the file as a standard MIDI file. Then have them open the MIDI file in a notation program, correct any mistakes that resulted from the translation process, and then enter the second line.

Using a Sequencer to Present Structural Elements

Using a sequencing program, have students create a multitrack sequence that illustrates the piece's structural elements. Putting each instrument onto a different track, the piece's construction can be shown by muting all tracks but one, then adding one track at a time to show the role each instrument plays. Alternatively, different tracks can represent hierarchical layers of a Schenkerian analysis. Muting or unmuting tracks can reveal the foreground, middleground, and background.

Exploring Sound Synthesis

Composition students can be led through an overview of the functions featured on synthesizers in an available music studio. How are sounds put together through combinations of samples, oscillators, filters, and envelope generators? What type of pieces may be constructed by starting from scratch—initial voices on an instrument—and creating original synthesizer patches that are used in a piece that is written with a MIDI sequencer?

Alternative Tunings

Some synthesizers have alternative tunings available, such as quarter-tone or just intonation. Have students experiment with the effects of creating music in alternative tunings. If other historical tunings are available, such as Pythagorean or meantone, it would be an interesting study to play Renaissance and Baroque music in the tunings for which they were originally written in order to compare the differences between the original realizations and contemporary realizations in twelve-tone equal temperament.

Music and Multimedia

These exercises incorporate elements of music software into other types of programs.

Placing a MIDI File on a Web Page

This exercise presupposes some knowledge of HTML or some Web page creation software.

Have students create a Web page that contains a MIDI file. MIDI files may be specified within HTML EMBED tags with the following format:

```
<EMBED SRC="[MIDI FILE NAME]" height="16"
width="160" autoplay="true">
```

Appendix 2 contains a template for a Web page document that may be used as a starting point.

Creating a Presentation with MIDI

Using presentation software, have students create a presentation (or slide) about a composer. Include a photo, text, a graphic of notated music, and a MIDI or audio file. Students will need to be comfortable either scanning photographs or downloading them from the Internet, creating graphics of musical notation from a notation program, and including a standard MIDI file as part of a presentation.

Creating a Graphical Music Illustration

Notation programs print musical characters using a music font. They come with a "cheat sheet" that indicates which keys produce which musical symbols. For example, a lowercase *q* may result in a quarter note in the notation font, and a lowercase *g* may produce a treble clef. Using a graphics program and a notation font, a number of useful applications may be explored. Different musical symbols may be entered and resized by simply choosing a smaller or larger font size for them. The characters may then be dragged to any location relative to each other. This may allow theorists to create Schenkerian graphs or educators to create colorful illustrations of songs for children to learn.

Digital Audio Exercises

A caveat must be stated before advocating too much work with audio files: doing so raises the question of copyright infringement, which is no joke. It *is* legal to purchase a CD and make copies of it for your own use. It is *not* legal to make copies to give to other people. Certain fair use principles may apply for classroom applications, but it is wise to double-check applicable copyright laws before making use of other people's music.

Assuming all legal questions have been satisfactorily addressed, students should feel comfortable editing digital audio. This includes, copying, deleting, and pasting, creating crossfades, volume envelopes, and pan envelopes. Most audio editors also have a variety of filters and effects available that students should familiarize themselves with. Students should also be comfortable exporting edited audio files so that they may be burned onto a CD.

Audio for a Music Presentation

Music classes frequently employ musical examples as an important feature. Many times, this affords students an opportunity to snicker at a hapless instructor searching for a desired spot on a cassette tape or vinyl LP, and inordinate amounts of time may be wasted with these attempts.

Using a digital audio editor, have students extract audio files from a CD they have purchased, and edit the files so that they have excerpts to present to the class. Have them put a volume envelope on the excerpt so that it gently fades in and out. Have them export the edited excerpt as an AIFF file and burn it onto a CD. Now class examples are a simple matter of selecting a CD track.

Creation of Radio Spots

Using available recording equipment and an audio editor, have students create a radio announcement that features an announcer's vocal, at least one sound effect, and background music. This project may be expanded by dramatizing a short story for radio broadcast that features a variety of actors, sound effects, and musical passages.

Web Page Template with MIDI File

```
<HTML>
<HEAD>
<TITLE>MIDI in Web Page</TITLE>
</HEAD>
<BODY>
<!-- CHANGE THE 'SRC' DEFINITION TO THE NAME OF YOUR
MIDI FILE YOU MAY PUT WHATEVER TEXT YOU LIKE ABOVE THE
EMBED TAG AND IT WILL APPEAR IN THE BROWSER -->
<EMBED SRC="[NAME OF MIDI FILE]" height="16" width="160"
autoplay="true">
</BODY>
</HTML>
```

References

Music and Acoustics

Blauert, Jens. *Spatial Hearing: The Psychophysics of Human Sound Localization, revised edition.* Cambridge, MA: MIT Press, 1997.

Bregman, A. S. *Auditory Scene Analysis.* Cambridge, MA: MIT Press, 1990.

Handel, Stephen. *Listening: An Introduction to the Perception of Auditory Events.* Cambridge, MA: MIT Press, 1989.

Helmholtz, Hermann. *On the Sensation of Tone.* London: Longmans, 1885. (Original English translation by Alexander J. Ellis, reprinted by Dover, New York, 1954).

Levarie, Sigmund, and Levy, Ernst. *Tone: A Study in Musical Acoustics, Second Edition.* Kent State University Press, 1980.

Minsky, Marvin. "Music, Mind and Meaning." *Computer Music Journal* V(3) (1981): pp. 28–45.

Moore, Brian C. J. *An Introduction to the Psychology of Hearing, Third Edition.* London: Harcourt Brace Jovanovich, 1989.

Moorer, James A., and Grey, John. "Lexicon of Analyzed Tones (Part I: A Violin Tone)." *Computer Music Journal* 1(2) (April 1977): pp. 39–45.

———. "Lexicon of Analyzed Tones (Part II: Clarinet and Oboe Tones)." *Computer Music Journal* 1(3) (June 1977): pp. 12–29.

———. "Lexicon of Analyzed Tones (Part III: The Trumpet)." *Computer Music Journal* 2(2) (September 1978): pp. 23–31.

Pierce, John R. *The Science of Musical Sound.* New York: Scientific American Books, 1983.

Roads, Curtis. *The Computer Music Tutorial.* Cambridge, MA: MIT Press, 1996.

Roederer, Juan G. *The Physics and Psychophysics of Music, Third Edition.* New York: Springer-Verlag, 1995.

Rossing, Thomas D. *The Science of Sound, Second Edition.* Reading, MA: Addison-Wesley Publishing Company, 1990.

Sundberg, Johan. *The Science of Musical Sounds.* San Diego: Academic Press, Inc., 1991.

Wessel, David. "Timbre Space as a Musical Control Structure." *Computer Music Journal,* 3(2) (June 1979): pp. 45–52.

Wilkinson, Scott R. *Tuning In: Microtonality in Electronic Music.* Milwaukee, WI: Hal Leonard Books, 1988.

MIDI

Chadabe, Joel. *Electronic Sound: The Past and Promise of Electronic Music.* Upper Saddle River, NJ: Prentice Hall, 1997.

Cutler, Marty, Robair, Gino, and Wilkinson, Scott. "In Control." *Electronic Musician* 17(5) (May 2001): pp. 64–109.

Loy, Gareth. "Musicians Make a Standard: The MIDI Phenomenon." *Computer Music Journal* 9(4) (1985): pp. 8–26.

MIDI Manufacturers' Organization, technical documents. http://www.midi.org/

Moore, F. Richard. "The Dysfunctions of MIDI." *Computer Music Journal* 12(1) (1988): pp. 19–28.

Raschke, Peter. *Exploring MIDI Web Site.* Northwestern University, 1997. http://nuinfo.nwu.edu/musicschool/links/projects/midi/expmidiindex.html

Rothstein, Joseph. *MIDI: A Comprehensive Introduction, Second Edition.* Madison, WI: A-R Editions, 1995.

Webster, Peter Richard, and David Brian Williams. *Experiencing Music Technology.* New York: Schirmer Books. 1999.

Digital Audio

Boyk, James, et al. "There's Life Above 20 Kilohertz! A Survey of Musical Instrument Spectra to 104.2 kHz." Published on-line at http://www.cco.caltech.edu/~boyk/spectra/spectra.htm

Deutsch, Diana (ed). *The Psychology of Music.* New York, Academic Press, 1982.

Hresko, Christian Adam. "The Internal Structure of Audio Files: RAW, NeXT/Sun, AIFF/AIFC, RIFF WAVE." In *Audio Anecdotes,* Ken Greenebaum, ed. Natick, MA: A.K. Peters, Ltd, 2001.

McClellan, James H., Schafer, Ronald W., and Yoder, Mark A. *DSP First: A Multimedia Approach.* Upper Saddle River, NJ: Prentice Hall, 1998.

———. The MiniDisc Portal. http://www.minidisc.org/

———. *Inside Macintosh: Sound.* Cupertino, CA: Apple Computer Co., 1999.

Moore, F. R. *Elements of Computer Music.* Englewood Cliffs, NJ: PTR Prentice Hall, 1990.

Oohashi, Tsutomu, et al. "High-Frequency Sound Above the Audible Range Affects Brain Electric Activity and Sound

Perception." *Proceedings of the 91st Audio Engineering Society Convention,* 1991. Preprint no. 3207.

Pohlmann, Ken C. *Principles of Digital Audio.* New York: McGraw-Hill Inc., 1995.

Smith, J. O. "Fundamentals of Digital Filter Theory." *Computer Music Journal* 9(3) (September 1985): pp. 13–23.

Steiglitz, Ken. *A Digital Signal Processing Primer.* Menlo Park, CA: Addison-Wesley Publishing Company, 1996.

Todd, Craig C., et al. AC-3: Flexible Perceptual Coding for Audio Transmission and Storage. *Proceedings of the 96th Audio Engineering Society Convention,* 1994.

Tsutsui, Kyoya, et al. "ATRAC: Adaptive Transform Acoustic Coding for MiniDisc." *Proceedings of the 93rd Audio Engineering Society Convention,* 1992.

Watkinson, John. *The Art of Digital Audio.* Oxford: Focal Press, 1999.

Yamamoto, Takeo. *Industry Seminar on DVD.* Presented at McGill University Faculty of Music, April 12, 1997.

Yoshida, Tadao. "The Rewritable MiniDisc System." *Proceedings of the IEEE* 82(10), 1994.

Audio Recording, Processing, and Synthesis

Apple-MPEG4-AAC Audio. http://www.apple.com/mpeg4/aac/

Beauchamp, James. "Will the Real FM Equation Please Stand Up?" in Letters, *Computer Music Journal* 16(4) (Winter 1992): pp. 6–7.

Chowning, John. "The Synthesis of Complex Audio Spectra by Means of Frequency Modulation." *Journal of the Audio Engineering Society* 21(7) (1974). Reprinted in *Computer Music Journal* 1(2) (April 1977): pp. 46–54.

Cleveland, Barry. "Mixed Signals." *Electronic Musician* 16(11) (November 2000): pp. 62–81.

de Campo, Alberto. *The CREATE Tutorial for SuperCollider 2.* Bundled with SuperCollider software, www.audiosynth.com

Dickreiter, Michael. *Tonmeister Technology: Recording Environments, Sound Sources and Microphone Techniques.* New York: Temmer Enterprises, Inc., 1988.

Dodge, Charles, and Jerse, Thomas A. *Computer Music: Synthesis, Composition and Performance.* New York: Schirmer Books, 1984.

Eargle, John. *Handbook of Recording Engineering.* New York: Van Nostrand Reinhold, 1992.

———. *The Microphone Book.* Boston: Focal Press, 2001.

Fukada, Akira. "A challenge in Multi-Channel Music Recording." In *Proceedings of the Audio Engineering Society's 19th International Conference on Surround Sound: Techniques, Technology and Perception,* 2001.

Keene, Sherman. *Practical Techniques for the Recording Engineer.* Sedona, AZ: S.K.E. Publishing, 1981.

Martin, Geoffrey Glen. *A Hybrid Model for Simulating Diffused First Reflections in Two-Dimensional Acoustic Environments.* Ph.D. thesis, McGill University Faculty of Music, 2001.

Mathews, Max V. *The Technology of Computer Music.* Cambridge, MA: MIT Press, 1969.

Pellman, Samuel. *An Introduction to the Creation of Electronic Music.* Belmont, CA: Wadsworth Publishing Company, 1994.

Philips Super Audio CD Web site. http://www.sacd.philips.com/b2b/format/index.html

Sony Super Audio CD Web Site. http://interprod5.imgusa.com/son-403/

Sound Peformance Lab. "Yes, You Can Mic Multichannel Music." Press release, SPL Electronics GmBH, Niederkrüchten, Germany, January 19, 1999.

Super Audio CD Web site. http://www.superaudio-cd.com/

Thiele, Günther. "Multichannel Natural Music Recoding Based on Psychoacoustic Principles." Extended Version 3 of Audio Engineering Society Preprint 5156, January 2001. Available at http://www.tonmeister.de/foren/surround/texte/multi-mr.pdf

Index